Oedipus Tyrannus

Tragic Heroism and the Limits of Knowledge

SECOND EDITION

Charles Segal

New York   Oxford
OXFORD UNIVERSITY PRESS
2001

Oxford University Press

Oxford   New York
Athens   Auckland   Bangkok   Bogotá   Buenos Aires   Calcutta
Cape Town   Chennai   Dar es Salaam   Delhi   Florence   Hong Kong   Istanbul
Karachi   Kuala Lumpur   Madrid   Melbourne   Mexico City   Mumbai
Nairobi   Paris   São Paulo   Shanghai   Singapore   Taipei   Tokyo   Toronto   Warsaw

and associated companies in
Berlin   Ibadan

Published by Oxford University Press, Inc.
198 Madison Avenue, New York, New York, 10016
http://www.oup-usa.org

Oxford is a registered trademark of Oxford University Press

Library of Congress Cataloging-in-Publication Data

Segal, Charles, 1936–
    Oedipus Tyrannus : tragic heroism and the limits of knowledge / Charles Segal.—2nd ed.
    p. cm.
    Includes bibliographical references (p.   ) and index.
    ISBN 0-19-513320-X. — ISBN 0-19-513321-8 (pbk.)
    1. Sophocles. Oedipus Rex.   2. Oedipus (Greek mythology) in literature.   3. Knowledge,
Theory of, in literature.   4. Heroes in literature.   5. Tragedy.   I. Title.

PA4413.O7 S52 2000
882'.01—dc21   00-032666

Printing number: 9 8 7 6 5 4 3 2

Printed in the United States of America
on acid-free paper

CONTENTS

ILLUSTRATIONS

PREFACE TO THE SECOND EDITION

This book is a revised and expanded version of the 1993 publication. The aim of the second edition remains the same as the first, to offer the nonspecialist, nonclassicist reader a lucid, in-depth analysis of the most famous of the Greek tragedies and one of the greatest masterpieces of world literature. I have tried to keep in mind the needs, questions, and interests of students at all levels who read this play in translation and have little or no training in classical studies. At the same time, I have tried not to falsify the richness and complexity of the material. My discussion includes both the classical background (the myth, historical, social, and intellectual influences, staging, etc.) and the play's later life in literature and art and in Western thought generally.

The responses to the first edition were gratifying. I have taken account of some helpful comments made by reviewers, updated and expanded the notes and bibliography, made a few corrections, added a new chapter (Chapter 11) discussing *Oedipus Tyrannus'* relation to *Antigone* and to *Oedipus at Colonus*, and made some new observations here and there. I have also tried to improve the volume by rearranging the order of the material. Following the format of the series in which it originally appeared, the first edition discussed the reception and later interpretations of the myth early in the book. I have now transposed much of this material to the last chapter and expanded and updated my account of recent trends in literary criticism. I have, however, left the discussion of Freud in its original early position in the volume (Chapter 4) because it bulks so large in contemporary readings. I have also made use of several recent books on the later adaptations of the play (Dawe, Frick, Halter, Paduano) but without losing sight of the book's primary aim, the interpretation of Sophocles' play.

The *Oedipus* perhaps indicates more clearly than almost any other work of classical antiquity how interpreters at different moments of cultural history and fashions in literary criticism find fresh possibilities of meaning. Recently, critics have been fascinated by the suspended quality of the ending and the indeterminacy and nonclosure of the plot. Sophocles does not tell us exactly what is going to happen to Oedipus or to plague-stricken Thebes. I have refocused some of my comments toward these concerns in the last two chapters. The new material also required some small excisions from previous chapters to avoid repetition.

In addition to renewing the expressions of gratitude tendered in the first edition, I would like to thank Stephen Scully for discussing some aspects of the play with me, David Mitten for help with the cover art, and Robert Miller of the Press for his good advice, his interest in this volume, and his encouragement toward the new edition.

Cambridge, Massachusetts
July 6, 2000

A NOTE ON REFERENCES
AND ACKNOWLEDGMENTS
(FROM THE FIRST EDITION)

The *Oedipus Tyrannus* of Sophocles is also called *Oedipus the King* and *Oedipus Rex*. As the Greek word *tyrannos* does not correspond exactly either to English "king" or Latin *rex*, I keep the Greek title. I refer to passages in the Greek plays by the line numbers of the Greek text, which are standardized in all modern editions. Of the two most widely used translations of *Oedipus Tyrannus*, David Grene in the University of Chicago series, *The Complete Greek Drama*, closely follows the line numbers of the Greek, and these are printed in the margin of his translation. Robert Fagles in the Penguin edition gives the original line numbers at the top of each page (his line numbers in the margin refer to his translation only).

I generally quote from the translations of Fagles or Grene, but in many cases I have made my own translation to bring out specific nuances in the Greek original, and in these cases no translator is indicated in the text. I cite other Greek authors according to the numeration of the Oxford Classical Texts, which English translations frequently indicate. I have used recent and available translations, as indicated in the text, but here too I have sometimes made my own. In some cases, as I note in the text, I have slightly modified existing translations to bring out aspects of the original. References to works cited in the Notes by author and short title may be found in the Selected Bibliography at the end of the volume. "Oedipus," unless otherwise noted, refers to the *Oedipus Tyrannus*. I refer to the *Oedipus at Colonus* sometimes as *Oedipus Coloneus* or simply as *Coloneus*.

I have profited greatly from the commentaries and the abundant scholarly literature on the play and the myth; and, even though I do not always agree, I am deeply indebted to the scholarly labors of Dawe, Edmunds, Jebb, Knox, Lattimore, Lloyd-Jones, Reinhardt, Moret, Vernant, and Winnington-Ingram, to mention only a few. Limitations of space do not permit me to acknowledge the many places in which I draw on previous scholarship or to discuss controversies or differences of interpretation.

I have concentrated on those aspects of the play that seem to me most meaningful to the nonspecialist, Greekless reader. Hence I have paid more attention to content than to form, to myth and meaning than to style or staging, although I occasionally touch on these areas of the play as well. I have tried to approach the text freshly and so have sometimes suggested interpretations that I have not found in the existing literature, which does not mean that someone else somewhere in the enormous body of scholarship on this play has not had the same idea.

ACKNOWLEDGMENTS

In the last section of Chapter 6 and in Chapter 10 I have drawn on my study, "Time, Theater, and Knowledge in the Tragedy of Oedipus," published in *Edipo: Il teatro greco e la cultura Europea*, eds. B. Gentili and R. Pretagostini (Rome: Edizioni dell' Ateneo, 1986), 459–84, which I have thoroughly revised and recast for this volume. I am grateful to the Edizioni del Ateneo for permission to reuse some of this material here.

   For helpful discussion I thank Albert Henrichs and Werner Frick. I am grateful to Lenore Parker for aid in the preparation of the manuscript. My greatest debt is to my wife, Nancy Jones, for sustaining patience and wise advice.

CHRONOLOGY

534   First tragic performance at Athens by Thespis at the Festival of Dionysus under the tyrant Peisistratus.

525   Birth of Aeschylus.

510–507   Expulsion of the tyrant Peisistratus and foundation of Athenian democracy under the leadership of Cleisthenes.

497/96   Birth of Sophocles, son of Sophillos, a wealthy inhabitant of the Athenian community of Colonus.

494   Birth of Pericles.

490   King Dareius of Persia invades Greece and is repulsed by the Athenians at Marathon, on the eastern coast of Attica.

480 (*approx.*)   Birth of Euripides.

480–478   King Xerxes of Persia invades Greece and is defeated by the Athenian fleet at Salamis and by a Greek land army at Plataea. Aeschylus is said to have fought at Salamis and Sophocles to have danced in the boys' chorus celebrating the victory.

477   Athenians found the Delian League, a naval alliance, to protect against further aggression by the Persians; it is a precursor of the Athenian naval empire.

472   Aeschylus presents *The Persians*, earliest extant complete tragedy, dramatizing the Athenian victory at Salamis. The young Pericles is the financial sponsor of the performance.

470/69   Birth of Socrates.

468   Sophocles wins his first victory at the dramatic competition with *Triptolemus*, defeating Aeschylus.

467	Aeschylus presents a trilogy on the House of Laius, including *Laius, Oedipus, Seven against Thebes*, and the satyr-play, *Sphinx*. Only the *Seven* survives.
461	Ostracism of Cimon, leader of the aristocratic party; increasing influence of the democratic party under the leadership of Pericles and Ephialtes.
460 (*approx*)	Birth of the historian Thucydides.
460–450	(?) Sophocles probably presents *Ajax* in this period.
458	Aeschylus presents *Oresteia*.
457–445	Expansion of Athenian power to Boeotia, the Megarid, and Euboea.
456/55	Death of Aeschylus in exile at Gela, in Sicily.
454	Treasury of Delian League moved to Athens; the defensive alliance is visibly transformed into Athenian maritime empire.
449	First victory of Euripides at the dramatic competition.
447	Periclean building program begins: a new temple to Athena, the Parthenon, is begun; construction of a monumental entrance to the Acropolis (the Propylaea) will soon follow.
447–45	Defeated in Boeotia, Athens cuts back her land empire and concludes a thirty years peace with Sparta.
444	Invited by Pericles, the Sophist Protagoras helps draft laws and a constitution for Athenian colony of Thurii in southern Italy, which the historian Herodotus also visits.
443–442	Sophocles serves as *hellenotamias*, supervising the amount of tribute to be assessed to Athens' island subject-allies.
442–441(?)	Sophocles presents *Antigone* at the City Dionysia in Athens and wins first prize.
441–440	Sophocles elected one of ten generals to serve in suppressing the revolt of the island of Samos. His election is supposed to have been due to the popularity of *Antigone* in the previous year (though this is sometimes questioned).
440-430 (?)	Sophocles probably presents *Trachinian Women* in this period.
438	Gold and ivory statue of Athena by Pheidias set up in the Parthenon; Euripides presents *Alcestis*, his earliest play to survive.
431	Beginning of Peloponnesian War. Athens and Sparta are the principals, but all of Greece is eventually involved. Except for a short interval of uneasy truce in 421–418, it is to continue until

	404, with frequent invasions of Attica by the Spartans and resultant crowding of Athenians from the outlying areas of Attica into the city. Euripides presents *Medea*.
430	Great plague breaks out in Athens.
429	Pericles dies in the plague.
429–425 (?)	*Oedipus Tyrannus* probably performed in this period.
428	Euripides presents revised version of *Hippolytus*.
428/27	Birth of Plato.
427	Aristophanes presents his first comedy at the dramatic competition. The celebrated Sophist and rhetorician, Gorgias of Leontini, visits and teaches in Athens. Possible service of Sophocles as a general in Peloponnesian War.
425	Aristophanes presents *Acharnians*, an anti-war play and the earliest of his comedies to be preserved.
423	Aristophanes presents *Clouds*, satirizing Socrates, the Sophists, and scientific speculation.
421	Aristophanes presents *Peace*; Peace of Nicias concluded.
421/20 (?)	Possible date for production of Euripides' *Electra*.
420	Sophocles chosen to receive the sacred snake of the healing god Asclepius in his home
419–410	Sophocles presents *Electra* sometime during this period.
416	Athens conquers the island of Melos, puts to death the men of military age, and enslaves the rest of the population.
415	Euripides presents *Trojan Women*, possibly reflecting on the Athenian harshness toward the Melians and similar events in the War.
415–413	Athenian expedition to Sicily under Nicias and Alcibiades. It ends in a serious defeat for Athens at Syracuse, with the loss of many men and ships. Athens never fully recovers.
414	Aristophanes presents *Birds*, a utopian comedy.
414–412	Euripides' *Ion*, *Iphigeneia among the Taurians*, and *Helen* fall in this period.
413	Spartans seize and fortify Athenian border town of Decelea, giving them a permanent foothold in Athenian territory.
411–409	Aristophanes' anti-war comedy, *Lysistrata*, presented in 411; Euripides presents *Phoenician Women* (*Phoenissae*) in this period, a play about the house of Oedipus.

411	Oligarchical coup at Athens; Sophocles chosen as one of the ten Probouloi or Commissioners. The democracy is temporarily replaced by a moderate and conservative oligarchy, but this latter lasts only a few months, and democracy is restored.
409	Sophocles, in his mid 80's, presents *Philoctetes*, which wins first prize.
408	Euripides goes into exile from Athens and takes up residence at the court of King Archelaus in Macedon; probably writes *Bacchae* and *Iphigeneia at Aulis* in this period, both performed posthumously.
407/6	Death of Euripides at the court of king Archelaus in Macedon. In response to the news, Sophocles is said to have dressed his chorus in black for his plays at the Dionysiac festival.
406	Death of Sophocles; said to have received a hero cult after his death as Dexion, the "Receiver," for having entertained the sacred snake of Asclepius.
405	Aristophanes presents *Frogs*, reflecting on the status of tragedy after the deaths of the great tragedians.
404–403	Surrender of Athens and establishment of a Spartan garrison there; rule of the Thirty Tyrants, supported by Sparta.
403	Restoration of the democracy; amnesty declared.
401	Posthumous presentation of *Oedipus at Colonus* by Sophocles' grandson.
399	Trial and death of Socrates.

LITERARY AND HISTORICAL CONTEXT

1

Introduction

WHY READ *OEDIPUS TYRANNUS*?

The place of *Oedipus Tyrannus* in literature is something like that of the Mona Lisa in art.[1] Everyone knows the story, the first detective story of Western literature; everyone who has read or seen it is drawn into its enigmas and moral dilemmas. It presents a kind of nightmare vision of a world suddenly turned upside down: a decent man discovers that he has unknowingly killed his father, married his mother, and had children by her. It is a story that, as Aristotle says in the *Poetics*, makes one shudder with horror and feel pity just on hearing it (14.1453b5–7). Tragedy stirs the deep emotions of pity and fear as it brings us face to face with suffering, strength, and courage at the outer limits of human experience; and *Oedipus* is Aristotle's favorite example for this tragic effect. We find the unexpected reversal in the lives of the great and fortunate deeply moving, both for individuals and for the state, as we know from contemporary responses to the deaths of famous people—our equivalent to the mythical kings of ancient Greece—such as that of Princess Diana of Britain. The stories of kings are themselves exemplary of the extreme limits of human criminality and human grandeur; and this play shows a great and passionate king confronting unspeakable horrors.

In Sophocles' hands this ancient tale also becomes a profound meditation on the questions of guilt and responsibility, the order (or disorder) of our world, and the nature of man. The play stands with the Book of Job, *Hamlet*, and *King Lear* as one of Western literature's most searching examinations of the problem of meaning and suffering. A life that seems happy, productive, and distinguished in the service of others suddenly crumbles into dust. The well-meaning king of Thebes—an effective, admired, and respected ruler—suddenly finds that he is not only the source of the calamity from which he has tried to protect his citizens, the plague with which the play begins, but also guilty of the two most horrible crimes imaginable: incest with his mother and the bloody killing of his father. The hero's determined march toward the horrifying discovery of these facts produces the feeling of an inexorable doom surrounding his life, as he recognizes that he has fulfilled prophecies that Apollo had given to him and his parents. In fact, the very attempts to avoid these prophecies seem to have brought them to pass. Thus, on one reading, the play is a tragedy of a destiny that the hero cannot evade, despite his best attempts to do so.

The play is a tragedy not only of destiny but also of personal identity: the search for the origins and meaning of our life, our balance between "one" and "many" selves, our recognition of the large areas of darkness about who we "really" are, and the effort to explore the essential mystery of our selfhood. It dramatizes the lonely path of self-discovery, as Oedipus separates his true self from an illusory self defined by the external status of his kingship, and retraces his existence from powerful ruler to lonely wanderer, without parents, city, home, or even a sure name. The hero chosen to perform exceptional deeds has also to undergo exceptional suffering as the polluted parricide and outcast who has infected his city.

Oedipus' story serves as the myth not only of Western personal identity but also of Western cultural identity. In this role he may be paired with the figure of Prometheus in Aeschylus' *Prometheus Bound*. Knowledge in *Oedipus* is the reverse of that in Aeschylus' play, in which the culture-hero Prometheus gives to man the boon of not foreseeing the day of his doom. Prometheus, benefactor of material progress, keeps technological man away from knowing his death and thus from contemplating the ultimate meaning of his life. To develop the arts and sciences necessary for the basic needs of society, introspective concerns with identity and ultimate meanings are an obstacle, and a certain degree of metaphysical blindness is an advantage. Hence Prometheus' gift that we not know the day of our death.

Prometheus places us close to the origins of the world; it takes us to a time of first beginnings still marked by man's primordial struggle with nature for survival. *Oedipus* describes the tragedy of humanity at a later stage, when a reflective awareness of the world within becomes more important than domination of the world outside. This post-Promethean knowledge is tragic rather than technological; it is a knowledge that looks to ends and ultimate reality rather than to means and immediate goals. Its hero has the fearful task, full of suffering, of unveiling the potential chaos of his world.

At the end of his life, in *Oedipus at Colonus*, Sophocles returns to Oedipus, whom he again characterizes as a paradoxical combination of knowledge, power, and weakness. Now in extreme old age, Oedipus appears as the wandering, defenseless exile from Thebes, a blind and homeless beggar. But he is also the vehicle of mysterious blessings that he will bring to Athens, the city in which he is to be buried and which he will henceforth defend through the magical power of his bones.

Freud saw *Oedipus* as a story of a man's deepest and most hidden sexual and aggressive impulses and made it the founding myth of psychoanalysis (see Chapter 4). For the general reader today, Oedipus' situation touches another

4

area of anxiety, existential rather than sexual or psychological, the fear of meaninglessness. Oedipus confronts the mystery of being alive in a world that does not correspond to a pattern of order or justice satisfactory to the human mind. He places us in a tragic universe in which we have to ask whether the horrible suffering we witness is all due to design or to chance, whether our lives are random or entirely determined. If everything happens by accident, a view to which the modern reader is probably more inclined than the ancient, then life seems absurd. If it is all by design, then the gods seem cruel or unjust, and life is hell. Sophocles does not give a final answer, any more than Shakespeare offers us a final answer for the tragic shape of Hamlet's life or for the death of Cordelia in *King Lear*.

If the play is the quintessential tragedy because of its content, it is also the quintessentially classic work in its form. It embodies the "classic" in its combination of intensely powerful emotions contained in an austere, controlled structure. This is not to say that there are not tensions and dissonances, but these are firmly contained within the design of the whole. Both plot structure and language operate within a severe economy that is both dense and lucid. The rhythm of Oedipus' search and discovery has no equal as sheer theater. The bits of information come naturally, randomly, and yet inevitably; and we watch with horror as Oedipus is forced to the terrible conclusion. Every detail, virtually every sentence, contributes to the dramatic effect; and nothing seems superfluous. The language is powerful in its immediate context but often carries a double or triple meaning.

Sophocles' play asks, Why do our lives turn out to have the shape that they finally have? He opens before us a kaleidoscopic configuration of different possibilities: the circumstances of our birth, our character, parental nurture or its absence, sheer luck, a mistake or miscalculation or wrong decision at a crucial moment, a mysterious doom or destiny, the will of the gods. The play brings together the question of how we make sense of our individual lives and how we make sense of our world given the elusiveness of final truth, the mysterious remoteness of the gods, and the slipperiness of language. The play adds the further question: even if we could know what "reality" is, that is, could discover the ultimate pattern determining the course of our lives, would this pattern offer us any hope or comfort, or would it turn out to be a kind of cruel joke, an "infernal machine," to cite the title of Jean Cocteau's Oedipus play?

Oedipus faces these questions both in macrocosm and in microcosm, both in reflecting on the world order and in assembling the minute details that make up the puzzle of a completed life. Over the centuries readers and audiences have faced these questions through the play and found different answers as they emphasize different aspects of the play. There is so much in Sophocles' dense weave of the simple and the complex that, as the classicist and translator Richmond Lattimore once wrote, "We can read *Oedipus* as many times as we like, and every time find new truths and throw away old falsehoods that once seemed to be true. There is always a dimension that escapes."[2]

Why the Title *Oedipus Tyrannus*?

Even in antiquity, *Tyrannus* in the play's title was a subject of learned discussion. The ancient summary that is prefixed to the play in the medieval manuscripts and draws on the scholarship of the centuries immediately after Sophocles explains that the title served to distinguish the play from *Oedipus at Colonus*. In the *Poetics*, Aristotle calls the play only *Oedipus*, which presumably was Sophocles' original title. Nevertheless, it is significant that Oedipus is a *turannos*, and the play so describes him repeatedly. For this reason the latinized form *Oedipus Rex* and the English *Oedipus the King* are misleading.

The term *turannos*, of unknown origin (possibly Lydian), describes the powerful rulers from the late seventh to the early fifth centuries B.C.E., like Polycrates of Samos, Peisistratus of Athens, or (in the fifth century) Hieron of Syracuse. By a combination of guile and force, such men emerged from the aristocratic oligarchy as sole rulers in their city-states, responsible only to themselves. They were known for currying favor with the populace by large civic projects and elaborate festivals, such as the Panathenaea and Greater Dionysia at Athens, the latter of which included the dramatic competitions. They were necessarily energetic, intelligent, confident, ambitious, and aggressive; they also had to be ruthless and suspicious of plots to overthrow their sometimes precarious position. Interpreters have sometimes looked for such "tyrannical" qualities in Oedipus; but, for the most part, the play uses the the term in a neutral sense of a ruler who is not a "king" (*basileus*), that is, one who has come to power without inheriting it from his family (ironically Oedipus is also the hereditary king). *Turannos* does not acquire a strongly pejorative meaning ("tyrant") in our sense, until the time of Plato, in the fourth century. But because the *turannos* had no legitimate, constitutional basis for his power and because he had greater opportunities for license and excess than others, the word can sometimes carry pejorative overtones, even in the fifth century. There may be hints of the pejorative meaning in the second stasimon (third choral ode, lines 872–96).[3]

Notes

1. Throughout the book I shall refer to *Oedipus Tyrannus* also as *Oedipus* and the *Tyrannus*.

2. R. Lattimore, *The Poetry of Greek Tragedy* (Baltimore: Johns Hopkins University Press, 1957), 99–100.

3. For a full discussion of Oedipus as *turannos* see Bernard Knox, *Oedipus at Thebes* (New Haven: Yale University Press, 1957), 21–25, 53–55; for a brief summary of recent views and a further bibliography, see Rebecca Bushnell, *Prophesying Tragedy* (Ithaca, N.Y.: Cornell University Press, 1988), 73; see also below, Chapters 2 and 8.

2

Historical and Cultural Background

PERICLEAN ATHENS AND THE FIFTH-CENTURY ENLIGHTENMENT

Sophocles wrote *Oedipus Tyrannus* during a period of both extraordinary intellectual and artistic energy and crisis. Under its astute and ambitious statesman, Pericles, Athens became the most powerful city-state (or *polis*) in Greece, and by 440 B.C.E. it was the acknowledged leader in almost every area of cultural activity and a center for philosophy, literature, architecture, sculpture, and painting at a level that is comparable to fifteenth-century Florence or seventeenth-century Paris.

Why such an outburst of creativity at this time and place? One can only guess at some contributing factors. At the very beginning of the century, Athens developed a stable democratic constitution. It gained both power and confidence from defeating the invading forces of the Persian Empire's attempt at westward expansion, first on land at Marathon (490), then at sea at Salamis (480). In this conflict (known as the Persian Wars), it built up a powerful navy, which gradually developed into a maritime empire that exacted tribute from the island and coastal cities of the eastern Aegean in return for protection against Persia. There are also more elusive factors, such as the native energy and initiative of the people, which the contemporary Athenian historian Thucydides contrasts with the conservative and slower temperament of Athens' great rival, the land-based city-state of Sparta.[1] Of no small importance too was the gifted leadership of Pericles, a man of wealthy and aristocratic origins who early in his career joined the democratic faction and guided Athens toward Hellenic leadership with a grand, if sometimes ruthless, vision of its cultural and political supremacy.

Pericles was and is controversial—cold, aloof, ambitious, but intensely patriotic. He sponsored the elaborate rebuilding of the Acropolis, which had been burned by the invading Persians in 480. The Periclean Acropolis contained the magnificent new temple of Athena known as the Parthenon, a grandiose entrance known as the Propylaea, and two other smaller temples completed after his death, the complex but graceful Erechtheum, with its famous caryatids (tall female figures who replace the columns in the south colonnade), and the exquisite, small Ionic temple to Athena Nike (Athena as Victory)—buildings whose beauty, even after the wear of twenty-five centuries, still astounds and inspires the visitor. Pericles was also the patron of the greatest sculptor of the age, Pheidias, who executed the famous gold and ivory statue of Athena for her temple, the Parthenon, and also designed and helped to carve the great frieze that adorns the inner colonnade.

The rebuilding of the Acropolis was only a small part of Pericles' program. He also oversaw the building of the massive temple to Athena and Hephaestus known as the Hephaesteum, which rises above the Agora or marketplace; the Odeion, or musical theater, beneath the Acropolis, adjoining the great theater of Dionysus, and the rebuilding of the theater itself; a new hall for the sanctuary of Demeter for the Eleusinian Mysteries just outside Athens; and several other temples in and around the city. He consolidated Athens' military security by building the Long Walls to connect the city with its harbors and thus make Athens as much of an island as its geography would permit. And Athens became a center for the manufacture of the elegantly painted vases in the style known as Attic red-figure, which were exported all over the Mediterranean. The celebrated painter Polygnotus worked at Athens and Delphi; although his work is not extant, we know it through later derivatives and the descriptions of later writers.

In addition to these visible achievements in art and architecture, Pericles brought to Athens the most inquiring minds of his time. He surrounded himself with poets and philosophers, thinkers and historians. Among his friends were Herodotus, whose *History of the Persian Wars* created history writing as we know it, and the Ionian philosopher-scientist Anaxagoras, who speculated that an ethereal substance called Mind (*Nous*) governed the world and that all of life could be explained by physical processes and the interactions of material substances.

Such rationalistic physical speculation, characteristic of Greek philosophy in the sixth and fifth centuries, naturally aroused suspicion among the more conservative Athenians, as it challenged the traditional anthropomorphic divinities of the Greek pantheon. Aristophanes, for example, made popular entertainment out of the novel scientific theories in his comedy the *Clouds* (423), which parodies thinkers like Anaxagoras for dethroning Zeus with a new god, the scientific principle Whirl or Vortex. The suspicion of intellectuals had more serious results, Pericles' political enemies tried to get at him by charging Anaxagoras with impiety and forcing him to flee Athens, sometime around the outbreak of the Peloponnesian War in 431. Some thirty years later, Socrates was put to death on a similar charge, and political motives were probably paramount with his accusers as well.

Such attacks on freedom of thought, however, were rare and generally were initiated by ulterior motives, such as political rivalries. Athens under Pericles was a place where many diverse currents of thought could mingle and conflict, as one can see in the comedies of Aristophanes, such as *Clouds* or *Birds*. The comic poets lampooned the city's leaders (Pericles included) with an exuberant license that was only occasionally checked. Athens' wealth and intellectualism drew the traveling teachers and thinkers known as the Sophists, who speculated and lectured (for pay) on a wide range of controversial subjects: religion, the origins of law and society, political and domestic management, and the skills in language and argument that assured success in the public assemblies and law courts.

Visiting Athens in 427, the Sicilian rhetorician and philosopher Gorgias made a sensation by displaying his intricate style of oratory. His two surviving speeches, quasi-playful works in defense of the mythical Helen of Troy and Palamedes, respectively, were showpieces of his skill in argumentation. Along with other contemporary orators and speech-writers, such as Antiphon and Andocides, he dealt with the questions of causality and responsibility that lay at the heart of many tragedies, including *Oedipus*. A few years later, the visit of another celebrated Sophist, Protagoras, provided the setting for Plato's dialogue of that name, *Protagoras*, which concerned the Sophist's claim to be able to teach civic skill or political virtue as a practical art or technique.

Protagoras was the best known of the Sophists, and his example is instructive. He ranged widely over many controversial areas and like his fellow intellectuals emphasized the power of human reason to confront and resolve the mysteries of existence. Among his sayings, two are particularly famous: "Of all things man [or, a man] is the measure, of the things that are, that they are, and of the things that are not, that they are not"; and "Concerning the gods I have no means of knowledge, either that they exist or that they do not exist; for many are the things that hinder knowing, the obscurity [of the subject] and the brevity of human life." Despite the uncertainties about these sayings' contexts and exact interpretation, both express a human-centered, rationalistic speculation that is embodied to some extent in the hero of *Oedipus*.

Besides its artistic merits, then, *Oedipus* is a major document in one of the most far-reaching intellectual revolutions in Western history, sometimes known as the Fifth-Century Enlightenment.[2] This period is marked by a shift from the mythical and symbolic thinking characteristic of archaic poets like Homer, Hesiod, and Pindar, to more conceptual and abstract modes of thought, according to which the world operates through nonpersonal processes that followed predictable, scientific laws. Instead of being regarded as an all-giving mother, for example, the earth is conceived of as a measurable surface that men mine and plow in their mastery of the world. The sun is not a god driving a blazing chariot across the heavens but (as Anaxagoras taught) a huge molten rock, about the size of the Peloponnesus. The gods may be regarded as psychological forces within man (as Euripides suggests for Aphrodite in his *Hippolytus*) or as an allegorical expression of the forces of nature. Religion itself is a human invention, a useful means of control in man's gradual creation of the social order necessary for his survival. Laws are not necessarily given by the gods but are the creations of human assemblies and councils. Cities are not the seat of divine powers rooted in a sacred landscape but human institutions, planned and placed by men in the environments best suited for human habitation. Disease is not the visitation of divine punishment or the manifestation of a pollution or a family curse but the result of an imbalance in the physical organism. As Hippocrates wrote at the opening of his treatise *On the Sacred Disease*, "In no way does this disease [probably epilepsy] seem to me more divine than other diseases or more sacred, but it has a physical basis and cause; out of inexperience and wonderment that it is unlike other diseases, men have supposed it to be a divine matter."

This new confidence in man's power to understand and shape his world finds visual expression in sculpture and painting and especially in a new exaltation of the human body (particularly the nude male body) as the ideal of beauty. In these works the human form often appears in movement or energetic action, but with a remarkable formal symmetry and equipoise that suggest dignity, calm, and confident control even in the most strenuous exertions. This style, known as classical, is best represented by the sculptures of Pheidias and Polyclitus. (From Argos, Polyclitus is one of the few major non-Athenian artists of the period; most of his work survives only in Roman copies). The Parthenon Frieze, designed and partly executed by Pheidias, is the greatest surviving masterpiece of the period. Depicting the citizens of Athens and their gods in a religious procession, it is the fullest realization of that mixture of harmony, energy, grandeur, simplicity, and idealized human beauty that constitutes the classical style.

The fullest literary expression of this humanistic confidence is the famous first stasimon of Sophocles' *Antigone*, which begins, "Many the wonders but nothing walks stranger than man. / This thing crosses the sea in the winter's storm, / making his path through the roaring waves" (332–35, Grene's translation). The ode goes on to celebrate man's domination of earth and its creatures, and his discovery of the arts of sailing, politics, and medicine. In fact, this Ode on Man, as it is often called, only scratches the surface of the Periclean achievement, which laid the foundation for Western conceptions of astronomy, mathematics, physics, city planning, architecture, musical theory, science, philosophy, politics, and history.

Philosophers roughly contemporary with Sophocles, like Parmenides of Elea and Empedocles of Acragas, speculated about perception and the relation among the senses in constructing reality. Parmenides in particular made a radical division between Being and Nonbeing: with Being belong light and truth; with Nonbeing, night, darkness, opinion, and error. The deceptiveness of the senses and the concealment of ultimate reality beneath false appearances are dominant themes throughout the period in both philosophy and literature. *Oedipus* shares this concern with finding truth in a world of appearances and is influenced, even if indirectly, by the new theories about language that pose the problem of the relation of words to reality and emphasize the power of words to deceive, to win unjust causes, and to confuse moral issues.

Interest in the potential ambiguity of language parallels interest in the deceptiveness of appearances. In Euripides' *Hippolytus* of 428 B.C.E.—a play that is in a way the *Oedipus* in reverse—the hero is falsely accused of incest with his stepmother and is killed by the curse of his enraged father, Theseus, who complains bitterly, "Alas, mortals should have clear evidence to show who are their friends, and also a means of distinguishing their hearts, to see who is truly friend and who is not. And all men should have two voices, one of justice and one as it happens to be, so that the voice of unjust thoughts would be tested and refuted by the just voice, and so we would not be deceived" (925–31).

Skeptical and rationalistic explanations of oracles, of the nature of the gods, and of the origin of religion find echoes in the historians Herodotus and Thucydides and in Sophocles' younger contemporary, Euripides. To take one example, Hecuba in Euripides' *Trojan Women* wonders whether Zeus may be the "necessity of nature or the mind of mortals" (884–85). Euripides is here drawing on a philosophical view of the gods as impersonal governing forces ("nature's necessity") rather than anthropomorphic beings. The questions about the validity of oracles in the *Oedipus* obviously belong to this intellectual ferment.

In a society as deeply traditional as that of ancient Greece, old ways of thinking often persist alongside the new. Thus Greek tragedy, and particularly Sophoclean tragedy, is a kind of dialogue between the older and newer ways of looking at the world. Indeed, much of the creative energy in Periclean art and literature derives from this transition between different conceptions of reality. *Antigone* and *Oedipus* raise questions about the power of Enlightenment Man and suggest that his life is still surrounded by the mysterious forces of the archaic world view, forces less amenable to human understanding and control. According to this older paradigm, nature is not merely an inert, passive object for human domination but an organically connected network of animate beings that stand in delicately balanced, mutually responsive relations to one another. Imbalance or violation in one area will produce some kind of disturbance in another; and the resultant disaster and its ramifications may be on a far greater scale than the original crime. Such is the plague that sets the tragic action of *Oedipus* into motion.

The Plague, the War, and the Tragedy of Athens

Among the unforseen catastrophes of the Peloponnesian War that broke out between Athens and Sparta in 431 was the great plague that ravaged Athens between 429 and 425. It spread quickly among both country and city people, who were crammed together behind the walls of Athens when the Spartans invaded, and it destroyed a quarter of the population. The victims included Pericles himself in 429, a loss that the city was to feel keenly as men of lesser intelligence and foresight succeeded him. The *Oedipus* is generally regarded as a response to events of this period.[3] An unexpected, supernatural-seeming disaster suddenly sweeps away brilliant hopes; confidence in human reason and calculation is shattered, and greatness swiftly turns into misery.

Thucydides, the Athenian general and historian who lived through the war and the plague and chronicled both, attributes to Pericles a brilliant speech that sets forth that leader's idealized vision of Athens (*History of the Peloponnesian War* 2.35–46). Known as Pericles' Funeral Oration because its occasion is the commemoration of the soldiers who died in the first year of the war, the speech is an encomium to Athens, a "hymn" to the city, as Pericles himself calls it (2.41.4–42.2). He contrasts Athens' free inquiry, individual initiative, democratic openness, cultural vitality and diversity to Sparta's closed, suspicious militarism. "Love of the beautiful with a spare toughness, love of intellectual pursuits without softness" is his famous phrase for his beloved city's spirit (2.40.1). In its energy in war and peace, its festivals open to everyone (and Pericles is surely thinking of the dramatic festivals too), its welcoming of leading intellectuals from all over, and its democratic institutions, Athens is "the education of Greece" (2.41.1).

Having achieved so much, says Pericles, the Athenians have more at stake than others in the war, for they have more to lose (*Peloponnesian War*, 2.42.1). Yet lose they did, though only after more than twenty years of fighting. By the end of the next year, the great plague broke out, and Pericles was dead. "In name it was a democracy," Thucydides says, summing up Pericles' years of power, "but in fact it was rule under the first man" (2.65.9). By juxtaposing Pericles' idealized Athens in the Funeral Oration with the fearful moral and psychological disintegration brought by the plague (2.53), Thucydides himself imposes a tragic structure on the events, a reversal from high to low. It would be surprising if other contemporaries—like Sophocles—did not also see a tragic pattern.

The breakdown of law and respect for the gods that Thucydides describes as taking place during the plague may find resonances in the second stasimon of *Oedipus*, in which the chorus complains of declining reverence for the gods (883–910). The crises and anxieties of the war, Thucydides reports, bring an increasing interest in oracles;[4] and this atmosphere too may have contributed to *Oedipus'* concerns. The mixture of helplessness, desperation, superstition, and religiosity that followed on the outbreak of the plague (*Peloponnesian War*, 2.47.4) is not far from the atmosphere that Sophocles creates in Thebes in the opening scenes of *Oedipus*.

Another circumstance connects Pericles and Oedipus. Pericles' ancient and powerful family, the Alcmaeonids, had been under an old curse for blood pollution; and one of Sparta's opening moves in the war was to demand that the Athenians drive out the accursed clan—a ploy that only endeared Pericles all the more to his fellow citizens.

Sophocles was a close friend of Pericles and held important posts during his ascendancy. But his more conservative religious spirit may well have made him uneasy about his friend's free-thinking intellectualism and his association with philosopher-scientists like Anaxagoras. It would be reductive to read *Oedipus* as a pietistic critique of Pericles' humanism or even as an expression of anxiety about his approximation to the power of a "tyrant."[5] Yet Sophocles' conception of Oedipus probably owes something to the life of a man famous for the dispassionate rationalism that won him the nickname, "the Olympian."

Pericles' death from the plague may have inspired the theme of Oedipus' fall. Events beyond human control thwart a leader's victory for his city, as with Pericles' careful planning for Athens' victory over its enemy Sparta in the Peloponnesian War and Oedipus' salvation of Thebes with his victory over the Sphinx. The play could, then, have been seen by Sophocles' contemporaries not just as a warning against pride or confidence but as a compassionate recognition that a great man's noble enterprise can collapse because of unforeseen events, or simply as an objective statement of life's uncertainties, of which Pericles was the most striking recent instance.

As Bernard Knox has brilliantly argued, the figure of Oedipus may also be a distillation of Athens at the height of its power, energy, daring, intellectual curiosity, and confidence in human reason.[6] Athens, rather than Pericles, is the "tyrant," holding its maritime empire with an iron fist when necessary, as it did during repeated attempts by the subject "allies" to revolt. In the last of the three speeches that Thucydides attributes to Pericles, the Athenian leader warns that Athens holds its sea empire as a "tyranny," the surrender of which "is as dangerous as its possession, in the eyes of many, is unjust" (*Peloponnesian War*, 2.63.2). Thus the title *Oedipus Tyrannus*, as Knox suggests, may be due to this recognition of the potential tragedy of the "tyrant" city.

We may never know for certain the full extent of *Oedipus'* relation to contemporary events. It is even possible that Oedipus' search for who he really is reflects something of a communal identity crisis in a city that had undergone a massive transformation in a short time and had refashioned itself from a rather quiet, traditional aristocracy and tyranny in the sixth century into a radical, intellectualized democracy and a powerful empire.[7] Given the intensely political nature of life in Athens and in its dramatic competitions, some connection with politics is highly probable. Like every great work of art, however, the play transcends its immediate historical context. It is one of the great meditations on the mystery of our place in a world that, despite our enormous power and intelligence, we can only partially control and understand.

NOTES

1. For Thucydides' contrasts of Athens and Sparta see, e.g., his *History of the Peloponnesian War* 1.10, 1.18, 1.70–71, 5.105.4.

2. The term, Fifth-Century Enlightenment, which is in common use, is the subtitle of W. K. C. Guthrie's *A History of Greek Philosophy*, vol. 3 (Cambridge: Cambridge University Press, 1969). On the history and usage of the term, see Guthrie, 48.

3. The majority of scholars date *Oedipus* to the period 429–425, but it must be emphasized that there is no firm evidence for the date, and a few scholars place it later.

4. Thucydides, *Peloponnesian War*, 2.17.2, 2.21.3, 2.54.

5. Victor Ehrenberg, *Sophocles and Pericles* (Oxford: Blackwell, 1954), 67–69, 149–61, has made the strongest case for viewing *Oedipus* as a conservative Sophocles' warning against Periclean rationalism.

6. B. Knox, *Oedipus at Thebes* (New Haven: Yale University Press, 1957), chap. 2, especially 64–106.

7. See Peter Euben, *The Tragedy of Political Theory* (Princeton: Princeton University Press, 1990), 99ff.

3

Performance, Theater, and Social Context

DRAMA AT THE FESTIVALS OF DIONYSUS

The ancient Greek dramas were performed each year in Athens as part of the festival of Dionysus, god of wine, vegetation, religious ecstasy, the mask, and the theater. Only two of the city's festivals featured dramatic performances, the Lenaea, which took place at the end of January, and the Great or City Dionysia, which took place at the end of March and lasted for five or six days. The festival of the Dionysia was by far the more important. Tragedies were introduced here at the end of the sixth century; they were introduced at the Lenaea relatively late in the history of Athenian theater, perhaps in the 440s, but performances were doubtless held in the Periclean theater of Dionysus after its completion.

During these festivals, all the male citizens and possibly (but not certainly) their wives, along with resident aliens and foreign visitors, gathered to watch twelve plays by three tragedians: each dramatist presented three tragedies and a satyr play. There were also five (later three) comedies and choral performances of dithyrambs (hymns in honor of Dionysus) sung and danced by men and boys. The plays to be performed were selected by a magistrate in a preliminary competition some months before the festival. At the festival itself five judges were selected by lot to award first, second, and third prizes.

The performances took place in the great open-air theater of Dionysus, which was built into the hillside in the precinct of the god on the southern slope of the Acropolis, where it can still be visited today. The plays began at dawn and continued throughout the day. The crowd sat on wooden benches like bleachers. Not until the fourth century B.C.E. were the stone benches built that survive today in the remains of the theaters at Athens, Epidaurus, Delphi, and elsewhere in Greece, Asia Minor, and Sicily. By the time of *Oedipus*, the Dionysiac festivals were famous, and many non-Athenians, especially those from Athens' subject allies, would attend. Plays were performed only once, at the Dionysiac festivals, although in some cases there would be repeat performances at the lesser Dionysiac festivals in the smaller towns outside of Athens. There were no private theaters or private companies. The performances were financed by the state, with the help of contributions from wealthy citizens for the cost of outfitting and training the chorus.

The festival was simultaneously a religious and a civic occasion. It began with a procession in honor of Dionysus, and various state functions also took place in the theater: the pouring of libations to the gods by the ten elected generals; the display of the tribute from Athens' subjects; the uniformed parade of the young soldiers who had been brought up at public expense because their fathers had been killed in war; and the reading out of the names and honors of those who had benefited the city.[1] The audience, therefore, was prepared to see a representation of events that had significance for the life of the community, especially in its relation to the gods, to public as well as private morality, and to the world order in general.

Staging was simple. The circular performance area, or orchestra, into which the audience looks from above, is backed by a long, low building (the scene building or *skênê*), which was probably of wood in the fifth century but was constructed of stone in major fourth-century theaters like that of Epidaurus. The action of the plays requires easy communication between the protagonists and the chorus, as is clear from the opening scene of the *Oedipus*. Some scholars have argued for the existence of a low, raised platform in front of the scene building as the protagonists' main playing area, with a step or two or a ramp affording access to the orchestra. The issue remains highly controversial, and the evidence for such a low platform in the fifth century is tenuous.[2] The scene building serves for the entrance and exits of characters through the front door, which in this play represents Oedipus' palace. Its roof can also serve as the place where a divinity can appear as the *deus ex machina*, a device rare in Sophocles and not used in any of the Theban plays. Characters also enter and exit from the side passages of the orchestra, the *parodoi*.

The circular space in front of the scene building is called the orchestra or "dancing place," and it is here where the chorus and probably the actors also perform. It probably has an altar of Dionysus in the center. In the opening scene of *Oedipus*, this altar is probably the gathering place for the procession of suppliants. It should be noted that there are no stage directions in our texts; we have to infer all stage business from the play itself, and many details of Sophocles' staging remain uncertain.

By modern standards, the stage is bare. There are few props. All the roles are played by male actors, who wear stylized masks and elaborate costumes. Only three actors per play are allowed, and these take different roles. Thus the actor who plays Creon in the first half of *Oedipus* returns later in the role of the Corinthian Messenger; and the actor who plays Jocasta returns as the Old Herdsman after Jocasta exits for her suicide. There are also supernumeraries for nonspeaking roles, like the suppliants in the opening scene of *Oedipus* or the guard whom Oedipus tells to bind the Old Herdsman. The chorus of fifteen members remains onstage during the entire performance and can interact with the actors like a regular character; at these times the chorus-leader, or *koryphaios*, speaks for the whole chorus. The odes, sung by the chorus as a whole, are accompanied by the *aulos*, a reed instrument more like our oboe than a flute, and the chorus also dances in accompaniment to these songs.

With the exception of a small bit of music for a chorus of Euripides' *Orestes*, nearly all of the music and all of the choreography of Greek drama are lost.[3] Every tragedy is composed in verse, and the language is lofty and poetic. The lyrics of the choral odes tend to be even more elaborate than the dialogue, and they often pose serious problems of interpretation because of their density and figurative language, abrupt leaps of thought, metaphors, and highly allusive style. The odes are written in the Doric dialect, slightly different from the Attic dialect of the Athenians, perhaps because of influences on the development of choral lyric in the Doric-speaking parts of the Peloponnesus. The dialogue (as opposed to the choral lyrics) is in a meter known as iambic trimeter, which consists of six iambic feet. It is a supple meter, and it allowed the tragedian both to approximate the rhythms of ordinary speech and to attain a dignity above the everyday. The effect is analogous to the blank verse in Elizabethan drama or the Alexandrines in the classic French drama of Corneille and Racine.

Each play is performed from beginning to end without intermission. There is no curtain and no formal division into acts or scenes. The choral odes, at more or less regular intervals, mark pauses in the action; they often follow after a crisis or climax and thus allow us to absorb what has happened and to reflect on the meaning of the events. Sophocles generally begins his plays by showing his main characters in action in the prologue, the section before the entrance of the chorus. The chorus members then enter from the wings at either side of the scene building to sing their first ode, known as the parode or *parodos*. Subsequent odes are called *stasima* (singular, *stasimon*). The odes are generally composed in pairs of strophe and antistrophe, stanza-like units that correspond to one another in meter, music, and choreography. Some odes have two or more pairs of strophe and antistrophe, and each one is generally in a different (though often related) metrical and musical form. Danced as well as sung, the odes have a solemn, ritualized effect. Indeed, the choruses themselves often consist in ritual actions like prayers to the gods, as is the case in the first ode of *Oedipus*.

The chorus is perhaps the hardest feature of Greek drama for modern readers to appreciate, just as it is the most perplexing for stage directors. It is a mistake to assume that the chorus is the mouthpiece of the playwright. Its statements are not to be taken at face value as an independent view of reality. The chorus, as Aristotle explained long ago, is a dramatic element, an actor among other actors. It shows us the communal background of the action, which is essential to this as to every other Greek play. Greek tragedy assumes that no life is entirely private, that the city's fortunes are inextricable from the individual's, and vice versa.

The chorus is so important to the play because Greek tragedy, unlike its modern counterpart, is a public art form. It is not just about individual lives; it reflects on such issues as the nature of authority, justice, and the worship of the

17

gods. And it does so in a wide framework of symbolic discourse made possible by myth, which connects matters of ethical and political life with questions about the world order on the one hand and with more personal matters—the relations between the sexes, tensions within the family, generational conflicts, the pull between public and private or between civic responsibility and individual desires or between family life and politics—on the other. Tragedy combines a public language of moral generalization and ritualized expressions of communal sentiment (generally by the chorus) within unusual (though not necessarily atypical) situations of personal emotion and intimate private life.

The chorus' collective response complements the individual responses of the main characters, but its response is not privileged just because it is collective. The chorus can be indecisive, as in Aeschylus' *Agamemnon*, or cowardly, as in Sophocles' *Antigone* or *Electra*; it can turn murderous, as in Euripides' *Bacchae*; and it can even lie and enter into deception, as in Sophocles' *Philoctetes*. In the *Tyrannus* it shows us, first of all, the terrible sufferings that result from the hidden pollution in the effect of the plague. Then, as the play goes on, the chorus is a vehicle for various hypotheses about what the events might mean and a sounding board for the emotions that they arouse.

Aristotle praises Sophocles for making his chorus participate directly in the action, in contrast to the more detached chorus of Euripides (*Poetics* 18.1456a). In *Oedipus*, Sophocles certainly uses the chorus to show the city's reactions to the events of the play, for example in its response to Oedipus' curse on the murderer of Laius (276–95) and later in its reaction to Oedipus' suffering after he blinds himself (1296–1368). This chorus too, unshaken in its loyalty to Oedipus, shows him to be a good ruler, valued for his ability and his devotion to the city.

The odes are always in character and so contain sentiments appropriate to the elderly citizens of Thebes. On the other hand, their intricate poetry and imagery often suggest more than the chorus itself knows and introduce a perspective that reaches beyond the human limitations of any single character. The odes of *Oedipus* contain no myths and almost no narrative (the only exception is the brief allusion to Oedipus' defeat of the Sphinx [507–10]). But they remind us constantly of the forces of nature outside the city, of the gods and their cults and oracles, and of the need to understand the sufferings of Thebes and of Oedipus in a wider philosophical and religious context.

THE MYTHICAL MATERIAL OF GREEK TRAGEDY

With a few exceptions, the classical Greek tragedians drew their plots from a body of inherited, traditional tales about gods and heroes that had taken shape gradually over many centuries. Most of these stories are about remote figures of the Mycenaean period, the great Bronze Age civilization that flourished in Greece from about 1600 to about 1200 B.C.E. Agamemnon, Achilles, Ajax, Oedipus, Theseus, to mention the most prominent, are legendary kings of great Mycenaean cities. The exact date when the stories about them developed cannot be determined with certainty, but it is probable that they were handed down from generation to generation in an oral tradition—modified, embellished, and endlessly varied—from the disintegration of Mycenaean civilization in the twelfth century to the beginnings of the Greek city-state in the middle of the eighth century B.C.E. These tales then continued to form the material of the epic and lyric poetry of the early Greek city-state as we see in Homer's *Iliad* and *Odyssey*, Hesiod's *Theogony* and *Works and Days*, and Pindar's *Victory Odes*.

This is a culture of song, performance, and oral recitation rather than of the written word. Indeed, books are relatively rare before the end of the fifth century. Because an oral culture has little concern for a fixed text, it also has no notion that a given myth must have one and only one definitive form. The bards would sing their mythic tales with many possible variants from performance to performance, and different versions would coexist from city to city and even within the same city. Hence, as we shall see in the next chapter, there are numerous variants in the myth of Oedipus.

In addition to the considerable body of epic and choral poetry that recounted the myths, sculptors and painters illustrated these stories, though to what extent they added their own interpretations and modifications is controversial. The pediments and metopes of the temples, terracotta tablets, sarcophagi, bronzes, and particularly the innumerable vases show how pervaded this culture was by its myths. As literary sources are often lost or fragmentary, these visual representations offer important evidence for early versions of the myths.

The myths had many functions in the cultural life of archaic and classical Greece (the period from approximately 750 to 350 B.C.E.). At a time when there is no other form of historical record, they are the repository of the past and retain the memory of great events and noteworthy deeds. These tales also embody the values and concerns central to the society. The Homeric epics in particular provide models for heroic behavior and for the ideal warrior and ruler, especially in an aristocratic society. Analogously, the tragedies, presented to the entire citizen body at the great civic festivals, are not just a major event in Athenian cultural life but a kind of mirror in which the city can view itself from the perspective of the whole heroic tradition and the values, ideals, and modes of behavior crystallized in the myths.

Although politics, in some form or other, is always in the background (see below), the tragedians are first of all mythmakers and storytellers as well as playwright-poets. They continue the work of Homer and Hesiod, speculating on the questions of the world order, divine justice, and human nature through their own versions of the ancient tales. They are thus part of the venerable tradition that runs from the *Iliad* through the *Argonautica* of Apollonius of Rhodes in the third century B.C.E. and on to Virgil's *Aeneid* and Ovid's *Metamorphoses* in the early Roman Empire. Neither they nor the poets who preceded them are interested in creating fictions; they prefer the traditional tales, with their centuries of encrusted meaning and authority.[4] The tragedies' mythical material gives them a perspective, seriousness, and universality comparable, say, to the historical themes of the Elizabethan theater. The grandeur and heroic elevation of the material are sustained by the lofty poetry, the elaborate costumes, and the intricate performance in dance and song by the chorus.

The convention of using mythical plots may seem constraining to us, but it probably did not feel so to a poet working in a highly traditional society whose members were accustomed to think in terms of the images and symbols of mythical narration. The tragedian could count on an informed and trained audience, and this fact doubtless contributed to the extraordinarily high quality of the works we have. During the great flowering of drama in fifth-century Athens, nearly a thousand tragedies were performed at the Great Dionysia, but of these only thirty-three survive complete. The audiences at the plays would know at least the outline of the plot, and they would both understand and delight in the special twists that each playwright gave his version. Many spectators, for example, knowing Aeschylus' plays, would appreciate Sophocles' innovations and understand why he told his Oedipus story in the way that he did.

TRAGEDY AND DEMOCRACY IN ATHENS

Drama is invented when the mythical tales are not just recited (as was the case with epic) but are acted out by living figures on the stage. This innovation is attributed to an obscure Athenian named Thespis and seems to have occurred in Athens at the very end of the sixth century. It meant a quantum leap in the immediacy and power with which the myths are felt by an audience. The new form is particularly well suited to the Athenian democracy, which began in the 490s, since the theater can publicly explore ethical and political controversies and reflect on the most urgent issues of the times. In adapting to a democratic audience the ancient tales about kings and proud aristocratic warriors obsessed with power, honor, and vengeance, the tragic poets transform them radically. This recasting of myth into dramatic form is unique to Athens, and it is surely not a coincidence that the democracy and the drama begin at about the same time.

By utilizing a structure of opposing characters, protagonist and antagonist, tragedy focuses the myths more sharply on conflict, on opposing principles and definitions, on questions of individual choice and responsibility, on the clash between public and private good and between competitive and cooperative virtues, and on the problem of the man of exceptional greatness in an egalitarian ideology. Both Aeschylus' Seven against Thebes and Sophocles' Oedipus, for example, open with a crisis for the city in which a leader standing before his citizens bears the responsibility for taking decisive action. Such situations would naturally appeal to an audience accustomed to seeing every major decision, whether political, legal, or financial, hammered out in debates and adversarial speeches in the assembly and the law courts.

20

Exactly how tragedy relates to the outlook of the democratic Athenian polis is controversial.[5] Whereas the comedies deal directly with political issues, the
mythical frame of tragedy establishes some distance from contemporary events.
It is sometimes claimed that the plays aim at reinforcing the democratic ideology of the city, but in the extant corpus only a very few plays seem to have an
overtly political agenda as their primary concern.[6] Most of the surviving plays,
though generally pro-Athenian and pro-democratic, present conflicts and problems for debate rather than clear ideological solutions or state propaganda. Euripides' *Hecuba* and *Trojan Women*, for example, must have raised questions about
the Athenian policy in conducting the Peloponnesian War. Several considerations bear on this more open and exploratory mood of tragedy. First, the festival of Dionysus has a carnival atmosphere in which the usual constraints on behavior and the normal structures of social life are suspended. Such an
atmosphere encourages thinking about the world in fresh ways and (as the comedies clearly show) radically questioning the existing order. Second, as Jeffrey
Henderson points out, the Periclean theater of Dionysus held an audience of
about 17,000, whereas the Pnyx, where the assembly of all the male citizens met,
could hold only about 6,000.[7] This fact suggests that those normally excluded
from full civic status and from full participation in running the state—women,
resident aliens, foreigners, slaves—might not only be present in the theater but
might even outnumber the male citizens. In that case the plays, both tragedies
and comedies, would be addressed in part to an audience of the excluded, the
"other," whose noncitizen point of view, for once, would be recognized. Third,
after a few experiments early in the fifth century (including Aeschylus' *Persians*),
the tragedians turned away from plays that dealt directly with contemporary
history and instead chose mythical subjects. The universalizing power of these
remote myths enables these works to transcend the contemporary issues that
may be in the background.

Whether or not women were present in the audience remains an unresolved
question, and the evidence is not decisive for the last half of the fifth century,
although it seems likely that by the early fourth century women did attend the
dramatic festivals.[8] Because women have no direct political power, are not supposed to be seen in public, and are regarded as inferior and subordinate to men,
they may well have been excluded from the dramatic performances. But if this
is so, why do women have such important and forceful roles in the tragedies?
Aeschylus' Clytaemnestra, Euripides' Medea, Sophocles' Deianeira and Electra
and, to some extent, Jocasta in the *Oedipus* would, one imagines, be of particular interest to women spectators. But of course the judges who decided on the
prizes were always men.

If the audience was entirely male, were these powerful female roles intended
to help men understand the women in their lives, or to bring into the open male
anxiety or guilt about their suppressed women folk, or to reinforce the preju-
dices about "bad women," or to help men explore their own masculinity, or to

21

reinforce or question the strong divisions between male and female roles in this gender-stratified society? These and many other solutions have been proposed, and discussion will continue to be intense, especially as our own sexual politics inevitably get engaged. The issue is not as central to *Oedipus* as it is to other tragedies, such as *Antigone, Trachinian Women, Medea,* or *Bacchae,* but it does color our view of Jocasta's role in the play.[9]

Nevertheless, if we view politics in the broad sense as concern for the nature of society in its relation both to the individual and the world order, then the political context is vital for understanding Athenian drama, and indeed all of Greek literature, and we shall see the implications for *Oedipus.*[10] When we go to the theater we expect an evening of private entertainment at a place and time of our choosing; in ancient Athens to go to the theater is to participate in a civic festival and to join with all of one's fellow citizens in probing the big questions of justice and injustice, evil and its punishment, social responsibility, the nature of the gods, the meaning of suffering. These are the issues that become the material of philosophy in the next century, but before the age of prose they still belong to the poets. In the centuries after Sophocles and Euripides, tragedies continue to be written and, along with the old plays, to be performed. The dramatic festivals are still elaborately supervised and eagerly attended. The proliferation of theaters throughout the Greek world in the fourth century and the frequent use of dramatic subjects to decorate vases, particularly in southern Italy, show that the popularity of tragedy has spread far beyond Athens. Yet the form has lost at least some of its innovative energy, and very little of postclassical tragedy survives.[11] Plato, who writes his dialogues in dramatic form, is in a sense the successor to the tragedians in a postmythical age.

NOTES

1. See Simon Goldhill, "The Great Dionysia and Civic Ideology," in John J. Winkler and F. Zeitlin, eds., *Nothing to Do with Dionysus?* (Princeton: Princeton University Press, 1990), 97–129, especially 98–106.

2. For a discussion of the problem of the low raised platform for the main actors see, for example, the summary in Arthur W. Pickard-Cambridge, *The Theater of Dionysus at Athens* (Oxford: Oxford University Press, 1946), 68–74; H.C. Baldry, *The Greek Tragic Theater* (London: Chatto and Windus, 1971) 43–45; Rush Rehm, *Greek Tragic Theatre* (London: Routledge, 1992), 34–36; Eric Csapo and William J. Slater, *The Context of Ancient Drama* (Ann Arbor: University of Michigan Press, 1995), 80. See also Stephen Scully, "Orchestra and Stage in Sophocles: *Oedipus Tyrannus* and the Theater of Dionysus," *Syllecta Classica* 10 (1999): 65–74, who argues for the raised stage. R. Drew Griffith, *The Theatre of Apollo: Divine Justice and Sophocles' Oedipus the King* (Montreal and Kingston: McGill-Queen's University Press, 1996), 14–28, has a useful scene-by-scene discussion of the staging of the *Oedipus.*

3. For a useful collection of the scraps of evidence and the bits of music that do survive, see Csapo and Slater (above, n. 2), pp. 331–48 and plate 21.

4. A few plays on contemporary subjects, however, were composed early in the fifth century, probably as a result of the stirring historical events of the Persian War. Aeschylus' *Persians* (472 B.C.E.) is the sole surviving example.

5. For a recent overview, with bibliography, see Suzanne Saïd, "Tragedy and Politics," in Deborah Boedeker and Kurt A. Raaflaub, eds., *Democracy, Empire, and the Arts in Fifth-Century Athens* (Cambridge: Harvard University Press, 1999), 275–95; for a more polemical discussion, see Jasper Griffin, "The Social Function of Attic Tragedy," *Classical Quarterly* 48 (1998), 39–61.

6. The most commonly cited examples of such political plays are the so-called patriotic plays of Euripides, such as the *Erectheus*, *Children of Heracles* (*Heracleidae*), and *Suppliant Women*. Yet, as recent interpreters have noted, even these plays are not so straightforward in their endorsement of Athenian civic ideology as they might at first seem; see, for example, Stephen Scully's Introduction in S. Scully and Rosanna Warren, trans., *Euripides: Suppliant Women* (New York: Oxford University Press, 1995), 3–18, especially 10–18.

7. See Jeffrey Henderson, "Women and the Athenian Dramatic Festivals," *Transactions of the American Philological Association* 121 (1991), 136–37. One can, however, argue that the size of the theater was intended to accommodate only the entire male citizen population (adult free Athenian males over 18), whose number is estimated at about 30,000.

8. A strong case for women's presence in the theater is made by Henderson, 133–47. For recent discussion, see also Anthony J. Podlecki, "Could Women Attend the Theatre in Ancient Athens? A Collection of Testimonia," *Ancient World* 21 (1990), 27–43; Synnøve Des Bouvrie, *Women in Greek Tragedy. Symbolae Osloenses*, Supplement 27, (Oxford, 1990), 86–90; Simon Goldhill, "Representing Democracy: Women at the Great Dionysia," in Robin Osborne and Simon Hornblower, eds., *Ritual, Finance, Politics: Athenian Democratic Accounts Presented to David Lewis* (Oxford: Oxford University Press, 1994), 347–69.

9. See below, Chapter 12, end.

10. For this broad sense of the political meaning of Greek tragedy, see Christian Meier, *The Political Art of Greek Tragedy* (Baltimore: Johns Hopkins University Press, 1994), and the books of Peter Euben and Christopher Rocco cited in the Bibliography.

11. For postclassical tragedy, see P. E. Easterling, "From Repertoire to Canon," in P. E. Easterling, ed., *Cambridge Companion to Greek Tragedy* (Cambridge: Cambridge University Press, 1997), 211–27.

4

The Oedipus Myth and Its Interpretation

The Myth before Sophocles

The myth of Oedipus is very old and formed part of a series (or cycle) of epics about Thebes In *Works and Days* (between 740 and 700 B.C.E.) Hesiod refers in passing to the heroes of old who fought "at seven-gated Thebes over the flocks of Oedipus" (lines 162–63), a possible reference to the struggle between Oedipus' two sons for the throne after their father's death. In the *Iliad*, Homer mentions "the grave of Oedipus who had fallen in battle" (23.679–80), a version of the story that suggests that Oedipus continues to rule in Thebes and is honored at his death. Presumably too he is not blind.

Our fullest early account of the myth occurs in the *Odyssey*. Odysseus, recounting his adventures in the palace of the Phaeacians, tells how he saw the famous heroines in the underworld, among whom is Jocasta, here called Epicaste:

> And I saw the beautiful Epicaste, Oedipus' mother,
> who in the ignorance of her mind had done a monstrous
> thing and married her own son. He killed his father
> and married her, but the gods soon made it all known to mortals.
> But he, for all his sorrows, in beloved Thebes continued
> to be lord over the Cadmeans, all through the bitter designing
> of the gods; while she went down to Hades of the gates, the strong one,
> knotting a noose and hanging sheer from the high ceiling,
> in the constraint of her sorrow, but left to him who survived her
> all the sorrows that are brought to pass by a mother's Furies.
>
> (Lattimore's translation, 11.271–80)

This version says nothing about the oracles, the self-blinding, or the couple's children, but it does give a prominent place to the gods' intervention, with suggestions of divine malevolence or cruelty. It vividly depicts Jocasta's suffering in the "sorrow" that accompanies her suicide, a small anticipation of the tragic form that her story would find in the hands of the dramatists. The Furies (in Greek, the Erinyes) are dreaded underworld deities who fulfill family curses and are the avengers of murder within the family. Their presence here does not necessarily mean that Jocasta curses Oedipus at her death, but the family curse is there as a motif for Aeschylus to develop. Homer may have deliberately omitted the incestuously born children; his epic grandeur tends to shun such ugly details.

The family curse, as we shall see, will be important for Aeschylus, but it is already prominent in the epics about Thebes, which were composed between the seventh and fifth centuries B.C.E. but drew on older material. In these poems, Oedipus' two sons, Eteocles and Polyneices, quarrel bitterly over the kingdom of Thebes when he leaves the throne. Polyneices enlists the help of Adrastus, king of Argos, and returns to Thebes with six other chiefs to take the kingdom by force. The expedition fails, and in the attack the two brothers kill one another at the gates of Thebes. Their fratricidal self-slaughter is the result of a curse from their father.

One of the Theban epics, the *Oedipodeia*, known only from late summaries and a few fragments, told how Oedipus has his children by a second wife, Euryganeia. Another Theban epic, the *Thebais*, also lost, told how Oedipus in anger curses his sons because he feels that they dishonored him by giving him a meaner cut of meat at a sacrifice and wine in the cup of his murdered father, Laius. A recently recovered papyrus fragment attributed to the lyric poet Stesichorus (who flourished in southern Italy at the beginning of the sixth century B.C.E.) contains a speech in which a mother (who may be Jocasta) tries to dissuade her sons from civil war by suggesting that one take the kingdom, the other the movable property.[1] Here too the prophet Teiresias foretells the sons' doom from oracles of Apollo. If the woman speaking is indeed Jocasta, not Oedipus' second, nonincestuous wife, Euryganeia, the passage shows the beginnings of the tragic conception of this figure, already implicit in the *Odyssey* passage above, that Sophocles will develop.

The most important pre-Sophoclean treatment of the myth is Aeschylus' trilogy of 467 B.C.E., which comprised *Laius*, *Oedipus*, and *Seven against Thebes*, the last referring to the warriors whom the exiled brother, Polyneices, leads against the city. The accompanying satyr-play, *Sphinx*, dramatized Oedipus' victory over that monster. Only the *Seven against Thebes* survives, but references and quotations in later writers provide evidence for the first two plays. In *Laius*, Aeschylus probably told the story of Laius' love for Pelops' son, Chrysippus. Laius carries the boy off, and Chrysippus, in shame, commits suicide, whereupon his father calls down on Laius the curse that eventually destroys his house.[2] Aeschylus traces this curse over the three generations of Laius' family, with one generation per play. His *Oedipus* probably covered much of the same ground as Sophocles' play, and we shall turn to it soon. The *Seven* ends with the death of the two brothers at one another's hands and the resolve of Antigone to defy Creon's decree forbidding burial of Eteocles—an ending sometimes suspected of having been added to the play much later, under the influence of Sophocles' *Antigone* of 442 B.C.E.

Whereas Aeschylus emphasizes the Fury and the family curse (the Fury is the "all-true evil prophet" of disaster for the house of Oedipus, *Seven against Thebes*, 720–26), Sophocles has only a passing reference to the Fury, and even here he subordinates supernatural agency to the play of human emotions. At the peak of his anger Teiresias alludes to the Fury as he shouts to Oedipus, "The double-smiting, dread-footed curse of your mother and father will drive you from this land" (417–18). The language recalls Aeschylus' *Seven against Thebes* (70, 791), where curse and Fury are closely associated. Sophocles, however, does not actually mention the Fury by name; he instead emphasizes the oracles and brings their mysterious power onstage in the person of Teiresias, whose seeing blindness also keeps the problem of knowledge in the foreground.[3]

The only acts common to all the early versions of the myth of Oedipus are the killing of his father and the incestuous marriage. Stesichorus may be the first poet to make Oedipus and Jocasta the incestuous parents of the children; as we have observed, Homer omits any reference to the children; and the Theban epics have them born from his second wife, Euryganeia.[4] Oedipus' self-blinding appears for the first time in Aeschylus' trilogy and was probably described in its second play, the lost *Oedipus*. This detail adds to the horror of the discovery and the destructive power of the family curse. The chorus in the *Seven against Thebes* is probably referring to the preceding play of the trilogy when it tells how Oedipus blinded himself when he became aware of his past:

> But when in misery he knew
> the meaning of his dreadful marriage,
> in pain distraught, in heart distracted
> he brought a double sorrow to fulfillment.
> With patricidal hand
> he reft himself of eyes
> that dearer to him were than his own children.
> And on those children savage
> maledictions he launched
> for their cruel tendance of him
> and wished they might divide
> with iron-wielding hand his own possession.
> And now I fear
> that nimble-footed Fury bring those wishes to fulfillment.

> (Grene's translation, 778–91)

In Aeschylus' *Oedipus* the climax seems to have been the hero's curse on his sons rather than the self-blinding, but the self-blinding implies a new conception of Oedipus' story. Homer's Oedipus, despite suffering, is able to continue as king and even as warrior. Aeschylus' Oedipus is not allowed to continue his life in undiminished power. The incest and parricide arouse a horror and a guilt that drive him to this terrible self-mutilation.

The plague is not mentioned in the myth before Sophocles, and it may well be his invention. It too attaches a strong feeling of horror and pollution to Oedipus' deeds. Incest and parricide, though committed in ignorance, are so deep a violation of the world order that nature responds with sterility and disease. This is a logical development of the Aeschylean view, but it also focuses more sharply on the individual hero. Sophocles may have been influenced as well by the plague that broke out in Athens in 430.

Oedipus' unique intellectual power and his mysterious god-given destiny, enunciated in the oracles, belong to his individual situation as Sophocles conceives it. Blindness and vision, the recognition of ignorance, knowledge, and discovery are also part of Sophocles' distinctive slant on the myth. As in Aeschylus, however, the hero's suffering is not just a personal tragedy; through the crisis in the city and in nature caused by the plague, it is inseparably linked to the political order and the world order.

Although the oracles are important both in Aeschylus and in the lyric poet Pindar, Aeschylus' contemporary, Sophocles is the first to make them a leitmotif of the plot. He is also the first to make the road between Delphi and Thebes the setting for the fatal encounter. Aeschylus, too, used the motif of the ominous triple road, but he located the killing of Laius not on the way to Apollo's oracles at Delphi but at a place called Potniae, south of Thebes, in the direction away from Delphi, where there was a shrine of Demeter and Kore and possibly of the Furies.

The Furies may have had an important role in Aeschylus' *Oedipus*, as they do, for instance, in his *Oresteia*. But he did not invent this part of the myth. The Fury, as we have seen, already occurs in Homer's version in the *Odyssey*. About ten years before Aeschylus' *Seven against Thebes*, the Theban poet Pindar in his *Olympian Odes* alluded to a version that combines the oracle and the family curse:

> And so Moira [the assigned portion], who holds the kindly destiny that belongs to this paternal line, brings some woe too along with the god-sent wealth, which reverses itself in turn at another time; from the time *when the destined son [Oedipus] killed Laius, when he encountered him,* and so he brought to fulfillment *the ancient oracle spoken at Delphi.* But the *keen-eyed Fury destroyed his warlike race in mutual slaughter;* yet to Polyneices when he fell there was left behind [his son] Thersander, who gained honor in the youthful athletic contests and in the battles of war . . . (Pindar, *Olympian Odes* 2.35–45 [my emphasis]).

Pindar here closely associates the oracle given to Oedipus at Delphi with the continuation of the family curse, from which result the fratricidal deaths of Oedipus' two sons, Polyneices and Eteocles. Sophocles mentioned the family curse in *Antigone*, some twelve to fifteen years before *Oedipus*. The *Oedipus* changes this part of the myth not only by suppressing the old family curse but also by having the hero respond to his discovery of the truth with tenderness and concern for his children, not with a curse (*Oedipus* 1459ff.). Sophocles' change here may even imply a deliberate criticism of Aeschylus' work.

Although Sophocles does not neglect the divine background (no Greek dramatist does), he is more interested than Aeschylus in purely human motivation. Telling the myth in a single play rather than through a trilogy, he cannot trace the continuity of a family curse over three generations as Aeschylus does. He must concentrate on the events in the foreground and can only suggest or hint at the past or the future. Telling the story across a trilogy, Aeschylus draws on the archaic belief, emphasized by the poets Hesiod and Solon (late eighth and late seventh centuries B.C.E., respectively), that the gods will eventually punish transgression but no one knows how long this may take or who may be the ones to pay. Sophocles, treating the myth in the single play, turns this mysteriousness of divine justice and punishment into a tense drama of personal discovery.

For this reason too, Sophocles' treatment of the oracle to Laius is very different from Aeschylus'. In Aeschylus' play, Laius seems to have received the oracle many years before the birth of Oedipus, and it takes the form of a warning that he must remain childless if he wishes to save his city. But as Aeschylus' chorus reviews the tale in *Seven against Thebes*, Laius "was mastered by loving folly / and begot for himself a doom, / father-murdering Oedipus. / [...] Madness was the coupler / of this distracted pair" (Grene's translation, 740–57).

Sophocles narrows the temporal perspective of the oracle, eliminates any reference to the curse on the house of Laius, and so makes the oracle a purely personal matter involving only the father and son. Instead of being a warning, the oracle is an inescapable fact of Laius' life: "His portion will come, to meet death from a son who is born from me and him," is Jocasta's report of the oracle in *Oedipus* 713–14. She repeats this formulation some hundred lines later : "Apollo said that he (Laius) must meet death from his son" (854). When Oedipus defies Teiresias' prophecy of doom with the line, "But if I saved this city I do not care" (*Oedipus* 443), there may be an intentional contrast between the civic concern of the son and the foolish and imperious self-centeredness of Aeschylus' Laius.

The oracle makes its first appearance in Sophocles' play as a feature of Jocasta's skepticism, and this is in keeping with Sophocles' interest in character. Recalling the oracle about her lost son, Jocasta wants to prove Delphi's unreliability (711–12). Here too Sophocles focuses on human responses rather than on divine power. But it is noteworthy how little Jocasta says about the circumstances in which Laius heard his oracle. Because this oracle does not involve a choice, as it does in Aeschylus, Sophocles can be deliberately vague about the details. With the severe economy that is the hallmark of his art—and of classical art generally—Sophocles restricts the oracle to its most essential effect, driving the parents to put their child out to die. At the same time, Sophocles' use of the oracular motif leaves the role of the gods suggestively and mysteriously

28

in the background. Sophocles, moreover, as we shall see, combines this oracle to Laius with several other prophecies in the play, the oracle about the plague at the beginning, Teiresias' prophecies about Oedipus' future, and Oedipus' own fearful oracle foretelling his incest and parricide.

A chance quotation by an ancient grammarian and a line in Aristophanes enable us to see another Sophoclean innovation, namely the manner of Oedipus' exposure. In Aeschylus, the baby is put out in a terra-cotta pot—at the time a not-uncommon way of practicing this cruel form of population control.[5] Sophocles adds the detail that Laius pierces the feet, presumably to discourage passersby from rescuing the child, and this is the first time that this motif appears in the myth.[6] It brings into the story the Old Herdsman and the Corinthian Messenger, both essential to Sophocles' new focus on the search for a hidden truth about the hero's identity. Perhaps too it emphasizes the futility of the parents' attempt to prevent the saving of the child by this disfigurement and hence to evade the oracle.

The emotional charge that Sophocles gives to the motif of exposing the infant suggests that he may be exploring the guilty feelings that parents would have over this practice. In Euripides' *Ion*, some fifteen years later, a mother's self-accusation and remorse lasts all her life. The young Ion, like Oedipus, is intensely concerned about his mother's exposure of him as a newborn, and, like Oedipus at the discovery, he also calls attention to what the mother's feelings would have been (compare *Ion* 1369–79 and *Oedipus* 1173–75). Both of these passages, so concerned with maternal emotions, might have more point if women were present at the dramatic performances. Sophocles, like his contemporary and friend Herodotus in his accounts of infanticide, allows pity for the exposed infant.[7] From the parents' point of view, the oracle that their child will commit incest and parricide may reflect the natural anxiety about producing a son with criminal tendencies (in contemporary terms, a sociopath) in a time when rearing any child meant risk and hardship.[8]

OEDIPUS TRAGEDIES IN THE LATE FIFTH CENTURY

Sophocles was not the last tragedian to put the myth of Oedipus on the stage. We know of at least six other plays about Oedipus by fifth-century dramatists; all of them are lost.[9] Euripides wrote an *Oedipus*, probably a dozen or so years after Sophocles, but only fragments survive. He seems to have opened the play with the Aeschylean motif of Apollo's forbidding Laius to beget a child. He also has Oedipus blinded by the escort of Laius, presumably in punishment for his killing of the king.

Euripides' *Ion* (414–412 B.C.E.), as we have observed, has many points of contact with Sophocles' play. The plot tells how the foundling Ion, now an adolescent temple servant at Delphi, discovers his parents, but this story ends happily and has a much lighter tone than *Oedipus*. Apollo is also present in the back-

ground and is also ambiguous, but in a very different way from Sophocles'
Apollo. He is shown both as a cruel and selfish rapist who attacked Creusa in
the cave of Pan on the Acropolis and as a helpful savior god who saw to it that
their child, Ion, would survive and gain his royal heritage. Euripides changes
the focus of his foundling story to the instinctive feeling that the separated pair
have for one another at their first meeting and to the mother's life-long grief
over the loss of her son. He thus explores just the features of the mother's story
that Sophocles leaves vague, the painful decision to expose her infant and the
emotional price she pays for this act.

Like Oedipus, Ion eventually learns the truth about his paternity, but his relation with his mother dominates the action. The aggressiveness between parent and child also focuses on the mother rather than the father, first in Creusa's
unsuccessful plot to poison Ion, when she thinks that he is her husband's bastard and not her own child, and then at the end, when Ion accuses her of the
murder and is about to have her put to death. Fortunately, their true relation is
revealed by birth tokens, and the catastrophe is averted. In many places, the *Ion*
seems to be harking back self-consciously to Sophocles' play. Through these verbal echoes Euripides may be trying to call attention to his very different han-
dling of a tale of exposure and discovery.[10]

In his comedy *Frogs* (405 B.C.E.), Aristophanes presents a literary competition between Euripides and Aeschylus in Hades, in which Euripides' *Oedipus*
figures prominently. Euripides quotes the first line of his play, "Oedipus at the
outset was a fortunate man," which Aeschylus then criticizes as follows:

> By god, he was not. He was the most *un*fortunate
> from birth. Before birth, since Apollo prophesied
> before he was even begotten, that he would kill his father.
> How could he have been, at the outset, *fortunate*?[11]

Euripides then quotes his second line, "But then he became the wretchedest of
humankind." And again Aeschylus offers criticism:

> He didn't *become* the wretchedest. He never stopped.
> Look here. First thing that happened after he was born
> they put him in a broken pot and laid him out in the snow
> so he'd never grow up to be his father's murderer.
> Then he went to Polybus, *with swollen feet*, wasn't that luck?
> and then he married an old lady, though he was young,
> and also the old lady turned out to be his mother,
> and then he blinded himself . . .

The phrase "with swollen feet" (*oidôn tô pode*) is a pun on the name "Oedipus"
and confirms the importance of this kind of wordplay in Sophocles' play. In
addition to offering the detail about the exposure in the pot, this passage also

shows the popular view of the Oedipus myth as the tale of the greatest possible misfortune.

In one of his last plays, the *Phoenician Women* (ca. 409 B.C.E.), Euripides returns to the myth of Oedipus, but his main subject, like Aeschylus' *Seven against Thebes*, is the murderous struggle for Thebes by Oedipus' two sons. It is now many years since Oedipus' discovery of the truth and his self-blinding, but Jocasta has not committed suicide, and Oedipus is living in the palace. Jocasta speaks the prologue and summarizes the past. Though basically following the Sophoclean version, Euripides adds some new details. As in Aeschylus, Laius is warned by the oracle not to beget a child or he will destroy both himself and his house; but he yields to "drunkenness and pleasure" and sires Oedipus (*Phoenician Women*, 18–22).

Like Sophocles, Euripides makes father and son meet at the crossroads, but he adds the vivid detail that Laius' horses trample and bloody Oedipus' feet. Thus he follows Sophocles in making the father initiate the aggression, but he replaces Laius' blow at the son's head (*Oedipus* 807–09) with another wounding of his feet—an act that suggestively repeats Laius' violence against the infant Oedipus. Oedipus then brings Laius' chariot back to Corinth as a gift for his supposed father, Polybus (*Phoenician Women*, 42–45). Such examples show how much freedom Greek dramatists could take with the details of a myth and how much they enjoyed adding small variations. Euripides also fills in the details about Laius' oracle that Sophocles omits. He has Laius consult Delphi because he and Jocasta have been childless for many years (14–16). He is also more precise about how the exposed infant is adopted by King Polybus, adding the detail (possibly borrowed from Herodotus' story of Cyrus the Great) that Polybus' wife passed the baby off as her own.[12]

Almost a century afer Sophocles' play, the famous Cynic philosopher Diogenes (around 350 B.C.E.), takes an irreverent view of the Oedipus myth. Advocate of a life of unencumbered, primitive simplicity, even at the cost of uncouth or unconventional behavior, Diogenes uses Oedipus to shock his audience out of complacency. Oedipus, he suggests, should have just kept quiet about the incest or else made it lawful in Thebes. Diogenes then goes on to point out that animals commit incest all the time—to which Sophocles might reply that the point is precisely that we are not animals.[13]

Diogenes' remark reminds us that Oedipus is not the only myth about incest in Greek literature. In the myths about the early phases of the world order in Hesiod's *Theogony*, for example, incestuous unions and offspring are common and express the still evolving state of the world order. Many of these incestuous unions, moreover, produce monstrous creatures, like the Sphinx. Although Homeric epic tends to avoid the kind of pollutions and familial violence that incest brings, Phoenix in the *Iliad* tells of his violent quarrel with his father because (at his mother's request) he slept with his father's concubine (*Iliad* 9.448–77). A controversial passage in Phoenix's tale even has him come close to parricide (9.458–61).[14] Incest and parricide also come together in the (probably) late sixth-century continuation of the Odysseus myth, the *Telegoneia*, attributed to Eugammon of Cyrene. Here Telegonus, son of Odysseus by Circe, unknowingly kills his father and then marries his father's wife (but not his own mother), Penelope.

Closer to Sophocles's play is Euripides' *Hippolytus* of 428 B.C.E., possibly influenced by the *Tyrannus*, which tells of Phaedra's passion for her stepson, the virginal hunter Hippolytus. This is, in a sense, the *Oedipus* in reverse: the criminal passion (which legally is incest) is focused primarily on the woman; and it is the father, in his wrathful vengeance, who brings about his son's death. A number of Greek tragedies recounted the incestuous union of Thyestes, brother of Agamemnon, with his daughter. In Euripides' *Andromache*, produced around 425 B.C.E. and so roughly contemporary with *Oedipus*, Hermione, the spoiled and shrewish Spartan wife of Neoptolemus, Achilles' son, attacks her rival, the Trojan captive Andromache, now Neoptolemus' concubine, with the accusation that incest and murder within the family are common practice among "barbarians" (i.e., non-Greeks): "The father has intercourse with his daughter, the son with his mother, the sister with her brother, and the closest kin murder one another, and no law prevents any of this" (173–76). Euripides is exploiting the Athenians' anti-Spartan feelings, as well as their full awareness that this girl's family includes Atreus, Thyestes, Agamemnon, and Clytaemnestra.

In the centuries after Sophocles, Hellenistic writers were fond of illicit and pathological love stories involving incest. Drawing on Hellenistic writers, Ovid's *Metamorphoses* relates the incestuous love of Byblis for her brother Caunus and of Myrrha for her father Cinyras (9.450–665, 10.298–518). The collection of *Erotic Adventures* (*Erôtika Pathêmata*) by the Greek writer Parthenius, contemporary of Virgil, relates the incestuous love affair between Periander, tyrant of Corinth in the sixth century B.C.E., and his mother (Chapter 17). Indeed incest was commonly attributed to tyrants, as a mark of their excess and license, from Periander to the Roman emperor Nero. These stories, like the Oedipus myth, usually end in disaster. According to Parthenius, for example, Periander goes mad, and his mother commits suicide.

RIDDLE, KINSHIP, AND LANGUAGE IN THE OEDIPUS MYTH

For Aeschylus and Sophocles the riddle of the Sphinx is a fundamental part of the Oedipus myth. The earliest reference to the Sphinx, however, is in Hesiod (end of the eighth century, B.C.E., who describes the Sphinx as a monster that afflicts Thebes (*Theogony* 326–32); but in his account its slayer is Heracles, and there is no riddle. The connection of the Sphinx with Oedipus cannot in fact be found any earlier than about 525 B.C.E., judging from vase paintings. The story of his encounter with the Sphinx seems not to have become popular in Athens before the period 470–450 B.C.E. (see Figures 1 and 2). In another version of the story that also may be relatively late (i.e., not much before the fifth century B.C.E.),

Hera sends the Sphinx to punish Thebes for Laius' rape of Chrysippus. It has been argued that the Sphinx is a sixth-century addition to the kernel of the Oedipus myth, perhaps added under Delphic influence, which would emphasize the motifs of oracle, knowledge, and intelligence. Against this view is the new evidence of a black-figure vase from around 520 that not only shows the scene but also gives the text of the riddle in archaic language that suggests the antiquity of both riddle and Sphinx.[15]

In various versions of the myth, both literary and pictorial, the Sphinx preys on young men, carrying them off in a deadly, quasi-erotic embrace and devouring them. Thus she is a particular danger in the male passage to adulthood. In other tales of this kind, however, the solver of the riddle wins a royal bride and lives happily ever after. By succeeding against the Sphinx, Oedipus wins a bride and kingdom, but he also gains bitter unhappiness. Some versions of the story have the defeated Sphinx plunging from a high place to her death, and some interpreters have suggested parallels between this and Jocasta's suicide, viewing the Sphinx, therefore, as a figure for the evil, devouring mother who blocks the son's path to maturity. The word *sphinx* may be related to the Greek verb *sphingein*, to "constrict" or "strangle" (see *sphincter*). The etymology would be appropriate to her function as a demon of death. Little of this aspect of the myth is visible in Sophocles, however, although he does suggest parallels between the supernatural sayings that Oedipus can solve (the Sphinx's riddle) and those that he cannot (Apollo's oracles).

Sophocles' version of the Oedipus story is built in part on a structure of opposites that fuse into one another. He exploits a certain logic encoded into the myth and expressed through the succession of generations. From Oedipus' father, Laius, to his sons, Polyneices and Eteocles, the myth moves from homosexual rape to threatened childlessness and then to incest and the father's deadly curse on his sons. The open prohibition of marital intercourse in Laius' generation leads to excessively fertile intercourse in the next generation and then to a surplus of children in the incestuous begetting of two sons who fight for what only one can inherit. Oedipus' marriage contrasts with Laius' (overabundance of children versus threatened childlessness), but is also parallel to it in the transgressive nature of the sexual union it contains: the oracle to Laius prohibiting children is analogous to the oracle to Oedipus foretelling his crime against father and mother that will produce incestuous children.

This is a family whose closeness can only turn inward, against itself. The members are either too close (Oedipus and Jocasta) or too distant (Oedipus and Laius). Indeed the brothers, Polyneices and Eteocles, become simultaneously too close *and* too distant, for each claims his father's heritage within the house, and each treats the other as an enemy in a mutually destructive battle at the gate just outside the city. Laius' line appropriately comes to an end in the third generation when the brothers turn their "excess" of kinship to fratricidal slaughter, which is equivalent to incest in its violation of blood bonds. The two sisters, Antigone and Ismene, behave in a way parallel to the two brothers: Antigone

Figure 1 Oedipus and the Sphinx. Nolan Amphora, 450–440 B.C.E. Courtesy, Museum of Fine Arts, Boston. Bequest of Mrs. Martin Brimmer.

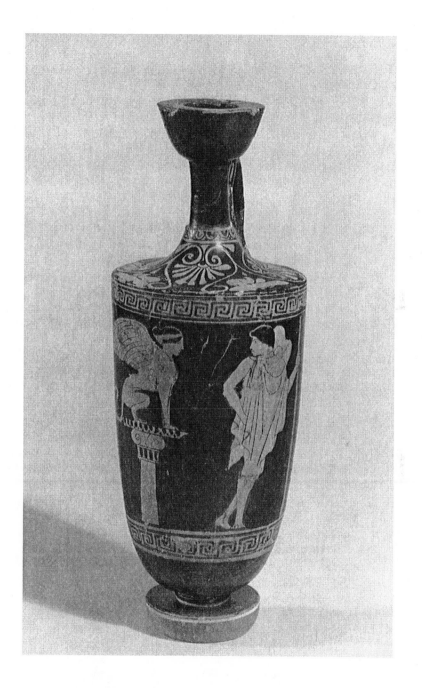

Figure 2 Sphinx and Youth (Oedipus?). Attic Red-figured
Lekythos, ca. 460 B.C.E. The Art Museum, Princeton University.
Gift of Edward Sampson for the Alden Sampson Collection.

commits suicide after her determined attempt to bury one of her fallen brothers in defiance of Creon's decree (the subject of the *Antigone*); in other early versions of the myth both Antigone and Ismene are killed. The *Antigone* also tells how Creon's son, in love with Antigone, turns against his father in a parricidal gesture that harks back to Oedipus and Laius (*Antigone* 1231–34), as if contact with Oedipus' house brings the same destructive pattern into Creon's.

The myth offered rich possiblities for exploring the analogies between kinship and language as parallel forms of order and stability, which the tragic events of Oedipus' life destroy. In Oedipus' life story the ambiguity of language is both causally and metaphorically related to the confusion of kinship, since Oedipus' multiple generational ties confuse his kin roles (son and husband to his mother, father and brother to his children), and these are a model for linguistic ambiguity in general. Both in its overall pattern and in its specific incidents, Oedipus' life is an anomalous coincidence of progress and regress. This is expressed through the repeated motifs of feet and movement. Instead of simply passing by his father on the road (of life) and letting the older man follow his own road (see *Oedipus* 800–12), Oedipus stopped his father's journey and replaced him, making his own journey forward to a new home, wife, and kingdom coincide with his father's uncompleted journey back to his old home, wife, and kingdom.

The Sphinx, possessing wings, paws, and a human face, is herself a living riddle and so is the appropriate figure to stand over the confused locomotion of Oedipus' life. The earliest form of the riddle that comes down to us uses feet to ask about the different generations of mankind: "There is on earth a being two-footed, four-footed, and three-footed that has one name [literally, one voice]; and, of all creatures that move upon earth and in the heavens and in the sea, it alone changes its form. But when it goes propped on most feet, then is the swiftness in its limbs the weakest." The riddle points to the precarious, changing nature of man: of all creatures he alone uses his intelligence to change his mode of locomotion as he progresses through life. As the very existence of the riddle implies, he alone is conscious of his uniqueness in nature. Oedipus, as self-aware, intelligent Man, is the solver of his own riddle. Indeed his name, in one possible etymology, suggests the meaning "Know Foot" (*oida*, "I know," and *pous*, "foot")—that is, "He who knows the riddle of the feet."

The riddle also combines man's power and weakness and so points to Oedipus in a very different sense, because he is the most contradictory of men in his combination of intelligence and ignorance. His essence, therefore, is even more unstable than the shifting identity of generic "man." He can answer the riddle because he is its hidden subject. Indeed, the Sphinx's word for "two-footed," *dipous*, the riddle's first item, evokes the name of Oe-*dipous*. But even his two-footedness is precarious, for he walks through life on the pierced feet that were "yoked" together to prevent him from walking at all, and he struck his father down with the staff that is his "third foot" (see Oedipus 810–12).[16]

Only Sophocles presents his hero struggling with riddles, and these are essential to the Sophoclean interpretation of the myth. Oedipus both answers and acts out the riddle's answer, for he is himself the quintessence of the being to whom the riddle points. The answer to the riddle is both "Man" and "Oedipus." Oedipus gives the first answer to the Sphinx in the events before the play begins, and he gives the second answer to us, the audience, within the play. But of course both answers are intertwined, as Oedipus is Sophocles' model of Tragic Man. It is his—and Man's—fundamental nature always to be a riddle to himself and never to be reducible to a single, sure meaning. Hence the riddle-like ambiguities of language in the play are not just a surface effect of Sophocles' poetry; they are also an expression of the tragic meaning. Sophocles' genius lay in his ability to crystallize the myth's tragic paradoxes in the ambiguities and ironies of his language and plot and to interweave these ironies so richly with the issues of knowledge and self-discovery, illusion and reality, and the meaning or nonsense of life.

SOME MODERN INTERPRETATIONS OF THE OEDIPUS MYTH

The systematic study of myth in the nineteenth century brought a number of interpretations to the Oedipus myth, including the famous interpretation of Sigmund Freud, which we shall presently discuss. Only some of the nineteenth-century readings are relevant to Sophocles' play. Interpreters do not always distinguish clearly between the play and the myth as it occurs outside the play. This distinction becomes even harder to make because we must recognize that the Oedipus myth today is to some extent a modern construct produced by synthesizing and analyzing the total narrative pattern that emerges when we put all the variants together into a single, composite story. Furthermore, many of the older versions have been lost or have left only scant traces. Sophocles' three Oedipus plays, *Oedipus Tyrannus*, *Antigone*, and *Oedipus at Colonus*, have become *sources* for the myth as well as *versions* and even *interpretations* of the myth. Additionally, in a living oral culture like that of early Greece a given myth has many possible forms: it is a configuration of narrative elements that lends itself to a different selection and elaboration of details each time it is told. For these reasons, it is probably futile to try to reconstruct the "original myth." These considerations, however, have not stopped scholars from speculating—a harmless enough activity, as long as one is clear about whether the *play* or the *myth* (or both) is the subject of speculation.

Hegel, the nineteenth-century German philosopher, approached the myth in terms of the development of human consciousness and saw in the figure of Oedipus Western man's dawning moral and intellectual self-awareness. Oedipus shows the emergence of an ethical sense and an acknowledgment of guilt after the lack of consciousness of committing a crime.[17] Friedrich Nietzsche viewed Oedipus as the paradigm of man's guilt about his power to dominate nature. To solve the riddle of the Sphinx, he suggests, is to solve "the riddle of nature." The "unnatural acts" of incest and parricide show wisdom itself as an "unnatural crime," through which man does violence to nature, forcing her to "yield up her secrets" (*Birth of Tragedy*, section 9).

Both the Hegelian and Nietzschean positions share a view of Oedipus as emblematic of the progress of Western consciousness. In his quest for self-knowledge and his destruction of the Sphinx by answering her riddle, Oedipus embodies the intellectual and moral courage to break with a sacral, traditional past, which Freud will view as the act of killing the father. Oedipus thereby embarks on a journey of moral and rational independence that will lead to a human-centered definition of knowledge and so to the development of Western science and philosophy.

Both Hegel and Nietzsche also hint at the other, negative side of this development in the residue of tragic guilt, which is the area of the myth that Freud will develop. As Jean-Joseph Goux, elaborating on the Nietzschean view suggested recently, Oedipus' break with traditional, sacral patterns and his human-centered solution to the Sphinx's riddle constitute an act of intellectual hubris that is all the more violent because it is without help from the gods (*Oedipus* 393–98). Hence it will lead to a divided consciousness, to the division between the conscious and unconscious. When Freud, therefore, "discovers" the oedipus complex, he is in fact discovering the "oedipal" condition of the Western psyche after the Greeks.[18] Oedipus, then, is the model for the liberation from an archaic dependency on a god-centered, hieratic worldview and also for the conflicted, guilt-ridden, divided mental condition that results from that liberation.

These symbolic interpretations place the myth in the broad perspective of the history of Western consciousness. At the opposite extreme are attempts at a more specific historicization in the past. The British historian of classical religion, H. J. Rose, finds in the myth the kernel of a historical narrative about kings in Mycenaean Thebes. The Russian folklorist Vladimir Propp suggests that the myth reflects the transition between a matrilinear and a patrilinear mode of succession. It develops, he argues, at a point of historical change from inheriting the kingship through the mother to gaining it through the father. The killing of a king by the husband of his daughter is a common folklore motif (e.g., in the hero myths of Pelops or Perseus, which we shall discuss in Chapter 5). In stories of the Oedipus type, however, the son, not the son-in-law, is the subject of dangerous omens and prophecies and the one who is feared as the old king's killer.[19]

Looking to an even more remote past, some have seen in Oedipus the remnants of an ancient fertility god or a pattern of sacred kingship, of the type familiar from Sir James Frazer's vast survey of myth and ritual, *The Golden Bough*, wherein the old king has to be killed and replaced by a younger and more potent successor.[20] Others have brought Oedipus closer to earth as a figure of folklore, stressing the affinities with folklore motifs like the riddle and the transparently significant name, but recast into a moralized form by a patriarchal society that stigmatizes crimes against the father as the worst of all possible deeds.[21]

The most influential reading of the myth and the play in our century has come not from classical studies or myth criticism but from psychology, from the work of Sigmund Freud, founder of psychoanalysis. The play fascinates us so much, Freud suggested, not because it dramatizes "the contrast between destiny and human will," but because "there must be something which makes a voice within us ready to recognize the compelling force of destiny."[22] This "destiny" is the universal necessity to which all of us (or at least all males) are subject—namely the wishes that remain from our buried animal nature to kill the father and possess the mother.

For Freud, the oracle that Oedipus receives about his life from Apollo contains the repressed wishes of the unconscious. Because we cannot escape having these wishes, deny them though we will, they constitute our secret destiny. Freud set forth his view of Oedipus succinctly in *The Interpretation of Dreams*:

> His destiny moves us only because it might have been ours—because the oracle laid the same curse upon us before our birth as upon him. It is the fate of all of us, perhaps, to direct our first sexual impulse towards our mother and our first hatred and our first murderous wish against our father. Our dreams convince us that this is so. King Oedipus, who slew his father Laius and married his mother Jocasta, merely shows us the fulfilment of our own childhood wishes
> . . . Here is one in whom these primaeval wishes of our childhood have been fulfilled, and we shrink back from him with the whole force of the repression by which those wishes have since that time been held down within us. (Freud, 296)

Freud continued to reflect on the play throughout his life and to refine his interpretations. In his late essay "Dostoevsky and Parricide," he suggests that the external objectification of Oedipus' crime in the oracle is a way of "projecting the hero's unconscious motive into reality in the form of a compulsion by a destiny which is alien to him."[23] And in one of his last works he speculates that this disguising of Oedipus' unconscious desires in the form of an oracle from the gods not only lets the unconscious become visible but also accounts for the feeling of guilt that we have about these unconscious desires, even though we are not guilty of any crime. He paraphrases the play as telling the viewer, "In vain do you deny that you are accountable, in vain do you proclaim how you have striven against these evil designs. You are guilty, nevertheless; for you could not stifle them; they still survive unconsciously in you."[24]

Freud addresses the issue of guilt in a slightly different way in his essay on Dostoevsky, in which he suggests that Oedipus' eagerness to punish himself, with no attempt at self-defense, corresponds to the inner conviction of guilt that stems from these unconscious desires: "The hero makes no attempt to exculpate himself by appealing to the artificial expedient of the compulsion of destiny. His crime is acknowledged and punished as though it were fully conscious—which is bound to appear unjust to our reason, but which psychologically is perfectly correct."[25]

The central role of Sophocles' Oedipus as a model for the unconscious, in Freud's thinking, led him to give the name "oedipus complex" to a major tenet of psychoanalytic theory. The oedipus complex denotes each person's attitudes and behavior in his or her most intimate family relationships, especially to mother and father. To mature as an emotionally healthy, nonneurotic adult, the child, according to Freud, must somehow come to terms with the residue of repressed infantile hatred and desire for his or her parents.

The mixture of primordial, hidden desires and aggressions that belong to the oedipus complex, and the guilt that derives from living with them in the unconscious, are, in Freud's view, what create the sexual dynamics of the personality. This view, however, has been increasingly questioned and modified in recent years. Critics of Freud's theories have objected to his mechanistic and deterministic approach to human behavior, his extreme concentration on sexuality and sexual repression, his neglect of gender differences and of the role of culture in forming the human personality, and his tendency to universalize factors that may belong to a specific historical moment and society. Revisionist followers of Freud also place greater emphasis on the pre-verbal and pre-oedipal stages of the child's life in the first two or three years and on separation from the mother. On the other hand, the widespread popularity of tales of the Oedipus type throughout many parts of the world does lend support to the basic validity of Freud's theories.

While Freud's oedipus complex may now seem to be a rather limited way of understanding Sophocles' play, there is more promising material in his sensitive remarks on the process of discovering unconscious knowledge enacted in *Oedipus*. In *The Interpretation of Dreams*, Freud observes, "The action of the play consists in nothing other than the process of revealing, with cunning delays and ever-mounting excitement—a process that can be likened to the work of a psychoanalysis—that Oedipus himself is the murderer of Laius, but further that he is the son of the murdered man and of Jocasta" (Freud, 295). Whether or not Freud's theories about infantile fantasies stand the test of time, there is profound truth in his insight about the way in which *Oedipus* takes its audience through a deeply involving process of uncovering hidden truths about the self. It was an important insight to relate this process to the uncovering of the unconscious, whatever the exact contents of the unconscious may be.

In dramatizing the discovery of a hidden truth about oneself, the play may be said to anticipate the model of psychoanalysis. Its powerful effect, Freud once suggested, lies in the viewer's reacting "as though by self-analysis he had detected the oedipus complex in himself and had recognized the will of the gods as glorified disguises of his own unconscious."[26] But the opposite is also true: psychoanalysis is a systematic technique for reaching the kind of knowledge that the play can bring to a fully involved spectator. Analytical and descriptive language (like mine in this book) can attempt to re-create or account for this experience after the fact but cannot reproduce the living power of the effect itself. As Freud once observed, the unconscious was discovered long before psychoanalysis; Freud was merely the first to give it a name. Both Sophocles and Freud are concerned with forcing into conscious speech and, in the case of the *Oedipus*, into clear, theatrical vision knowledge that has been repressed into the darkness of the unknowable and unspeakable.

It is important to confront honestly and undogmatically the limitations of a Freudian analysis of classical (and other) literature—limitations that Freud himself acknowledged.[27] A Freudian reading is often unhistorical and inattentive to esthetic form and tends to disregard cultural differences. Freud's critics, especially feminist critics, have objected (among other things) to the view of desire in terms of limited quanta of libidinal energy; to a reductive phallocentricism, focused on castration for males and penis-envy for females; and on the deterministic role of infantile sexuality.[28] As an interpretive tool, a Freudian approach runs the risk of merely interposing an intertext from contemporary culture between ourselves and antiquity. As Jean-Pierre Vernant and others have pointed out, Oedipus does not have an "oedipus complex," at least as far as Jocasta is concerned, for his infantile emotional involvement is entirely with the woman he assumes to be his mother, Merope.[29] It is only later writers, like John Dryden and Nathaniel Lee in their *Oedipus*, who suggest the erotic side of the bond between Oedipus and Jocasta and some kind of latent, unconscious sexual attraction between them, albeit two centuries before Freud.[30] Greek tragedy, moreover, does not allow us to enter its characters' private moods and impulses to the degree that, say, Shakespearean drama does in the case of Hamlet and Gertrude. In Freud's defense, it should be noted that the play, both through Oedipus and the chorus, fully expresses the horror of the incest, although the emphasis is on the pollution rather than on the interior realm of emotion. Nor is the sexual element entirely absent. It appears, however, not in overtly erotic terms but obliquely in the recurrent images of earth, plowing, seeds, and gates.

Freud uses the play, as so many writers have done, as a springboard for his own ideas and theories. His most interesting contribution, here and elsewhere, lies in his conception of the unconscious: a realm of primordial desires, fears, and impulses that the censorship of our conscious mind allows to appear only through the distorting mechanisms of symbol-making, condensation, displacement, splitting, and the like, that clothe the contents of the unconscious in forms acceptable to our conscious minds. Even if we do not accept the Freudian unconscious, Freud suggests a way of looking at the play as offering a model of a kind of knowledge, and indeed a kind of world, that does not correspond to the logic that we think of as normal reality, and the glimpse of this kind of nonrational world is terrifying.

A Freudian reading illuminates the *Oedipus* because it points to the central theme of concealing and revealing terrible knowledge. It may be objected that Oedipus' passion for knowledge, his determination to discover his past, is at least as strong as his blindness to the clues in his path. But the tragic situation and its ironies lie precisely in this discrepancy between the will to know and the long persistence in ignorance.

The Freudian critic operates with the hypothesis that the subject refuses to know what he (unconsciously) knows, and, furthermore, that this process of paradoxical knowledge-in-ignorance is enacted in language.[31] Thus Oedipus not only refuses to "hear" the truth that Teiresias plainly speaks to him but repeatedly gives details about himself that he does not recognize as truth. In the prologue, for example, he seems to say, by a typical "Freudian slip" of the tongue, that a single robber, not "many robbers," killed Laius (124). Later, with the same "innocence," he offers to fight for Laius as if "for my own father," since he and Laius, as he says, possess a "wife of common seeding" and children "in common" (260–65). This inability to acknowledge the truths about himself that his own language utters exemplifies the resistance to knowing consciously what lies buried in his unconscious.

One could go even further and suggest that Oedipus has defended himself against his incestuous and parricidal wishes by splitting each mother figure and father figure into two—the consciously acknowledged parents at Corinth, Merope and Polybus, from whom he must be separated forever by the oracle's prohibition against incest and parricide, and the unacknowledged parents at Thebes, against whom he unknowingly commits just these crimes. Our pleasure in the irony for which the play is famous lies in the shiver of excitement and recognition that we feel when the unconscious tries to surface to the conscious mind, that is, when we can see acted out in language before us the usually invisible processes of denying unconscious knowledge. This is the effect that Freud described as "the uncanny." Indirectly, Freud's reading of *Oedipus* suggests how a literary work uses the processes of disguise, gradual revelation, and symbolism to make us experience areas and forms of knowledge to which we can have access in no other way.[32]

There is, however, a major difference between the Sophoclean and the Freudian irrational. For Sophocles, the irrational lies outside as well as within. It is embodied in the gods, in the mysterious ways of Apollo, and in the gods' messages to men: the oracles and the plague. The Sophoclean oracle is not an interior voice that proclaims a universal and inevitable destiny; it belongs to a religious institution in a society that has prophets and believes in mantic utterances from the gods.[33] Nor does Oedipus assume that the fulfillment of the oracle is inevitable. He immediately takes steps to avoid it. For Freud, the irrational is our "fate" or destiny in the sense that it is built into our emotional makeup as this evolved with the development of human civilization. For Sophocles, the surd, the irrational, really is an *other*, an aspect of the divine outside of and apart from man. For Freud this *other* is projected inwardly, as a part of our own mind, something hidden within ourselves. Nevertheless, even in Sophocles the oracle to Oedipus does not just drop unbidden into his lap. Oedipus goes in search of it at a moment of trouble and perplexity about who he is, when a drunkard at Corinth taunts him about his birth. Although the oracle belongs to an established religious procedure (the consultation of Apollo at his sanctuary at Delphi), Sophocles does not report it merely as a statement of objective fact but makes it part of the emotional turbulence and self-questioning that Oedipus feels at that moment.

CURSES AND BLESSINGS

The myth of Oedipus, like many Greek myths, is concerned with the mystery and danger of power. The hero is the conduit of powerful energies of creation and destruction, and he brings these into his city as a result of his special closeness to the gods. More exposed than other men and women to such numinous power, the hero can reach the highest or lowest points on the scale of human values. Not only in Sophocles' play but also in related mythical patterns, the hero of the Oedipus type becomes both a wondrous savior and a wicked criminal. In medieval legend the Oedipal pattern—oracle, exposure in infancy, killing the father, and marrying the mother—applies to the diametrically opposite figures, Judas and Saint (later Pope) Gregory. In the one set of legends the Oedipus figure becomes the most accursed of men, Judas Iscariot, who betrays Christ and finally hangs himself in despair. In the other set he attains the highest sanctity: Saint Gregory, on discovering the truth of his incestuous marriage, is overwhelmed by guilt and has a fisherman lock him up in a cellar, where he lives in solitary penance, is miraculously found, and named pope.[34]

Oedipus at Colonus (also called *Oedipus Coloneus*), which Sophocles wrote in the last years of his life, shows how the coincidence of accursed outcast and holy man already exists in the paradoxes surrounding the ancient hero. Oedipus is now an old, blind exile and wanderer (in contrast to the Homeric versions, in which he rules and is buried in Thebes). Sustained through years of misery by his faithful daughter Antigone, he eventually arrives at the grove of the Eumenides in Colonus, on the outskirts of Athens. He knows of a prophecy that this is to be his final resting place, and he soon hears of another mysterious oracle that his bones will protect whatever city receives him for burial. But Creon, now king of Thebes, who also knows this latter oracle, tries to seize Oedipus and bring him back to his old city by force. Oedipus refuses, and Theseus, king of Athens, protects him. The play ends with the gods suddenly calling Oedipus to his resting place. Henceforth his body, from its tomb known only to Theseus, will protect Athens from foreign invaders.

The classical play, however, unlike the medieval legends, does not allow so complete a polarization of the hero's numinous power, the total evil of the traitor and the penitential sanctity of the future pope. Despite the blessings that the old Oedipus will bring to his adoptive city, he still arouses awe and horror in those who meet him; he still curses, angrily and bitterly, the sons who drove him out. For all his special gifts from the gods, he is not saintly in the Christian sense, like Gregory. He remains a dangerous and violent figure, the source of maledictions as well as of blessings.

The ambiguity that continues to surround Oedipus is marked in the transgressive act that opens *Oedipus at Colonus*: he reenacts the danger of his special relation to divinity by entering the heavily tabooed grove sacred to the dread Eumenides. These goddesses are a somewhat gentler form of the Furies, but they are still awesome powers, the daughters of Earth and Darkness. The play takes its name from the setting of this grove, at the edge of Athens, near the Athenian locale of Colonus, where Oedipus is also to be buried. In Sophocles' time Oedipus was worshipped there as a local divinity.

In entering this shrine and steadfastly refusing to leave, Oedipus reenacts a version of his initial crime, trespassing in a sacred female space forbidden to him. As in the earlier phase of his life, he is again the stranger and intruder who claims a place in a foreign city. To find his way into this new home, he must also pass through trials, as he did at his first arrival at Thebes in his youth (see Chapter 5). But his entrance into Athens also contrasts with that earlier entrance into Thebes. At Athens he resolves his ambiguous status as both insider and outsider.

Athens often functions in classical tragedy as the place for the recovery and reintegration of a conflicted personality and for the successful resolution of familial conflict, whereas Thebes (as we also see in *Seven against Thebes*, *Antigone*, and *Bacchae*) is the place for disastrous confusions of identity and unresolved family conflicts.[35] Thus at Thebes, in the *Tyrannus*, Oedipus is pulled back into his family's self-destructive, accursed past, and can only repeat it, even though he is under the illusion that he is finding a new identity. At Athens, in the *Oedipus Coloneus*, he begins with full clarity about the relations of past and present, wanderer and citizen, weakness and strength, and he escapes all the attempts to drag him back to Thebes.

Oedipus' apparent trespass into the Eumenides' grove at the beginning of the *Coloneus*, then, proves to be part of a divinely sanctioned plan to give him rest, not to force him out of an illusionary security. Whereas the remote gods of *Oedipus Tyrannus* reveal his terrible "sickness" of pollution beneath an apparent power to cure, now they reveal the feeble, battered body as a source of mysterious power. In the *Tyrannus* the unraveling of Oedipus' present power and confidence begins with Jocasta's account of Laius' death, when he cries out, "O Zeus, what have you planned to do with me?" (738); in the *Coloneus* it is thunder from Zeus, albeit the Zeus of the lower world, that marks the completion of his sufferings on earth and ushers him into his future numinous existence as a heroized inhabitant and protector of the Athenian land (1606). Now it is the onlookers, his daughters, who "shudder" in terror and grief (1607–9), whereas Oedipus remains calm and in control. Yet Oedipus still remains a living contradiction. What is more paradoxical than a miserable, blind beggar who can defend a city from powerful armies? The terms are almost exactly the reverse of those in the *Tyrannus*, in which the king, soon to be this blind beggar, is in fact the criminal and pollutant of his land.

Despite the two plays' differences, the later shares the earlier's pattern of the hero who combines the extremes of power and weakness. *Oedipus at Colonus*, however, reinterprets the pattern from the perspective of the end rather than the beginning of Oedipus' life. Where *Oedipus Tyrannus* traces the process of uncovering a hidden past, the *Coloneus* begins with a hero who already holds the secrets of his life's beginning and end, has a privileged knowledge of his contact with divinity, and is fully aware of his special power for the future.[36]

NOTES

1. *Papyrus Lille* 73 and 76 (1977) contain these fragments of Stesichorus. They are now available in David A. Campbell, ed. and trans., *Greek Lyric* III, Loeb Classical Library (Cambridge, MA: Harvard University Press, 1991), 136–43. For interpretation, see Charles Segal, "Archaic Choral Lyric," *Cambridge History of Classical Literature*, I, P. Easterling and B.M.W. Knox, eds., (Cambridge: Cambridge University Press, 1985), 197–200. See also below, note 4.

2. Euripides also wrote a play based on this myth, the *Chrysippus*, now lost. It was probably presented along with the *Phoenician Woman* in 409 B.C.E.

3. The fact that the only reference to the Fury in *Oedipus* comes from Teiresias (417–18) may be a trace of Sophocles' substitution of the prophet, who after all is still a human figure, for the supernatural and demonic power of the Fury.

4. Jennifer March, *The Creative Poet, University of London, Bulletin of the Institute for Classical Studies*, Supplement 49 (London 1987), 126–33, 139–38, argues vigorously that the woman speaking in the Stesichorus fragment (see above, note 1) is Euryganeia, and not Jocasta (or Epikaste), trying to save her own children, so that the incestuously begotten children would be Aeschylus' creation (139–48). If the speaker is Jocasta, Euripides is following this tradition in his *Phoenician Women*, keeping Jocasta alive after the discovery of her incestuous marriage, although she commits suicide after the fratricidal deaths of her sons. The Stesichorus fragment gives a possible indication of this later suicide, for Jocasta says that she does not want to survive the death of her two sons (lines 211–17, "But if it is the destined portion for my sons to be subdued by one another and the Fates [Moirai] have spun it out so, may I have at once the fulfillment of hateful death before ever looking upon these grievous, tearful sorrows amid [?] woes, my sons dead in the halls or the city taken"). Given the likelihood that this threat of suicide was fulfilled in the lost subsequent portion of Stesichorus' poem, the congruence with Euripides suggests that the speaker is indeed Jocasta. But the fragment does not explain the admittedly unexpected fact that Jocasta (if it is she) has decided to live with the double pollution of incestuous marriage and children. This latter point is the strongest argument in favor of March's thesis. If Stesichorus' speaker is Jocasta, which still seems to me the most likely interpretation, the incestuous birth goes back to at least the late seventh or early sixth century. See also Anne Burnett, "Jocasta in the West: The Lille Stesichorus," *Classical Antiquity* 7 (1988), 107–54, who argues for Jocasta as the speaker.

5. For the exposure in the pot, see Aeschylus, fragment 122 in Stephan Radt, ed., *Tragicorum Graecorum Fragmenta*, vol. 3, *Aeschylus* (Göttingen: Vandenhoeck and Ruprecht, 1985) and Aristophanes, *Frogs* 1190.

6. The piercing of the feet has never been fully explained. Vladimir Propp, "Oedipus in the Light of Folklore," in L. Edmunds and A. Dundes, eds., *Oedipus: A Folklore Casebook* (New York: Garland, 1983), 93, suggests that it serves to place the marks of death upon the child. The motif occasionally surfaces in later adaptations of the Oedipus myth, for example in a twelfth-century Latin version of the life of Judas Iscariot: see L. Edmunds, *The Ancient Legend and its Later Analogues* (Baltimore: Johns Hopkins University Press, 1985), 61. But this is probably derived ultimately from Sophocles' version.

7. See Herodotus, *Histories*, 1.112 and 5.92; also Euripides, *Ion* 954–63. See in general Robert Garland, *The Greek Way of Life* (Ithaca, N.Y.: Cornell University Press, 1990), 84. The baby's arousal of pity in its would-be executioners reappears, doubtless independently, in the *Roman de Thèbes*, see Léopolde Constans, *La Légende d'Oedipe* (Paris, 1881; Geneva: Slatkine Reprints, 1974), 172–73.

8. Garland, *Greek Way of Life*, 86.

9. These are (in addition to Euripides) Achaeus, Carcinus, Philocles, Theodectes, and Xenocles. Versions are also attested by later writers such as Lycophron, and the rather dubious Nicomachus. See Augustus Nauck, *Tragicorum Graecorum Fragmenta*, 2d ed. (Leipzig: Teubner, 1889), s.v. "Oedipus."

10. Parallels between *Ion* and *Oedipus* include the motif of fitting together times and stages of life (*Ion* 352–54, 547 and *Oedipus* 740ff., 1112–13); the praise of the quiet life (*Ion* 585–647 and *Oedipus* 584–99); the motif of compelling the gods to reveal the truth before its time (*Ion* 377–79 and *Oedipus* 316–29, 341; cf. *Oedipus* 1438–43); deriving one's name from a "chance" event in one's life (*tuchê, Ion* 661 and *Oedipus* 1036); an intense stichomythy on the fate of a lost child (*Ion* 344–54 and *Oedipus* 1142–81); the concern with being found out a slave (*Ion* 1382 and *Oedipus* 1062–63); the cry to Zeus at the prospect of a sudden reversal at the moment of recognition (*Ion* 1422 and *Oedipus* 738), where the Ion's cry, "O Zeus, what destiny is tracking us down," also uses the pervasive hunting image of the *Oedipus*). Oedipus stands at the point of "terrible hearing" when he is about to learn the truth of his birth from the Old Herdsman (*Oedipus* 1169–70); Ion awaits "something terrible" (*hôs echei ti deinon*, 1416) from Creusa's imminent revelation in the tense stichomythy of a recognition scene, but in the *Ion*, the "terrible" will turn to joy, not horror. Oedipus' cry, *tekousa tlêmon*, at his moment of the "terrible hearing" of the truth ("[did] the mother, wretched [or hard] woman, [expose the child]," *Oedipus* 1175), with its mixture of pity and condemnation, finds an echo first in the old servant's exclamation when Creusa reveals the secret birth ("O you so wretched [or hard] in your daring" (*tlêmon su tolmês*, 960) and later and more happily in Ion's cry, at the moment of recognition and reunion with Creusa, "O mother who endured terrible things" (*ô deina tlasa mêter*, 1496). For further discussion, see my essay, "Euripides' *Ion*: Generational Passage and Civic Myth," in Mark W. Padilla, ed., *Rites of Passage in Ancient Greece Bucknell Review*, vol. 43, no. 1 (Lewisburg: Bucknell University Press, 1999), 67–108, especially 100–2.

11. This and the following passage are from Aristophanes, *Frogs*, 1182–95. The translation is from Richmond Lattimore in William Arrowsmith, ed., *Aristophanes, Four Comedies* (Ann Arbor: University of Michigan Press, 1969), 74, which I have slightly modified.

12. See Herodotus, *Histories* 1.112–13.

13. Diogenes is quoted in Dio Chrysostom (also called Dio of Prusa), *Orations* 10.29–30. The idea of permitting incest because it occurs in "nature" belongs to an older debate, familiar to Sophocles and his contemporaries, contrasting "nature" and "convention": see, for instance, Aristophanes, *Clouds* 1427–29. The defense of incest by the appeal to animal behavior is taken up as a rhetorical ploy in Ovid's account of Myrrha's incestuous passion for her father, Cinyras, *Metamorphoses* 10.323–31.

14. The passage is omitted from our manuscripts of the *Iliad* and is known only from a quotation by Plutarch, who says that the Hellenistic Homeric scholar Aristarchus omitted it "out of fear" (Plutarch, *How the Young Man Should Listen to Poetry*, 8.27F).

15. See Jean-Marc Moret, *Oedipe, la Sphinx et les Thébains*, (Rome: Institut Suisse de Rome, 1984), vol. 1, p. 40 and vol. 2, plate 23; Jan Bremmer, "Oedipus and the Greek Oedipus Complex," in J. Bremmer, ed., *Interpretations of Greek Mythology* (London and Sydney: Croom Helm, 1987), 46–47.

16. Interpreters sometimes suggest that Oedipus was shown as limping because of the old injury to his feet, but of this there is no evidence at all in the play.

17. Hegel's views are easily accessible in Anne and Henry Paolucci, eds., *Hegel On Tragedy* (Garden City, N.Y.: Anchor Books, 1962), especially 279–80, 325–26.

18. See Jean-Joseph Goux, *Oedipus, Philosopher* (Stanford, CA: Stanford University Press, 1993). 140–81.

19. Propp, "Oedipus in the Light of Folklore," 84–89.

20. For versions of this approach, with discussion of previous scholarship, see Edmunds and Dundes, *Oedipus: A Folklore Casebook*, 161–64; also Propp, "Oedipus in the Light of Folklore," 85.

21. See Propp, "Oedipus in the Light of Folklore," 76–121, especially 149. A useful, brief survey of various interpretations of the myth may be found in Lowell Edmunds, *Oedipus: Ancient Legend* (Baltimore, MD: Johns Hopkins University Press, 1984), 1–46; see also Martin P. Nilsson, *The Mycenaean Origin of Greek Mythology* (Berkeley and Los Angeles: University of California Press, 1932), 101–12.

22. Sigmund Freud, *The Interpretation of Dreams*, trans. and ed. by James Strachey, 3d ed. (New York: Basic Books, 1955), 296. References to this work are henceforth given in the text.

23. S. Freud, "Dostoevsky and Parricide," in, James Strachey, ed., *The Standard Edition of the Complete Psychological Works of Sigmund Freud* (London: Hogarth Press, 1961), vol. 21, 188. The essay dates from 1928.

24. S. Freud, *A General Introduction to Psychoanalysis*, trans. Joan Riviere (New York: Liverwright, 1935), 291.

25. Freud, "Dostoevsky and Parricide," 188.

26. Freud, *A General Introduction to Psychoanalysis*, 291.

27. See the discussion in Walter Kaufmann, *Tragedy and Philosophy* (New York: Doubleday, 1968; revised rpt., New York: Anchor Books, 1969), 124.

28. For some of the feminist critiques of Freud see the well known works of Juliet Mitchell, *Psychoanalysis and Feminism* (New York: Pantheon, 1974) and Luce Iri-

garay, *The Speculum of the Other Woman* (1974), trans. G. C. Gill (Ithaca: Cornell University Press, 1985), 13–129. For further discussion and bibliography see Gayle Rubin, "The Traffic in Women," in Joan Wallach Scott, ed., *Feminism and History* (New York: Oxford University Press, 1996), 125–37.

29. See J.-P. Vernant, "Oedipus without the Complex," in Jean-Pierre Vernant and Pierre Vidal-Naquet, *Myth and Tragedy in Ancient Greece*, trans. J. Lloyd (New York: Zone Books, 1990), 85–111. For further discussion, see my chapter, "Freud, Language, and the Unconscious," in my *Sophocles' Tragic World* (Cambridge, MA: Harvard University Press, 1995), 161–79, especially 163ff.; also Pietro Pucci, *Oedipus and the Fabrication of the Father* (Baltimore, MD: Johns Hopkins University Press, 1992), 44–48.

30. On this post-Sophoclean eroticization of the myth, see G. Paduano, *Lunga storia di Edipo Re* 15–19, 66–70, and his Chapter 3, passim; also below, Chapter 12.

31. The refocusing of the work of the unconscious on the processes of language is implicit in Freud (see, for example, his famous essays, "The Antithetical Sense of Primal Words" and "Negation," and the analysis of language practiced in *Psychopathology of Everyday Life* and *Jokes in their Relation to the Unconscious*); but it is especially developed in the work of Jacques Lacan: see J. Lacan, *Ecrits. A Selection*, trans. A. Sheridan (New York: Norton, 1977) and *Speech and Language in Psychoanalysis*, trans. A. Wilden (Baltimore, MD: Johns Hopkins University Press, 1968).

32. See Paul Ricoeur, *Freud and Philosophy*, trans. D. Savage (New Haven: Yale University Press, 1970), 519.

33. On the importance of oracles in the religious thought of the Greeks, see A. D. Nock, "Religious Attitudes of the Greeks," in Zeph Stewart, ed., *Essays on Religion in the Ancient World* (Cambridge, MA: Harvard University Press, 1972), 2.534–42.

34. These legends may be found in Edmunds, *Oedipus: Ancient Legend*, 61–93, 144–48, 155–60; and cf. the parallel story of St. Andrew of Crete, 186–97. See also Propp, "Oedipus in the Light of Folklore," 114–18.

35. See Froma I. Zeitlin, "Thebes: Theater of Self and Society in Athenian Drama," in John J. Winkler and F. Zeitlin, eds., *Nothing to Do with Dionysus?* (Princeton, NJ: Princeton University Press, 1990), 130–67, especially 144–50.

36. See Bernard Knox, *The Heroic Temper* (Berkeley and Los Angeles: University of California Press, 1964), 148–49; see also below, Chapter 11.

5

〰〰〰〰

Oedipus and the Trials of the Hero

The Myth of the Hero

Viewed in its simplest form, the Oedipus myth is a version of the myth of the hero. It resembles the stories of Perseus, Jason, Theseus, Cyrus the Great, Moses, Romulus and Remus, Siegfried, and many others. Persecuted by a hostile father or father figure (uncle, grandfather, king) because of a warning or omens at or before his birth, the hero is threatened with death as an infant—left to die in the woods or set adrift in the sea or a river. In some myths the real father is a god; in others, the child is born of incest. Rescued from death and raised by foreign parents or sometimes by animals, he gives signs in his youth of remarkable powers. When he grows up, he performs great deeds, often killing monsters (as did Theseus, Perseus, Jason, and Oedipus). Through his prowess, he regains his kingdom, wins a bride, punishes the evil father figure, and discovers and restores his lost parents. Heroes often receive cults as minor divinities in the places where they are buried; and this pattern applies to Oedipus too, and underlies Sophocles' later play, *Oedipus at Colonus*, which describes Oedipus' last days on earth.

In the *Oedipus Tyrannus*, however, the hero myth is enacted in reverse. Whereas the other heroes are confirmed in their adult status and power when they discover their true birth, Oedipus' move back to his infancy is disastrous. Sophocles' hero calls on the place where he was left to die as an infant, Mt. Cithaeron (1391–93, 1451–54). In other hero myths the protagonist proves to be the son of a god; in *Oedipus* the chorus *hopes* that Oedipus will prove to be the son of a god (1098–1109) but immediately afterwards discovers the opposite, that he is is the land's pollution.

The Sphinx corresponds to the dragon or monster in other myths of the hero, such as the dragon that guards the Golden Fleece in the Jason myth, or the dragon that guards the accursed gold in the tale of Siegfried, or the sea-serpent or Chimaera in the myths of Perseus and Bellerophon, respectively. The Sphinx seems, in fact, to combine the "princess who sets the task" with the "dragon who demands tribute in human blood" in the familiar tales of the fairy tale hero.[1] But in the Oedipus myth the Sphinx always appears in high places, on a hill,

49

mountain, or column, never in a cave, and Oedipus combats it by solving a riddle, not by a sword or spear (Figures 1 and 2). Oedipus, victorious by intellect rather than force, is unusual in this kind of hero myth. Perseus and Heracles, for instance, have bloody battles with the monsters they subdue; Oedipus does not lift a finger.[2] The few vases that do show him in martial combat probably represent a later, secondary development, following the more common type of hero myth.[3]

TRIALS OF THE HERO

As a series of trials characteristic of the myth of the hero, the story of Oedipus has the following form. (1) The young man is challenged about his birth, and (2) goes on a journey to discovery his true origins. (3) He makes inquiry of a god, and (4) receives a mysterious answer. (5) Instead of returning home, he continues his journey into a strange land, where (6) he meets his first challenge, an older, regal figure who stands in his way, blocking his road. The encounter with this blocking figure is his first heroic combat (7), and he defeats and kills his opponent. He then meets a second trial on his path, the Sphinx (8), whom he also defeats and kills, thereby (9) winning the queen and (10) gaining the throne.

Sophocles has made this hero myth one of tragedy instead of triumph by making the prophecy (no. 4) so horrible and by combining the meeting with the father (7) and the meeting with the Sphinx (8) into a composite first trial. Sophocles in fact blurs the separate stages of defeating the monster and winning a bride and a throne into a composite victory whose obscure chronology is of a piece with the darkness of Oedipus' origins and also contributes to the problem of discovering the truth about past events. This fusion of usually clear and separate moments of the hero's success into a single, blurred event is also characteristic of Oedipus' whole life-pattern.[4] Recast into its tragic mode, the myth is dominated by anxiety, uncertainty, mystery, lack of control, and the problem of self-knowledge. In the life crisis dramatized in *Oedipus*, the hero can move forward only by reaching backward to the past. And so Sophocles' plot unfolds as the recovery of lost knowledge and a lost past.

As an inverted form of the hero myth, Oedipus' success at each stage really hides a terrible failure. His strengths are eventually revealed as sources of defeat and weakness, culminating in his self-blinding. This pattern is replicated in Oedipus' trials within the play, of which the first is the plague. Both the priest in the opening scene and the chorus in the first ode describe its devastations. Even before the midpoint of the action, however, it is simply forgotten. Oedipus' search for his origins completely overshadows the sufferings of the city that have set the plot in motion. We hear of the plague for the last time when Jocasta reproaches Oedipus and Creon for quarreling in private while "the land suffers from such a disease" (635–36).

The hero's trials that follow from the plague take the form of a series of personal encounters. These are almost juridical inquiries, and they fall into two groups of three meetings each. All six show Oedipus' keen intelligence in action as he tries to solve the murder of Laius and the mystery of the plague by careful cross-examination, often in line-by-line exchange.

The first three tests are, respectively, Oedipus' meetings with Creon, Teiresias, and then Creon again. In each case, Oedipus is pursuing the killer as someone whom he assumes is *other* than himself (87–131, 316–462, 513–630). The second series begins with Jocasta and continues with the Corinthian Messenger and Laius' Herdsman. Now Oedipus is pursuing the killer as possibly the *same* as himself (726–862, 954–1085, 1119–85). In this set of encounters, his goal shifts gradually from uncovering the murderer to discovering his own parents. The confidence and power that he demonstrated in the first series of encounters gradually erode into anger, loss of control, and fear.

This second series of tests comes not in personal encounters with men onstage but from the remote past and from the gods. Oedipus swings between fear and hope as he encounters unknown figures from his past, first the Corinthian Messenger and then Laius' Old Herdsman. Oedipus will now have to make the final decision, whether to cross the hair-thin line from uncertainty to certain knowledge (1169–70). By introducing this hesitation at the moment of discovery, Sophocles makes the truth emerge as a deliberate act of will: Oedipus takes on himself the decision to cross the divide that henceforth separates him from all men.

After this climactic moment, Oedipus' encounters belong to a more private realm and are dominated by emotion rather than intellectual inquiry. Instead of a king addressing subjects in the civic space outside the palace, he rushes within to find Jocasta, already dead by her own hand in the most intimate chamber of the palace. Meeting Jocasta both begins and completes the process of self-discovery. Whereas the previous meetings have consisted of dialogue and argument, this one, which we learn of only through the report of the Messenger, consists of the violent act of self-blinding.

How will Oedipus confront the world after these discoveries and these sufferings? The remainder of the play pursues this question and completes the hero's trials. Again there is a series of three meetings, each a test of the new non-King Oedipus. First he encounters the chorus of his citizen-subjects, then Creon, and finally his two young daughters, Antigone and Ismene. Like the tests of the first series, these three encounters move from Oedipus' public to his personal life, but now they try his courage, endurance, and capacity for learning through suffering, rather than his intelligence or competence.

Oedipus' strength of spirit determines the quality of the play's final test, his last meeting with Creon. Oedipus is troubled and embarrassed as the chorus announces the approach of this man whom Oedipus had almost condemned to death for his own crime (1419–21). Creon's pity and moderation make Oedipus' situation easier, but the mood of the scene shifts surprisingly. Oedipus turns from his utter desolation and abasement to something of his old air of command, albeit in a chastened and softened tone. He asks Creon to expel him from Thebes as quickly as he can and gives orders for Jocasta's burial (1446–54), a gesture of concern and responsibility characteristic of the Oedipus we saw in the opening scenes. The conflict of authority with Creon changes to a gentler, more personal, and more intimate tone as Creon, anticipating Oedipus' wish, brings him his daughters.

Crosscurrents of anger and conflict between Oedipus and Creon still threaten the stability of the last scene in a way reminiscent of Achilles' precarious self-control before Priam in *Iliad* 24. For a moment, Oedipus vacillates between his old, hasty imperiousness and his present acceptance of helplessness, between wanting expulsion from his human community and wanting closeness to his family. This is a test of Oedipus very different from that of the opening scene. Creon too keeps a delicate balance between generosity and rebuke.

The entire action of the play may be viewed as one huge, collective test, a reenactment of Oedipus' contest with the Sphinx. In the course of the play, Oedipus increasingly directs the intellectual power that made possible his external victory over the monster to the harder riddles of his own origins and the horrible secrets of his life. The result seems to be defeat rather than victory—or is it defeat after all? Oedipus does succeed: he solves the riddle of who he is, and he has the strength to endure the suffering that he has found: "No man but I can bear my evil doom" (1415). The Oedipus who emerges from this final trial is more like a prophet than a king. He has lost his eyes but gained something of Teiresias' vision of truth.

The chorus had introduced Teiresias as the only man who had truth "inborn, as part of his nature" (299). Having become blind, like Teiresias, to gain a new kind of sight, Oedipus will now live a life of truth rather than illusion. But his truth is gained through painful effort, not given as an inborn quality like the truth that Teiresias possesses (299). What Oedipus was "born" with leads him into darkness, illusion, and deception. After confronting this truth Oedipus finds his trials coming from within rather than from the outside, and here the issue is neither victory nor defeat, only understanding and endurance.

NOTES

1. See Propp, "Oedipus in the Light of Folklore," in L. Edmunds and A. Dundes, eds., *Oedipus: A Folklore Casebook*, 109.

2. On this anomaly, see Jean-Joseph Goux , *Oedipus, Philosopher*, trans. C. Porter (Stanford, CA: Stanford University Press, 1993), 16–18, 25–27, but I cannot always agree with the conclusions that he draws from this situation. We should also recall the parallel pattern of the trickster-hero, like Odysseus.

3. See Moret, *Oedipe, la Sphinx et les Thébains*, vol. 1, pp. 81–90 and vol. 2, plates 62 and 63.

4. For this blurring of the stages of the heroic quest, but with a very different view, see Goux, *Oedipus, Philosopher*, 15–16.

6

Life's Tragic Shape: Plot, Design, and Destiny

REMOVING PRECONCEPTIONS

One of the hardest problems in approaching the *Oedipus Tyrannus* is trying to look at it freshly. To do that, one must remove a few layers of misconception; so I have to begin with a few "nots." This is *not* a play about free will versus determinism. The Greeks did not develop a notion of a universal, all-determining Fate before the Stoics in the third century B.C.E. The human characters are not mere puppets of the gods; no figure in Greek tragedy is. To be sure, the supernatural elements are important: Apollo, the plague, the oracles, Teiresias' prophetic knowledge. But the play does not label any of these as the certain *causes* of suffering. There are no gods on stage, as happens regularly in Aeschylus and Euripides, nor is there the direct confrontation of powerful god and crushed mortal victim that occurs at the end of Euripides' *Hippolytus* and *Bacchae*. For all its concern with prophecy and oracles, the *Oedipus* has a startling modernity precisely because these supernatural elements are not only kept in the background but are also hidden and mysterious.

The issues of destiny, predetermination, and foreknowledge are raised as problems, *not* as dogma. How much control do we have over the shape of our lives? How much of what happens to us is due to heredity, to accidents, to sheer luck (good and bad), to personality, to the right (or wrong) decision at a particular crossroads in life, or to the myriad interactions among all of the above? These are the questions that the play raises, and it raises them *as questions*. It shows us men and women who are both powerful and helpless, often at the same moment. Oedipus embodies the human condition in just this paradoxical relation to both open and closed conceptions of life. He is both free and determined, both able to choose and helpless in the face of choices that he has already made in the past or circumstances (like those of his birth) over which he had no power of choice. The play, as one interpreter remarks, shows us the issues of choice and predetermination as "a box of mirrors to bewilder each new generation; the whole tangle is here in this story. . . . The play offers to each spectator as much as he is capable of seeing."[1]

Although it is customary to group *Antigone*, *Oedipus Tyrannus*, and *Oedipus at Colonus* together as the three Theban plays because they deal with the royal house of Thebes, the three works were not conceived as a trilogy. *Antigone* was written more than a decade before *Oedipus Tyrannus*, and *Oedipus at Colonus* was composed some twenty years after. There are numerous verbal echoes of *Antigone* in *Oedipus Tyrannus* and of both plays in *Oedipus at Colonus*, which self-consciously looks back to these two works. It is helpful, therefore, to have the earlier works in mind when reading the later ones, but esthetically the three works are independent.

Oedipus does *not* have a tragic flaw. This view rests on a misreading of Aristotle (see Chapter 12), and is a moralizing way out of the disturbing questions that the play means to ask. Sophocles refuses to give so easy an answer to the problem of suffering. Oedipus' haste and irascibility at crucial moments (particularly in the killing of Laius) contribute to the calamity but are not sufficient reasons for it nor its main cause.

Finally, the play does *not* end with the self-blinding of Oedipus, but continues afterwards for nearly three hundred lines. These closing scenes are essential for understanding how Sophocles conceives of his hero and should not be neglected.

The tragic effect of the *Oedipus Tyrannus* lies in part in its dramatic irony, long ago observed by Aristotle: what seems to be bringing salvation in fact brings destruction. In the very first scene the Theban priest invokes Oedipus as the "savior" from the plague, when in fact he is its cause. Later, Oedipus will curse his savior, the man who saved him from death when he was exposed on the mountain in infancy (1349–54). Despite all the attempts to avoid the three oracles—the oracles given to Laius in the remote past, to Oedipus some twenty years ago at Delphi, and to Thebes in the present—they all come true. In this perverse-looking situation, every would-be savior in the play is also in some sense a destroyer: Creon with his news from Delphi, the prophet Teiresias, Jocasta in the past, the two herdsmen, Apollo, and of course Oedipus himself.

The plot that unfolds these events may look like a diabolical trap set for Oedipus by the gods (which is the direction that Jean Cocteau follows in his reworking of the play, *The Infernal Machine*), but Sophocles lets us see these events as the natural result of an interaction between character, circumstances in the past, and mere chance combinations in the present. Nevertheless, by placing the oracles in so prominent a position in the action, Sophocles, from the first scene, makes the question of divine intervention unavoidable. The play forces us to ask where the gods are in this tale of extraordinary coincidences and extraordinary suffering. Even the supernatural element of the oracles operates in a human way.

Typically in Greek tragedy, the gods work through normal human behavior and motivation. They are, one might say, an added dimension of our reality, not an arbitrary negation of reality. What we mean by calling *Oedipus Tyrannus* a tragedy of fate might be more accurately phrased as Sophocles' sense of the existence of powers working in the world in ways alien to and hidden from human understanding. Karl Reinhardt has put the ancient view very well: "For Sophocles, as for the Greeks of an earlier age, fate is in no circumstances the same as predetermination, but is a spontaneous unfolding of daimonic power, even when the fate has been foretold."[2] The play leaves it an open question whether Laius, Jocasta, or Oedipus might have prevented the fulfillment of the prophecies if they had simply done nothing: not exposed the infant, not consulted Delphi, not avoided Thebes, not married an older woman, and so on.

Oracles, moreover, like dreams, are traditionally elusive, and even dreadful prophecies may prove innocuous. Herodotus, for example, tells how the expelled Athenian tyrant Hippias, accompanying the Persian invaders at Marathon in 490 B.C.E., had the "oedipal" dream that he would sleep with his mother. He interpreted the dream to mean that he would be restored to his ancient mother, his native land of Athens, but the vision is fulfilled in a very different way when he loses a tooth in the Athenian soil (Herodotus, *Histories* 6.107). Actual incest is never at issue.[3]

In contrast to Aeschylus, as we have seen, Sophocles' oracles to Laius and Oedipus do not give commands or advice; they simply state the way things are. How things got that way we do not know. All we can say, and all the play shows us, is that the events do work out as the god said they would and that the human figures bring about these events through a chain of actions that contains some striking coincidences but is nevertheless within the realm of possibility. The oracle to Thebes that sets the action in motion, to be sure, does have the form of a command: "Lord Apollo ordered us clearly to drive out the land's pollution," as Creon reports from Delphi (96–97). Yet even this command is not an arbitrary intervention but a statement about the disorder that has spread from the polluted royal house to the whole kingdom. The reasons behind the older oracles that resulted in this disease are left obscure. Equally obscure is the god's choice of the time to reveal the truth. Why did the plague not break out immediately after Oedipus' marriage to Jocasta or after the birth of his children? The chorus asks this question later in its own poetic terms (1211–13): "How, how could the plowed furrows of your father have been able to bear you, miserable man, in silence for such a long time?" We are given no answer other than the fact that such is the shape that Oedipus' life is to have, and in that intermingling of guilt and innocence, responsibility, chance, and character lies the quality that we (following Aristotle) have come to call "tragic."

Sophocles' plot has some faults, which must be confronted frankly. To achieve his dramatic effects he has had to pay a certain price in terms of verisimilitude. We have to accept that Jocasta never before discussed with Oedipus the child she and Laius exposed, that Oedipus never mentioned the encounter at the crossroads, that neither of them ever talked about the scars on his feet, that the sole witness to Oedipus' killing of Laius was also the Herdsman to whom the infant was given for exposure, and that the Messenger from Corinth who reports Polybus' death had received this child from the Herdsman. Critics have also been troubled by the fact that a man of Oedipus' intelligence takes so long to put two and two together to discover the truth, especially after Teiresias has told him that he was the killer early in the play. Modern playwrights, from Corneille to Cocteau, have recast the plot to answer these questions (see Chapter 12).

We also have to accept the facts that the sole survivor and witness simply lied about how many attackers there were (118–19) and that Oedipus is mistaken in thinking that he killed "all" the men escorting Laius (813).[4] And we have to admit that Sophocles has left vague the amount of time that had elapsed between the killing of Laius and this witness' return to Thebes to find Oedipus already in place as king (758–62). During this unspecified interval (see 558–61), Oedipus has managed to defeat the Sphinx, marry Jocasta, and become installed as king of Thebes.

A play is not a novel, and the *Oedipus*' rhythm of action is so gripping, the movement of human emotions so convincing, that these problems do not bother us while we watch or even read the play. If we do stop to think about them (as most viewers or readers do not), they all have plausible answers. Laius' trusted Herdsman who received the child for exposure would be a likely escort for the king on his journey to Delphi. A man who "fled in fear," as Creon says (118), at the attack on Laius would be likely to keep quiet out of fear after finding Laius' killer established as the ruler of Thebes. Being a slave, he is at Oedipus' mercy, and his timidity and vulnerability are clear when we see him interrogated by Oedipus later. Knowing that he failed in his duty to protect his king, he might well have lied about the number of assailants and have taken his time in returning to Thebes to give his report of the event. We may compare the Guard of the *Antigone* (223–36), who makes a point of his reluctance to report to an irascible King Creon the bad news that his orders have been disobeyed and the corpse of Polyneices has been buried.

Oedipus might be faulted for having neglected to investigate Laius' killing and for not even knowing where it happened (113–14). Yet the play shows that the old king's death was primarily the Thebans' concern in the period before Oedipus assumed the throne, and that they were too preoccupied with the Sphinx to carry out a full inquiry. Oedipus asks why they did not investigate more thoroughly, and he receives a satisfactory answer (128–31, 558–67). Newly installed as king of a country ravaged by a monster, involved with a new marriage and new duties, he would naturally have been far more concerned about the future than the past. By the time of the present action, Laius' murder was regarded as past history, and this is clear from the way Oedipus speaks of the event. The Sphinx is gone; orderly succession to the throne has occurred; and Thebes has been happy, so far, with its new ruler. The old king is dead; long live the king!

Teiresias' prophetic powers also raise questions. If he has such foreknowledge, why did he not intervene to stop the marriage of Oedipus and Jocasta? Why could he not answer the riddle of the Sphinx himself, and why did he wait so many years to declare Oedipus the killer of Laius? Oedipus raises these last two questions (390–98, 558–68), and they are never answered explicitly. When Oedipus asks Creon point blank why Teiresias delayed so long in naming Laius' killer, Creon merely says that he does not know (569). This is probably Sophocles' way of telling us to leave the matter there; the ways of prophets are obscure, after all, and especially the ways of prophets as awesome as Teiresias.

Teiresias' foreknowledge suggests the existence of forces and patterns in our lives beyond the limit of ordinary human knowledge. As to his failure to help Thebes earlier, we have to accept it as a given piece of background detail that the Sphinx could be defeated only by the young hero from outside, not an old prophet within. Monsters too have ways of their own, and Sophocles, in any case, is careful to keep details about this fabulous beast very vague.

Teiresias' silence, however, is a more interesting matter. Even in the play's present action, Oedipus has to force him to speak; so it is not surprising that he volunteered no information in the past, assuming that he knew the truth even then. Even if Apollo had revealed the truth to Teiresias long ago (a fact that we have no right to assume), presumably the god also revealed that he, Apollo, would bring it to light in his own sweet time.

Speculation along these lines is fruitless, and one runs the risk of disregarding the conventions of the literary form and falling into the so-called documentary fallacy, treating the events as if they occur in real life and not as part of a literary construct that creates a circumscribed, artificial world. For the artifice to work, however, it has to be plausible, and the meeting between the king and the prophet is indeed plausible, both dramatically and emotionally. They interact as two such leaders might be expected to respond in a crisis involving power and authority. They are both proud, stubborn, and hot-tempered men; both are defensive, and both are led to say more than they initially intended. Oedipus, we know from the prologue, will be energetically exploring every means available to do what Apollo has commanded, and find the killer. The unsolved murder of his predecessor makes him uneasy and suspicious about a conspiracy to overthrow his own regime. Teiresias too is not used to being contradicted, let alone accused. We may compare the irascible Teiresias of *Antigone* (1048–94) and the aged and blind Oedipus himself in *Oedipus at Colonus*.

It is part of the tragic pattern that Teiresias' very silence raises Oedipus' suspicions of his collusion with Creon, as we see when Oedipus interrogates Creon about Laius' death, the inquiry to Delphi, and Teiresias' silence in the past (555–65). Here again possible divine causation interacts naturally and plausibly with human motivation. Viewed as part of a divine plan, Teiresias' silence can be attributed to his knowledge, as a divine prophet, of what is bound to happen, regardless of whether he speaks. Viewed in terms of normal human behavior (especially in the volatile political atmosphere of a late fifth-century *polis*), Oedipus is justified in assuming that Creon and Teiresias have conspired to accuse him of the murder and seize power for themselves.

The silence of Teiresias has another and perhaps more profound meaning, and this relates not so much to character as to moral structure. His presence, like that of the oracles, implies the existence of some kind of order operating mysteriously in our world. The most general Greek term for this order is *dikê*, often translated as "justice" but actually connoting something like "path of retribution." It implies a process that undoes violence by violence. It restores a balance in the world order that has been upset by action beyond the limits of allowable human behavior, and this restoration of order may bring with it even greater suffering than the original crime. In simplest terms, the crimes of Oedipus, regardless of his moral guilt, are a source of this kind of disorder, and the violence that he has released will return to his world and his life.

The stain of blood that Oedipus carries from killing Laius, even though he acted in self-defense, is the source of a pollution that results in the plague. Sophocles' audience would naturally assume that the plague was sent by the gods, and Apollo's command, which Creon reports from Delphi in the first scene, confirms this. Sophocles, however, never actually says that the gods have sent the plague. In its mysterious and probably supernatural origin, the plague is both the causal agent of the process of purging disorder that the Greeks called *dikê* and the sign that this process is under way.

Oedipus' pollution would normally require ritual purification and exile from his city, at least for some years. As Bernard Williams has recently suggested, the Greek view of this aspect of Oedipus' situation may be compared with our law of torts rather than with criminal law.[5] According to criminal law (both ours and the Greeks') Oedipus is not a criminal, for he acted in self-defense in the one case and in ignorance in the second. Yet his actions (which would correspond to his liability under the law of torts) have caused serious damage, in the form of the pollution, from which individuals and the community have suffered, and he must make some kind of requital. In the *Oedipus at Colonus*, Oedipus will in fact successfully argue the legal basis of his innocence before the citizens of Colonus (258–74, 960–99). Unlike the later play, however, *Oedipus Tyrannus* stresses the sheer misfortune and unpredictability of Oedipus' situation rather than questions of legality.

The play clearly distinguishes between the parricide and incest that Oedipus committed in ignorance and the willed act of self-blinding when he discovers the truth (1329–46). This willed and self-chosen punishment also contrasts with his involuntary curse on himself as Laius' killer, which he pronounced early in the play (246–51). At the same time this curse becomes another of the tragic coincidences that stretch Oedipus' sufferings to their fullest possible pitch, for his own zeal to help his city dooms him even more horribly, "to wear out his wretched life wretchedly in utter doom" (248).

At a time of intense interest in issues of causality, motivation, and legality, the play explores the shadowy areas between involuntary crime, religious pollution, moral innocence, and the personal horror in feeling oneself the bearer of a terrible guilt. Oedipus is not completely innocent, but, as a court of human law might measure it, his suffering and the suffering of those around him (Jocasta, their children, and all those who have died in the plague) are far out of proportion to the degree of guilt. Like every great tragedy, the play forces us to rethink our comfortable assumptions about a just world order. Oedipus' tragic heroism consists in taking on himself, by his own hand, a punishment far greater than what the law would require.

The irreducible discrepancy here between what a man has done and what he suffers makes up the play's tragic view of life, a view that presents our control over our circumstances as precarious and our grasp on happiness as always uncertain. Teiresias, in his paradoxical vision-in-blindness, knows this truth but is reluctant to tell it, partly because we do not want to hear it. It is a characteristically tragic wisdom, and as such it must be wrested from him forcibly and received reluctantly, if at all.

In an old tale we find a mythical paradigm for this kind of knowledge and its difficult reception among men. Silenus, a satyr and companion of the god Dionysus, is captured and forced to reveal his knowledge. "Why do you force me to tell what it is better for you not to know?" he asks his captors. "For life is freest of pain when it is accompanied by ignorance of its own suffering . . . For mortals, best of all is not to be born" (Plutarch, *Consolation to Apollonius*, 115D). The reluctant silence of Teiresias is akin to the reluctance of this wise demigod of nature; Sophocles echoes the sentiments in a choral ode in his last play: "Not to be born wins every accounting; and by far second best is when born to return there whence one has come as quickly as possible" (*Oedipus at Colonus* 1224–28).

What is at stake in Oedipus' inquiry, then, is not just his personal situation—it is also the makeup of the world and its bearing on the possibility of happiness in human life. Through Teiresias, the oracles, and the puzzlement of the chorus, questions about the orderliness, justice, or chaos of our world will be framed not in the small, petty circumstances of daily life, but in the large civic arena and against the background of the vast natural world. The mountains—especially Cithaeron, which reappears throughout the play, and also Parnassus and Olympus—are in the background, part of the outer frame, as are the places beyond the limits of the mortal world mentioned in the odes, especially the far western realm of death in the first ode (the parodos) and the eternal realm of the gods and their laws in the third (the second stasimon).

STORY AND PLOT

In looking at the remarkable design of the *Oedipus Tyrannus*, we must distinguish not only between the play and the myth but also between the *story* (the totality of the events as they might be told in chronological order) and the *plot* (the events as they appear in the order shown in the play). This play does not tell the whole myth of Oedipus, nor even the whole story of his life; it unfolds as a *plot*, a carefully chosen and constructed sequence of events at one brief, though decisive, crisis in the hero's life. From that point, the play moves both backward and forward to other parts of the myth as a whole. The plot does not give us all the details at once, nor does it present them in a continuous order or as a single, linear development. It reveals fragments, and we, like Oedipus, have to piece these together to make up a coherent narrative.

It is characteristic of Sophocles' selective narration that he reserves his most focused, continuous account of events for the few tense moments surrounding Jocasta's death and Oedipus' self-blinding (1237–85). There is no connected story of Oedipus' life, from his birth to his rule at Thebes, such as Euripides provides in the prologue of his *Phoenician Women*. Instead, the past of Oedipus is a shadowy area of elusive facts submerged in what seems to be remote, mythic time.

The plot structure has two other related effects. First, the events of the past are surrounded by mystery, both because they are so remote and so horrible and because they are recovered so gradually and so painfully. Second, the *process* of the discovery is as important as the *content* of what is discovered. This is a play about how we uncover a hidden, frightful, and frightening past. The rhythm of this process of discovery gives the play its unique power and fascination.

The play's most powerful moments come when the search for knowledge takes two different directions simultaneously. This happens first near the exact center of the play. Jocasta, intending to turn Oedipus away from further pursuit of Teiresias' prophecy, gives him the clue about the triple road that in fact intensifies his search. Later the pattern is repeated when the Corinthian Messenger inadvertently deflects Oedipus from the search for Laius' killer to the search for his own parents. At the end of this scene, Jocasta urges him not to carry his investigation any further (1056–68), but Oedipus is determined to press on, ignorant that the answer to both searches is the same. The following scene closes that gap between the two searches, but to reach that moment of "terrible hearing" (1169) Oedipus again has to wrest knowledge forcibly from one who refuses to tell. It is part of the play's irony that the same action that led to triumph in the past—namely overcoming the resistance of one who knows but won't tell (the Sphinx)—now leads to total disaster.

TELLING THE STORY BACKWARD: REVERSIBLE TIME

The *Oedipus* is almost unique among Greek tragedies in telling its story in reverse. Nearly every crucial event in the action has already happened. The action is therefore almost all retrospective action—that is, it depicts how the characters (and the spectators too) see and understand in the present events that took place far in the past. It is part of the same effect that the play uses and scrutinizes the different ways in which stories unfold, the different ways in which one may tell one's life story, and the different ways in which such stories are heard and understood. Akira Kurosawa's film *Rashomon* offers a modern analogy. The chief events of Oedipus' life history—his birth, exposure, victories over Laius and the Sphinx, and marriage—emerge piecemeal, from different points of view and in partial, fragmented perspective. Like Oedipus, we as spectators have to reconstruct a hidden past from hints, memories, glimpses.

The play's dislocation of the chronological order of the events makes it hard, if not impossible, for Oedipus to disentangle the riddles of his past.[6] This situation helps explain why a man of his intelligence cannot see the truth and at the same time supports his claims of moral innocence later. It is a subtle but important feature of Oedipus' innocent ignorance that, whenever he tells the oracle that has darkened his life, he reports its two parts in the order incest and parricide; and only after the revelation of the truth does he report the order in which these events actually occurred, parricide and incest.[7] A third conclusion also follows, namely that we have at least to consider the possibility that something in the structure of reality itself lies behind this innocent suffering. This mysterious agent Oedipus calls "Apollo" and modern interpreters call "fate." The play, however, leaves the matter as a question, unresolved but important. Rather than giving a final answer, it shows us the hypotheses of the various characters, including the chorus, to try to account for the suffering.

Because of this way of telling its story, the play is also about narrative. It uses the special privilege of literary texts to reflect on their own artifice and to remind us of the ways in which they can suspend reality to offer an enhanced vision of reality. One of Sophocles' contemporaries, the philosopher and rhetorician Gorgias, wrote, apropos of the effect of tragedy, "He who deceives is more just than he who does not deceive, and the one deceived is wiser than the one who is not deceived."[8] In the case of *Oedipus*, the "wisdom" that we (the "deceived" audience) get comes from accepting the dramatic illusion (the "deception" of the plot) and participating in the special vision of the world that we thus receive. At the same time we know that this vision is real only in a particular sense, as a model of a problem or a hypothesis about our world that we rarely see so sharply focused in our everyday reality.

As part of its wise deception the play also exploits its freedom to tell its story in fragments, in scenes taken out of chronological order, with omissions that are filled in later, and in flashbacks. Art has the power to reverse time and so to let us see, and question, modes of causality that are invisible in "real" life. We are forced to think about the role of the gods and, especially, about the mixture of free choice and necessity in the oracles. If Laius, Jocasta, and Oedipus, for example, had done nothing to avoid the oracles, would they have come true anyway? Or by taking their evasive action did they in fact play into the hands of the gods and bring about the very events that they were trying to prevent? The literary device of telling events out of their chronological order also creates much of Sophocles' celebrated irony: the discrepancy between the larger picture that we, the spectators, see and the small piece visible to the participants who are immersed in the stream of events.

It is revealing to compare Oedipus' story with that of Odysseus, another hero whose myth embraces the whole of a life cycle. The dominant feature of

Odysseus' story, as we see it in Homer's *Odyssey*, is commitment to his return from the Trojan War, a successful and ultimately happy journey home, with a clear goal and strong emphasis on the motifs of recovery and rebirth. The dominant feature of Oedipus' story is the tragic shape of a life that is always turning back on itself instead of going forward. He can realize his identity only by losing it, and then gaining it back under the sign of tragic truth.

The continuity of life-movement in the *Odyssey* corresponds to the clarity and forward movement of narrative in the epic form, in contrast to the halting, unpredictable, blocked movements of narrative in tragedy.[9] In the expansive epic frame, narrative is relatively unproblematic because time is unproblematic. Although the *Odyssey* uses retrospective narration (in the flashback of books 9–12), the hero's movement in time is steadily forward, toward his goal. In tragedy, and especially in *Oedipus*, time is constantly bending backward and forward with mysterious gaps and discontinuities. The dangers and limits that surround human life in tragedy make both generational time and narrative time uncertain, unreliable, and complicated. Even though the recognition of the limits of mortality is a major theme in the tale of Odysseus, he is always able to see, and ultimately achieve, his goal of returning to the full life that he left behind. For Oedipus past and future are always getting entangled with each other. In the terrible circularity of his life pattern, he can never pull free of the maimed life in the past.

The almost simultaneous return of the Corinthian Messenger and the Herdsman, who together saved the baby Oedipus many years ago, seems like pure coincidence, but, on reflection, it reveals a coincidence of another kind. Such returns are appropriate to a life story that cannot break free of its past. The past is always returning, in the wrong place. The child returns to the bed and to the "furrows" of his mother, "sowing" where he was "plowed," as Oedipus cries out in his agony near the end (1403–8). The son cast out by the father comes back to meet the father in just the wrong place, and so to kill him. The oracle originally given to Laius keeps returning, different yet always the same, to mark the different stages of Oedipus' life: in infancy, at the end of his adolescence, and in his maturity, when he is king of Thebes. Even a slave at the periphery of a famed king's' life turns out to be a part of a mysterious rhythm of fatally overlapping returns. The Herdsman who saved the infant Oedipus reappears at his passage between adolescence and adulthood to witness his killing of Laius, and then again at his tragic passage from full maturity to the blindness and debility of his remaining years. Sophocles does not use these coincidences as proof of a deterministic universe, but rather as the facts of an uncanny pattern of a life that is thus marked as tragic.

TIME, ORACLE, AND RIDDLE

The riddle has had the opposite role from the oracle in Oedipus' life: it is a source of pride and confidence, whereas the oracle is a source of anxiety and helplessness. Oedipus can resolve the simultaneity of the various stages of life intellectually, in the *verbal* play of the riddle; but he acts out the horror of that fusion of separate generational stages in living a *life* that fulfills the oracle.

While the answer to the riddle implies the complete span of a full life, from infancy to extreme old age, the oracle would prevent this life from getting started at all. In the form in which the oracle is given to Laius, it would first prevent a child's begetting and then prevent his growing up. Oedipus solved the riddle by seeing through its metaphor of feet for motion through life. But of course his own feet hold the secret or riddle of his life, and that is partly because of the oracle, which led his parents to bind his two feet together into one so that he, unlike the creeping, walking, and cane-using generic human being of the riddle, would never walk at all, never move through any of the stages of life.

The circular movement of time in the play itself is governed by the oracles. The first oracle is in the present: the command from Apollo at Delphi to drive out the land's pollution, the cause of the plague. It is a command and thus is directed to the future, but of course it points us back to the past, the killing of Laius nearly twenty years ago. The second oracle, given to Laius and Jocasta, referred to future events: the father will die at the hands of his son. But at the point when Jocasta tells Oedipus about this oracle, it belongs to the remote past (711–23). And Oedipus fears that his own oracle, the third, which he received at Delphi many years before, will point to his future, but when he relates it to Jocasta (787–93) it is in fact already part of his past: he has already fulfilled it in his journey from Delphi to Thebes.

Measuring and counting time is one of Oedipus' major actions onstage. But his attempts to organize time into logical patterns collapse in the terrible uncertainty of time in his own life. Rather than serving as something he can find out and know with certainty, time becomes an active force that finally has "found him out" as the one who "long ago" made that "no-marriage marriage" in which "birth and begetting," origins and maturity, were fused together (1213–15). Rather than becoming an aid to human understanding, time seems to have a kind of independent power that blocks knowledge. It blocks future knowledge because its course has been hidden from the actors. It blocks past knowledge because memory selects and filters. Both the Messenger of the blinding scene and the Old Herdsman attribute this failure of knowledge to erroneous or partial memory. Even Oedipus cannot accurately remember the details of his fatal encounter with Laius. As we now know, he did not kill all of the travelers.

Time in the play expands and contracts, producing effects of vagueness or density by turns. It is both the indefinite and inert passing of years and the single moment of crisis in decision and action, the irreversible turning point of a man's life. When he can still hope that the truth will leave his present view of himself intact, Oedipus describes himself as defined by his "kindred months" in a slow rhythm of waxing and waning, becoming small and great (1082–83).

But in fact he is defined by the abrupt catastrophe of a single day (351, 478) which makes him both "great and small," king and beggar, in one instant.

Time can have an unexpected fullness, as in Creon's account of past events in the prologue. Here there seems to be an indefinite interval between the death of Laius and the arrival of Oedipus to vanquish the Sphinx, an interval in which the Thebans cannot investigate the death of their king because the Sphinx compels them to consider only the immediate present, "to regard the things at our feet, letting go the things unclear" (130–31). It is as if this major crisis in the present life of the city retreats to the obscurity of remote happenings, far beyond living memory. But Oedipus, in his confident belief that he can overcome time, announces, "But I shall bring these things to light *from their beginning*" (132).

When Oedipus thinks that he has in fact reached through time to reveal this hidden truth, the time surrounding Laius' death again has the same vagueness and fullness. Interrogating Creon, whom he now takes to be the agent of the murder, Oedipus asks, "How much time before did Laius [die]?" and Creon replies, "Times [or, years] great and old would be measured" (561). As in the prologue, that critical event, the death of the king and the father, becomes surrounded by an aura of remote, almost mythical time, as if it were an act belonging to primordial beginnings (as in one sense it did) and not to a specific historical moment in the life of an individual and a city.

Oedipus is confident that he will uncover these "beginnings" (132), but origins are more mysterious and harder to fathom than he knows. At the climactic moment of discovery this vague temporal duration is suddenly ripped open by the electrifying flash of the single moment of "terrible hearing" (1169). In the relaxed seasonal tempo of the Herdsman's life on Cithaeron, before Oedipus' birth, only the changes of summer and winter, without events, mark the passage of time (1132–39). But tragic time has a wholly different aspect: it is the single instant of decision and recognition that suddenly overturns an entire life.

It is a gift of prophetic knowledge to see time past, present, and future in a single vision. Calchas, the prophet of the *Iliad*, "knew what is and what will be and what is before" (*Iliad*, 1.70), and the prophetess Theonoe in Euripides' *Helen* "understood the divine things, those now and all those to come" (*Helen*, 13–14). In *Oedipus*, we the audience first see Oedipus in the present as king and ruler, supplicated by his people because they hope he will save them. But Teiresias, a little later, sees the Oedipus of the future, a blind man tapping his way with his stick. Jocasta and the Herdsman see Oedipus as a helpless newborn, his feet pierced so that no one will take him up. Jocasta, again, in her last words on stage, sees the whole course of Oedipus' life as one of utter misery, which she marks in her final words for him, "ill-fated" and "ill-starred" (1068, 1071). The spectator at the play enjoys the omniscient perspective of the gods; like the gods, he or she can see Oedipus in all three roles at once: the powerful king, the accursed and helpless infant, and the blinded sufferer.

TRACKING THE PAST: THE RETURN OF THE REPRESSED

Knowledge in the play results from bringing separate, individual past events together into a single moment in the present. The major action of the play gets under way with Oedipus' inquiry about Laius' murder: "Where will be found this trace, hard to track, of the ancient crime?" (108–09). The investigation is like a hunt, and Oedipus assumes that he can follow a set of tracks that will lead smoothly from the present to the past, Laius' past. But the road into the past proves not to be single but manifold, just as Oedipus himself proves to be not one but many. Thus instead of the "track" leading to only one object of inquiry, Laius' killer, it in fact diverges into several different paths—triple roads, one could say: Oedipus' origins, his exposure by his parents, his marriage with Jocasta.

This collocation of the past with the present receives vivid dramatic enactment in nearly every scene of the play. Indeed, the very first line of the play, Oedipus' address to the suppliant citizens, juxtaposes old and new: "O children, of Cadmus old the newest brood." Visually too this scene displays a combination of ages in the onstage presence of youths, mature men, and elders, as the priest explains a few lines later (15–19). Oedipus is himself an anomalous composite of "young" and "old," since the incest makes him the member of two generations simultaneously.

This combination of past and present again becomes ominously vivid in Teiresias, the old man who belongs to the past and sees the "truth" that threads the past together with the future. "The future events will come of themselves," he says at the beginning of his interview with Oedipus, "even if I conceal them in silence" (341). Instead of thus "concealing" the future, he brings it visually before our eyes in his dreadful prophecies. Although he is not understood by Oedipus in the present, Teiresias warns him that he does not see "where he is" (367, 413–15) or the future sufferings that await him (427–29, 453–60). Those sufferings consist precisely in the fact that the incest makes the father "equal" to his children (424) and removes the boundaries that should separate those stages and activities of life. Oedipus, Teiresias reveals, unknowingly inhabits this fearful simultaneity of different generations (456–60).

Oedipus' intelligence, Jocasta suggests later, lies in "inferring the new by means of the old" (916). When Oedipus does in fact bring together the "old things" of his remote infancy and early manhood with the "new things" of his present life and circumstances, he knows himself as both king and pollution, both the savior and the destroyer of Thebes.

As Oedipus begins his "tracking" of Laius' killer (109), he needs, as he says, a *symbolon* (221), a word usually translated as "clue." But the word also means a "tally," one of two parts of a token that fit together to prove one's rightful place. In Sophocles' day Athenians used such "tokens" for admission to the law courts. The investigative skill that Oedipus will demonstrate, then, consists in fitting pieces together. The word *symbolon* also has another meaning, namely the "token" left with a child exposed at birth to establish later proof of his identity. The word carries this sense in the tale of Ion, another foundling, dramatized in Euripides' *Ion*, a kind of Oedipus story in reverse. Presented with an old basket that contains the secret of his origins, Ion hesitates to open it and examine the "tokens from his mother" (*Ion*, 1386) lest he turn out to be the child of a slave (1382–83: see *Oedipus* 1063, 1168). He finally decides to take the risk ("I must dare," *Ion* 1387), just as Oedipus does ("I must hear," *Oedipus* 1170), although with very different results. Oedipus' initial objective, the public task of "tracking down" a killer by a "clue" (*symbolon* in the juridical sense), turns into the personal and intimate task of finding the "birth token" (*symbolon* in the personal sense) that proves his identity.

As the forward rhythm of the push for knowledge begins to accelerate, there is a retarding movement that pulls back toward not knowing, toward leaving origins veiled in darkness. It is appropriately the mother who takes on this retarding role. She who stood at the first beginning of his life and (as we learn) was involved in a contradictory pull between the birth and the death of her new child (1173–75), would still keep him from the terrible knowledge and thus save his life. Like all great plots, the play combines forward movement to the end with the pleasure of delaying and complicating that end.[10]

This simultaneity of past and present belongs to the uncanny or the inexplicable, which is represented onstage in the blind prophet, behind whom stands the remote and mysterious Apollo. Although Oedipus' first act is to consult Apollo at Delphi, he never integrates what Apollo and Teiresias know into what he knows. Not until it is too late does he put the oracles together by means of that intelligence whose special property is to join past and present, to connect disparate events, facts, experiences, and stages of life. Oedipus' failure in logical deduction was one of Voltaire's objections to the structure of the play.[11] But what an Enlightenment rationalist would consider a fault the ancient dramatist would consider the very essence of the tragic element. Oedipus uses his human knowledge primarily in conflict with the divine, to block, deny, contradict, or evade it.

Knowledge veers not only between human and divine, but also between active and passive. Human knowledge is actively sought and willed as the achievement of man's intellectual power. The divine knowledge comes, it seems, by chance, on precarious and unpredictable paths. The mysterious divine knowledge is conveyed through the blind prophet, but its truth is confirmed only by sheer coincidence, through the arrival of the Corinthian Messenger and then the Old Herdsman, and it is the latter who provides the clinching piece of knowledge, Oedipus' identity as the exposed child of Laius and Jocasta.

This first mention of the one person who "knows" anything is as vague as possible: the man is only "some one man" (118). Oedipus makes no attempt to refine this description. Instead he shifts attention from "some one *man*" to "some one *thing*" in his next line: "What sort of thing [did he say]? For one thing would find out many things for learning" (120). The grammatical categories of language itself—the ease of shifting from masculine to neuter (one man, one thing) and from singular to plural (robber, robbers)—lead the investigators astray from what will finally solve the mystery. Language itself encourages their deception and leads them to pursue what will prove to be, in one sense, misinformation.

Forgotten for some six hundred lines, more than a third of the play, this individual resurfaces when Jocasta's reference to the triple roads (another numerical problem) arouses Oedipus' anxiety (see 730). "Alas, these things are now clear," he says. "Who was it who spoke these words to you, my wife?" (754–55). "A house-servant," Jocasta replies, "who arrived as the only one saved" (756). This last phrase is the other, objective side of Creon's more subjectively oriented description of the man as "having fled in fear" in the prologue (118).

"Did he then happen to be present in the house?" Oedipus presses on. "No," answers Jocasta, and she explains how the servant came to Thebes, found Oedipus already in possession of the royal power and Laius dead. Touching Jocasta's hand, he asked to be sent to the fields (761) and to the pastures of the flocks, so that "he might be as far as possible out of sight of the town" (755–82). The contrast between "house" and "field" (756–61) recalls Oedipus' first specific point of investigation of Laius' death: "Was it in the house or in the fields?" (112). The sole witness there was "some one man" (118); and Creon's phrase calls attention to his unitary identity.[12] His initial "oneness," like that of Oedipus, bifurcates ominously into two. He is both the house-servant (756) and the herdsman in the "pastures of the flocks" (761). He is both the man described by Jocasta and the man described by Creon, both the man who survived the attack on Laius and the killer/rescuer of the infant Oedipus on Cithaeron. Like Oedipus, he is both an insider ("reared in the house," as he describes himself later [1123]) and an outsider, one who was sent from the house to the fields or the mountains.

This figure of the Herdsman/escort plays an increasingly important role in giving different perspectives on what really happened in the past. He possesses "knowing" (*eidôs*) from a crucial "seeing" (*eide*, 119), a play on the similarity between the Greek words that is not easily translated into English. But here, as throughout the drama, this wordplay is charged with meaning. At this early point in the work, when Creon mentions this lone survivor for the first time, his reported story introduces the identification of knowing with seeing that is central to the play's concern with ignorance and perception. Later, Jocasta tells Oedipus that it was after the Herdsman "saw" Oedipus on the throne that he requested from her a kind of absence of vision, to be "out of sight of the house" (762). Like Oedipus in the future, he seeks a combination of negated vision ("out of the sight of the house") and exile from his place in house and city (see 1384–94, 1451–54).

Still confident as the king searching for the killer of Laius, Oedipus then sends for this only survivor of the attack on the former king (765–770). It is sheer coincidence that this man should also be the one whom Laius entrusted with killing the infant Oedipus. And yet that coincidence points to a deep necessity. Oedipus cannot progress in his role as ruler of the city, whose task it is to discover and expel Laius' killer, until he has solved the mystery of his own origins. He cannot solve the mystery of the plague until he solves the mystery of himself. To do that, he has to force the figure who holds the missing piece to recapitulate earlier stages of his life as well: when he changed from house-servant (756) to herdsman (761) and when, in that earlier role, he had brought Oedipus to both doom and salvation on Mount Cithaeron (see 1349–52). The philosopher George Santayana remarked that those who do not know history are compelled to repeat it. The Oedipus works out the truth of this statement on the level of personal history: not to know who you are is to be compelled to search ceaselessly for your origins.

The Herdsman's life also parallels Oedipus' in the spatial shift that he undergoes in the course of the play, from house to mountain, from a figure at the center of the palace life (756) to a figure at the margins of the city, in the mountains. The Herdsman's life, governed by such different rhythms of space and time, proves to be causally related to Oedipus' life and also similar to it in form, parallel in its course but also more vaguely outlined and set into a larger and remoter frame. The condensation of Oedipus' life into the hour or two acted out in the "real" time of the performance has behind it, like a larger shadow, the more expansive movement of the Old Herdsman's passage through time.

The Herdsman recurs as a figure dimly parallel to Oedipus in his life's movements and spontaneous impulse of pity and fear, but he is also in one essential point the opposite of Oedipus. The first specific detail given about him is his "flight in fear" in order to be "the only one saved" (118, 756). His characteristic mode of action in the play is evasion through running away. This is what he did when Oedipus attacked Laius at the crossroads and what he did again when he returned from that episode to find Oedipus ruling in Thebes. It is also what the young Oedipus did when he heard his destiny foretold him at Delphi (788–97). The Herdsman repeats the pattern a third and last time on the stage when Oedipus interrogates him. He tries to escape by evasion or denial (see 1129–31, 1146–59, 1165), but now Oedipus compels him to face and speak the "terrible" that is contained in the truth (1169–70).

This last scene brings Oedipus and his shadowy double together, finally, on the stage. Now neither of them can run away. Yet this coming together shows us their characteristic divergence. The Herdsman is a slave (see 1123; also 764, 1168), and he seeks survival by denying the truth. The king goes to meet his destiny head-on, confronting the "necessity" that comes from his oracles, even if that confrontation means his death. The Herdsman/slave at the crossroads was "the only one to be saved" (756). King Oedipus is ready to become the communal victim, the *pharmakos* or scapegoat, whose single death saves the whole city (see 1409–12), although his submission to Creon in the final scene prevents that pattern from being completely realized.[13]

NOTES

1. Philip Vellacott, *Sophocles and Oedipus* (Ann Arbor: University of Michigan Press, 1971), 108.

2. Karl Reinhardt, *Sophocles*, trans. H. and D. Harvey (Oxford: Basil Blackwell, 1979), 98.

3. In the *Dream Analysis* (*Oneirokritika*) of Artemidorus (second century C.E.) even intensely sexual incest dreams have nonsexual meanings: see John J. Winkler, *Constraints of Desire* (New York: Routledge, 1990), 37–44, with his translation of Artemidorus 1.79 on pp. 213–15.

4. The contradictions and problems of the plot have been observed as early as Voltaire's *Letters on Oedipus* (see Chapter 12). For a convenient list see John J. Peradotto, "Disauthorizing Prophecy: The Ideological Mapping of *Oedipus Tyrannus*," *Transactions of the American Philological Association* 122 (1992), 7–8, 13–14. The Old Herdsman's lie is rather unusual because when Sophocles lets his characters lie, he generally provides some hint in their manner of speech or some warning to the audience that a lie is being told. Presumably in this case he could assume that the story was sufficiently familiar so that the audience would know the truth and realize the falsehood of the Herdsman's statement. The reference to his "fear" here, as well as his frightened request of Jocasta of which we are told later (758–64), also helps us to recognize that he must be lying.

5. Bernard Williams, *Shame and Necessity* (Berkeley and Los Angeles: University of California Press, 1993), 62–67. R. Drew Griffith, *The Theatre of Apollo: Divine Justice and Sophocles' Oedipus the King* (Montreal and Kingston: McGill-Queen's University Press, 1996), especially 45–69, argues, unconvincingly, that Oedipus is justly punished by Apollo for killing Laius. No one would suggest that Oedipus is innocent, and he himself immediately recognizes his polluted state as Laius' possible killer (*Oedipus* 813–23). Yet an approach, like Griffith's, which focuses on this single act, leaves out all the overdeterminations and complications that the play interweaves as essential parts of Oedipus' life story (the oracles, the plague, the coincidences, the rhythm of discovery, the character of all the figures in the story, and so on). The fragmented reading of the type that Griffith proposes reduces the richness of the tragedy to a banal moralization. For the range of interpretation in this question of Oedipus' guilt, it is worth noting that Griffith's thesis is just the reverse of the theory of Frederick Ahl, *Sophocles' Oedipus: Evidence and Self-Conviction* (Ithaca, N.Y.: Cornell University Press, 1991), that Oedipus did not kill Laius at all.

6. See Brian Vickers, *Towards Greek Tragedy* (London: Longmans, 1979), 500–13; also Adrian Poole, *Tragedy: Shakespeare and the Greek Example* (Oxford: Blackwell, 1987), 100–104.

7. Incest and parricide: 791–93, 825–27, 994–96; parricide and incest: 1184–85, 1288–89, 1357–59, 1398–1408.

8. Gorgias, fragment 82 B23 in Hermann Diels and Walther Kranz, eds., *Die Fragmente der Vorsokratiker*, vol. 2, 6th ed. (Berlin: Weidmann, 1952), pp. 305–6. The fragment is quoted by Plutarch, *On the Glory of the Athenians*, chap. 5, 348C.

9. For some suggestive remarks on the differences between time and life patterns in epic and tragedy see Bennett Simon, *The Family in Tragedy* (New Haven: Yale University Press, 1988), 13–21, 59–60.

10. See Peter Brooks, "Freud's Masterplot: A Model for Narrative," in his *Reading for the Plot* (New York: Vintage Books, 1985), 90–112, especially 101–9.

11. Voltaire, *Letter on Oedipus*, Letter 3.

12. The phrase "Laius dead" (in the same metrical position) occurs in both Creon's account of the Herdsman/escort (in 126) and in Jocasta's tale of how this man came to her after he saw Oedipus on the throne (in 759). The verbal echo is another link between the two passages and perhaps also serves to remind us of the causal connection, still hidden from all but this herdsman, between Laius' death and Oedipus' "power" or kingship (*kratê*, 758).

13. On the scapegoat pattern, see below, Chapter 9, with note 11, and Chapter 12; also my *Dionysiac Poetics and Euripides' Bacchae*, 2nd ed. (Princeton, N.J.: Princeton University Press, 1997), 42–45.

READING *OEDIPUS TYRANNUS*

7

~~~~~~

The Crisis of the City and the King

Prologue and Parode (1–215)

The opening scene or prologue (i.e., everything before the entrance of the chorus at 151) is brilliantly constructed. Quickly and economically, Sophocles leads us into the city's crisis, provides the essential details to orient us in the present, and lets us see the chief protagonist in action. Nothing seems superfluous. The background emerges from the situation itself. But behind the clarity of exposition lie many unknowns: the remote death of Laius, the Sphinx, Apollo, and of course the awful truth that is hinted at in the ironies and the double meanings, as when Oedipus pledges that he will be "removing the pollution not on behalf of remoter kin but for my very self" (137–38).

The play opens with Oedipus standing before a group of citizens who carry the insignia of ritual supplication. They have come to him, their ruler and protector, for help against the ravages of the plague. The visual configuration shows him in his role as king, the protector of his people.[1] His brief speech of comfort, the first words of the play (1–13), establishes quickly and specifically some basic traits of his character: his concern for the city and its inhabitants, his reverence for the marks of supplication, his compassion for the young and helpless, his energy and good will. These impressions are confirmed by the Priest, the spokesman for the suppliants, who addresses the king with hope and confidence in his power, recalling his previous successes, particularly in defeating the Sphinx. The people regard him as their savior, almost as a god (48), and Oedipus responds to the challenge with compassion, commitment, and energy.

This is the only surviving play of Sophocles that begins with such a mass scene—an effect more common in Aeschylus and Euripides. Generally Sophocles begins with a quieter, more private setting, a monologue or a close conversation between two characters (as in *Antigone, Electra,* or *Oedipus at Colonus*). The public nature of the opening of *Oedipus,* with its ritual acts of supplicatory prayers, offerings, and laments, calls attention both to the danger facing the entire city and to Oedipus' responsibility as the leader who confronts that danger and takes it upon himself.

The opening scene has still another function. The rite of supplication implies the acknowledgment of another's greater power, in this case that of the gods, but that recognition of helplessness before the gods is combined with the city's confidence in the power of a mortal, Oedipus. The Priest, a man of traditional piety, carefully distinguishes his supplication of Oedipus from that of a god and thus introduces one of the central issues, mortal limitation and divine power:

> We have not come as suppliants to this altar
> because we thought of you as of a God,
> but rather judging you the first of men
> in all the chances of this life and when
> we mortals have to do with more than man.
>
> (Grene's translation, 31–34)

There is a warning note in the phrase "first of men in all the chances of this life" (33), for this can also mean, "first of men in the misfortunes of life." In fact, the word translated as "chances" (*symphorai*) refers to the "misfortunes" of Oedipus in its three later occurrences (833, 1347, 1527). Oedipus is thus "the first of men" in both success and misery, the extremes that he will span as the exemplar of mortal vicissitude.

Supplication is usually addressed to a god; this is one of the rare places in extant Greek tragedy where the protagonist is the one to be supplicated rather than the one to supplicate (as in Euripides' *Hecuba*) or merely to receive the suppliants (as in Aeschylus' *Suppliants*). This situation not only exalts Oedipus but also helps prepare for the major reversal in the plot, the shift from the collective crisis of Thebes to the personal crisis of its ruler.

At the same time the Priest's collocation of old and young, boys and mature men (16–19) sets forth that coincidence of different stages of life that will define Oedipus in his unique disaster. When he answers the Priest's appeal, he restates the combination of one and many, knowledge and ignorance, wholeness and infirmity, that eventually emerges as the tragic shape of his own life:

> . . . *I know* you are *all* sick
> yet there is *not one* of you, *sick* though you are,
> that is as *sick as I myself.*
> Your *several* sorrows each have *single* scope
> and touch *but one* of you. *My* spirit groans
> for *city and myself and you at once.*
>
> (Grene's translation, 59–64, my italics)

Oedipus' identification of his own suffering with the city's conceals his status as the polluted criminal who can heal the city's disease only by revealing the disease in himself. When he goes on to speak of the "many roads of thought" that he has traveled to arrive at the "only cure" for the plague (67–69), we are

74

prepared for the literal "roads" that he has traversed in reaching Thebes, especially the "road" where he met and killed Laius (801–4), thus bringing into the city its present "disease," which is himself.

Although Sophocles begins the play with Oedipus, he also makes us aware of the world around his protagonist, above all the city and the spaces of the city, both sacred and secular, both within and outside the walls. The Priest evokes the civic population gathered in the marketplace. He mentions the two temples of Athena and the oracular shrine of Apollo by the river Ismenos (20–21). He speaks of the fields and the fertile earth and the cattle in the pastures, all blighted by the plague. The words *city* and *town* recur repeatedly. But all of this human space is intersected by another realm, that of the gods above, who have sent the plague, and the gods below, to whom the Priest refers when he tells how "black Hades grows rich with the groans and cries of lament" (25–30). Images of the sea, which recur throughout the play, also suggest the great powers of nature mastered by human intelligence but always uncertain and dangerous (see 23–24, 50–51).

The Priest takes us beyond the present in his allusions to Oedipus' earlier liberation of the city from its troubles, when he defeated the Sphinx (35–36), the deed that gave him that universal "fame" which he proudly mentions in his opening speech (7–8): "I have come myself, I who am called Oedipus famous to all." Oedipus' announcement that he has already sent Creon to Delphi to seek a remedy from Apollo's oracle gives solid proof of his energy and concern (68–72), but throughout the speech (58–79) he also uses those images of walking, disease, time, knowledge, and revelation that will resonate ominously through the rest of the play.

Reckoning the time of Creon's absence, Oedipus gives a hint of his impatient energy. As Creon enters (for the play has no time to waste), Oedipus speaks of his eye and his walking, both images important for the meaning of the play, while the Priest points out the garlands of laurel, a sign of good fortune (78–84). Both men hang on Creon's words, but the Priest now steps aside, and Oedipus takes the commanding role, conducting the first of the several interrogations that make up the action of the play.

The little dialogue between Oedipus and Creon is a miniature instance of that "encounter with the divine," in which the Priest had just praised Oedipus, and the king lives up to his best hopes. He literally does not lose a moment. He is attentive and neither too confident nor too fearful (89–90)—a statement that provides a point of reference for his swings between these opposite moods later in the play (913–17). Concerned about his people, Oedipus insists that the oracle be announced publicly, to all, not kept as a state secret among the leaders (91–94). When he hears that Apollo's command is "to drive out the land's pollution and not nurture it unhealed," he at once searches for the remedy in clipped and eager questions (99): "By what purification? What is the character of the misfortune?" Yet the metaphor of "nurture" that Creon reports as Apollo's word ("the pollution nurtured in this land") points to that realm of birth and family that is so fraught with pain and peril for Oedipus.

The polluted killer, Creon reports, must be driven into exile or punished by death (100–1). The choice between exile or death will return later in the play, particularly when Oedipus accuses Creon of the crime and opts for the harsher penalty (622–23). Since Oedipus will not be put to death at the end, it is also necessary to have the lighter punishment in view. Oedipus himself envisages only exile when he refers back to this punishment later (823–24, 1379–82).

In reporting Apollo's reply, Creon also uses the language of retributive justice, expiating "killing by killing in return, since a storm of blood rages upon the city" (100–1). The solemnity of the repetition, "killing by killing," is appropriate to the god and evokes archaic notions of retribution: blood must be paid for by blood. The metaphor of the "storm of blood upon the city" also points to that interconnectedness of the human community ("city") with the mysterious forces of nature ("storm"), here evident in the plague. At the same time, it foreshadows the "black rain and bloody hail"—also metaphorical—that fall from Oedipus' eyes when he blinds himself in punishment for the pollution (1278–80), thus fulfilling the god's command of "blood for blood."

With the rapid exchange of Oedipus' questions and Creon's short replies, the play moves into its major mode of action, the recovery of a buried past (102–31). Oedipus swiftly elicits the scant but important details of Laius' death, and we see at once how he would have pursued such an investigation had he been asked earlier. As the dim and fragmentary facts emerge, the errors and omissions are intermingled with truth. Laius was killed on a sacred journey (114–15), Creon reports, but he mentions neither Delphi nor the crossroads.[2] Sophocles withholds these crucial details until later; to mention them now would precipitate Oedipus' discovery too soon. Particularly striking is the vacillation between singular and plural in the account of the event (97, 108, 118–24). Though Creon lays heavy stress on the plural, "robbers," referring to Laius' killers, Oedipus asks about a single "robber." The phrase can be read as Sophoclean irony or as a Freudian slip, the surfacing of something that Oedipus knows but has suppressed.

If Oedipus' insistence on the single "robber" belongs to the nonrational side of mental functioning, his rational intelligence is nevertheless fully in evidence. He makes a rapid calculation of possible intrigue within the city (125–26), which he realizes can be repeated against himself (139–41). These deductions are plausible and appropriate to a Greek city of Sophocles' time, and they explain the king's suspicions of Creon and Teiresias later. But Oedipus is not only an astute politician, he is also a decent, pious, and responsible ruler. He graciously thanks Creon, restates his determination to help, and in his exit line recognizes the need for the gods' aid (145–46): "For with the god we shall be shown as fortunate or as fallen low." The choice of words points ahead with tragic irony to his own fall, which of course takes place "with the god." "We shall be shown" also continues the imagery of revelation that so dominates the tragic reversal. "I shall show these things from the beginning," he had said confidently a few lines before, using the same word (132).

The strong echo of the opening in Oedipus' address to the Priest creates a formal closure (142ff.). The Priest, satisfied with Oedipus' response, leads the suppliants away and ends with a prayer to Apollo: "May Phoebus Apollo who sent these oracles, come as both savior and healer of the disease" (149–50). Thus both Oedipus and the Priest end with references to the god, but with a characteristic difference. Oedipus speaks in the first person of his own success or failure; the Priest utters a prayer for deliverance. How one fares in such "encounters with the gods," where the Priest had earlier judged Oedipus as "first of men" (34), frames the scene. By beginning and ending with the suppliants, the scene has shown the city poised between the human and the divine, protected by its temples but also at the limits of its ability to deal with the unknown forces of the gods and nature that threaten it.

The dangers and uncertainties of the realm beyond human control dominate the first ode, the parode, or *parodos*, sung by the chorus of Theban elders. The ode's lyrical form and language give emotional expression to the fears and anxieties revealed in the opening ritual of supplication. The chorus sings of the plague on crops, cattle, and human births and makes formal prayers to the gods. We see the entire community threatened by extinction as its environment refuses to support life. If Sophocles did indeed present *Oedipus* at the time of the great plague in Athens in the 420s, this choral song would have stirred intense emotions in his audience.

The ode has the structure and function of an apotropaic prayer, a prayer to turn away evil from the city. It thus reinforces the ritual quality of the first scene, heightens the seriousness of the city's crisis, and conveys the reality of powerful and dangerous divine forces interfering with human life. Ironically, what has to be driven away from the city is not the "raging" Thracian Ares (190–97) but the most respected man within Thebes.

In contrast to Oedipus' confidence, the elders feel defenseless: they have no "sword of thought" to fight off the disease (170–71). Their hope is almost wholly in the gods, as they take us from one sacred place to another, from their opening mention of Apollo's oracle at Delphi to the temples of Thebes (149–61). But they also evoke the demonic, hostile realms beyond the city: the western zone, beyond the sea, associated with Hades and death (175–79), and the remote northern seas of Ares, where they hope that the force of the plague may be deflected (190–99). They end with prayers to their local god, Dionysus, whose torchlight processions contrast with the destructive fires of Ares and the plague (213–15; see 27, 167, 175–77, 192).

First Episode (216–462)

Oedipus responds to the elders' prayers with a series of powerful curses on the killer or on anyone who shelters him. The curses afford ample scope for tragic irony. As in the prologue, he speaks of a single "killer," but he adds the quali-

fication, "whether it is one or many" (246–47). He will speak of a single perpetrator again in line 293.³ Oedipus extends his imprecation to include a possible
killer "from another land" (230) who is, of course, himself in his self–chosen exile from Corinth. This same phrase, "another land," will in fact recur, in exactly
the same verse position, when he learns how he owes his life to being sent away
"to another land" (1178). It is a still deeper irony that the "pollution nurtured
in this land," according to the oracle from Delphi (96–97), rests with the very
man who was sent away, without an infant's nurture, "to another land" to avoid
just such a pollution.

Just after pronouncing the curses, Oedipus criticizes the Thebans: "For even
if the matter had not been urged on by a god, it was not fitting for you to leave
it so uncleansed" (255–56). But Oedipus has lived uncleansed of his pollutions
for all these years of his rule and marriage at Thebes. He then goes on to allude
to himself, unwittingly, as the source of that pollution: he would have "children
of the same sowing" with Laius had he lived, and he fights for the dead Laius
"as for my father" (260–65). The irony is heavy, perhaps too heavy for our taste,
and rather gruesome, but the figurative language keeps the horror at an appropriate distance. The ironies also help prepare us for the scene with Teiresias,
who will speak openly of these hidden relationships.

In this irony-charged language of sharing "seeds," Oedipus makes his first
reference to Jocasta:

> . . . I possess his bed
> and a wife who shares our seed . . . why, our seed
> might be the same, children born of the same mother
> might have created blood-bonds between us
> if his hope of offspring had not met disaster.
>
> (Fagles' translation, 260–62)

The phrase "wife who shares our seed" is another relentless play on the incest.
It not only holds the truth that he and Laius have had children by "seeding" the
same woman but can also mean "woman" [or wife] who has her sowing in common with her child." Teiresias will use a similar expression, again with deliberate and horrible ambiguity, to mean "the one who sows the same woman as
his father did" (459–60).

The slowly built up ironies of the hidden truth explode in Oedipus' encounter with Teiresias (297–462). Strictly speaking, the scene is not necessary for
the plot, but it serves a number of purposes: it creates suspense, shows us a less
self-controlled Oedipus, awakens the anxieties that come to dominate the mood
of the second half of the play, and, most important, suggests the workings of
supernatural powers. Indirectly, it also motivates Jocasta's account of the oracle
to Laius (708–10, 723–25) and of his death at the crossroads that leaves Oedipus
so shaken. Just before Teiresias' entrance, Oedipus acknowledges the limitations
of mortals before the gods, for "no man would be able to compel the gods to do

what they do not wish" (280–81). The other side of that observation also holds true, namely that the gods reveal things in their own good time, as Oedipus will learn.

As the chorus watches the blind seer approach, it describes him as "the only man in whom truth is inborn by nature" (299). "Truth" dominates the scene, in its contrast both with the illusion that Teiresias reveals surrounding Oedipus and with the falsehood of which Oedipus will accuse him (386ff.). But if Teiresias is only a "man" with an inborn vision of truth, Oedipus nevertheless addresses him with extreme respect, almost as a god (300–15). The chorus refers to Teiresias as "the divine prophet" (298), and Oedipus likewise calls him "lord" and "savior." Indeed, he reminds us of the city's supplication to himself in the opening scene, for he approaches Teiresias virtually as a suppliant, with a triple repetition of the verb "save" (311–12). As Teiresias departs, "falsehood" is among his last words ("if you find me to have spoken falsehood," 461); and the ensuing choral ode begins with the Delphic oracle that has the power of "divine speech" (463–64). Oedipus opened his address to the prophet by praising his knowledge of "things teachable and unspeakable" (301), and that same opening passage of the choral ode immediately afterwards sings of the oracle's knowledge of the criminal who has done "unspeakable" things (464). Through this intricate framing pattern, Sophocles sets the Teiresias scene into a double axis, truth and falsehood (which is a variant of the dominant theme of reality and appearance) and divine and human knowledge.

When instead of offering help the famed prophet asks to be sent home again, Oedipus is naturally puzzled, and reiterates the city's need and supplication (322–27). "Do you plan, then, to betray us and destroy the city?" he asks finally. Only after Teiresias' point–blank refusal does Oedipus get exasperated. The change from respect to insult is very fast: "O you basest of the base," he cries to the prophet, "for you would anger even a stone, will you not speak? Will you show yourself thus unmovable and impossible?" (334–36). With effort Oedipus keeps his rising temper under control, until Teiresias again confronts him with a flat refusal (344-45). Oedipus has held back anger; Teiresias has held back "truth" (350, 356). Now they both let go. Oedipus makes his outrageous accusation that Teiresias was not only an accomplice in killing Laius but would have done it "alone" if he were not blind (346–49), whereupon Teiresias speaks out his equally outrageous-seeming "truth," namely that Oedipus is himself the source of the pollution.

The scene is often read as evidence of a "tragic flaw" of anger in Oedipus, or as a hint of the tyrannical behavior that the chorus warns against in general terms later, in the second stasimon (873–97), but this view is not tenable. To be sure, Oedipus is impetuous, quick-tempered, and emotional, but he behaves initially with restraint, and his anger, though unfortunate given the results, is pardonable. With the city in such danger, the prophet's refusal to speak looks incriminating, and Oedipus has already wondered about an earlier conspiracy (124–25, 139–41). He has also mentioned that the plan to call Teiresias originated with Creon (288), on whom Oedipus will now turn his suspicious eye. Teiresias, moreover, has been just as irascible as Oedipus. Indeed, angry old men are a common feature of Sophoclean drama: compare the Teiresias of *Antigone* and the aged Oedipus of *Oedipus at Colonus*.

Temperament and circumstances work together with the prophet's supernatural knowledge to shape the event. A calmer, more submissive, or more timid man—Creon, for example—might have taken Teiresias' refusal at face value and just let him go home. Oedipus is not the man to give up so easily. The irony of the situation is that with all their shouting these two gifted men speak past each other. When the truth is spoken, it cannot be heard. Oedipus is not yet ready to receive it, and the anger in Teiresias' telling sets up so much interference that Oedipus cannot "hear" logically. Anger, on both sides, obscures the truth that Teiresias possesses as an inborn gift (299).

Rather than providing a basis for a "tragic flaw," this scene is the most dramatic enactment to this point of the tragedy of knowledge: truth is trapped in illusion and in the disturbances of language and emotion. The scene also develops the contrast between divine and human knowledge. Oedipus boasts of having saved Thebes by the human skill that solved the riddle, while the prophet of the god could do nothing (390). But he asserts this claim to human knowledge just when his own ignorance has become clearest to us. When Teiresias says "Apollo," Oedipus replies with his accusation of "Creon" (377–78). The prophet looks toward the god whom he serves, the king toward the human realm and human motives that he can understand. Moments before Teiresias' appearance Oedipus had cautioned against forcing the gods to speak when they are unwilling (280–81), yet he does just this in pressing Teiresias, their mouthpiece. When the gods do speak, through Teiresias, Oedipus is unable to hear what they say.

With Teiresias there enters onstage something beyond the limits of human knowledge. Despite his all-too-human irritability, he possesses a vision that extends into both the buried past and the dark future. As his prophecy hints, he is himself a foreshadowing of what Oedipus will become (419, 454–56); but whereas these paradoxical collocations of sight and blindness, strength and weakness, are overt in Teiresias, they are still hidden in Oedipus.

Oedipus here resembles the Creon of the earlier *Antigone*: a ruler who denies the prophet's insight into sacred things and denigrates his vision by imputing to him merely secular motives (*Antigone*, 1033–63). But unlike Creon Oedipus is to evolve into a seer like Teiresias. In the later play, *Oedipus at Colonus*, Oedipus will be from the start the Teiresias figure that he is in the process of becoming here.

The clash between human and divine knowledge in this scene takes the form of the contrast between riddles and oracles, the two modes of knowledge that most sharply separate Oedipus and Teiresias. If Oedipus claims that the Sphinx's riddle needed a "prophecy" that Teiresias lacked (394), Teiresias gives Oedipus an oracle that poses a riddle: "How everything you say is too riddling and obscure," Oedipus complains after Teiresias foretells his horrible future (439). The oracle is a riddle that Oedipus cannot solve, as the chorus implies when it tries to intercede: "To us Teiresias' words seem to have been spoken in anger, and yours too, Oedipus. Of such words we have no need, but rather how best to consider *solving the prophecies* of the god" (404–407). Fair to both sides, the chorus perceives the anger in Teiresias as well as in Oedipus. What they cannot see is that this very anger is in fact helping to "solve the god's prophecies"—that is, to bring out the hidden truth of who Oedipus is.

The scene with Teiresias does advance the plot in one important respect: for the first time it raises the question of Oedipus' origins. "Do you know where you are?" asks Teiresias in the simplest possible language, just five monosyllables in the Greek (415). For the moment, the issue passes Oedipus by: the point is lost in the long list of mysterious horrors that Teiresias now utters and that Oedipus presumably regards as angry ranting (408–28). But a single word catches his attention in the line-by-line exchange immediately after. He dismisses Teiresias' doom-saying as "silly words," but Teiresias throws the insult back at him (435–42):

TEIRESIAS: Yes, silly, as you think, but full of understanding about the *parents* who begot you.
OEDIPUS: What *parents*? Wait. What parents gave birth to me?
TEIRESIAS: This day will give birth to you—and will destroy you too.
OEDIPUS: Very *riddling* all that you say, and all unclear.
TEIRESIAS: Are you not best at *finding out* such things as these?
OEDIPUS: You insult me in just these things where you will find me great.
TEIRESIAS: Yet it is just this fortune (*tychê*) that has destroyed you.

The passage is dense with ironies that echo throughout the play: the fortune/misfortune that makes Oedipus both "great" and small (1080–85); the motif of the single day, with its further associations of the precariousness of mortality; the mystery of Oedipus' origins; and the coexistence of his deep intelligence and his ignorance about the "riddle" of his past. Oedipus has directed all his formidable energy and intelligence at the search for Laius' killer. Except for his momentary distraction by Teiresias' word "parents," his thoughts are far from his own past.

This passage also shows how oracle and riddle complement one another as the two sides of Oedipus' tragic situation. The riddle points to his success and intelligence in saving Thebes and winning his high position. The oracle reveals his helplessness and ignorance before the larger powers that surround his life. In the prologue the Priest had said that Oedipus had solved the riddle "by the help of a god" (38). Answering Teiresias, Oedipus claims the superior power of his purely human knowledge. Your prophecy, he says in effect, could not solve the riddle when my own intelligence did, "without the help of any god" (394–98). But, as we have seen, Teiresias' prophetic language is a "riddle" of another kind (439), deeper than that of the Sphinx.

Sophocles has been taking risks in this scene, but he pushes the tensions even further in Teiresias' parting shot, his final prophecy to Oedipus:

> A stranger,
> you may think, who lives among you,
> he soon will be revealed a native Theban
> but he will take no joy in the revelation.
> Blind who now has eyes, beggar who now is rich,
> he will grope his way toward a foreign
> soil, a stick tapping before him step by step.
> Revealed at last, brother and father both
> to the children he embraces, to his mother
> son and husband both—he sowed the loins
> his father sowed, he spilled his father's blood!
>
> (Fagles' translation, 452–60)

How could Oedipus, famous riddle-solver, not grasp the truth when it is spoken so clearly? Teiresias' language is obscure, of course, as oracular language tends to be, and Oedipus also has the pressures of the city's crisis distracting him. Another answer is to suppose that Oedipus exits into the palace after he orders Teiresias' attendant to lead the old prophet away (445–46). In that case Teiresias would speak his prophecy to a retreating figure who does not hear him.[4] We have little solid evidence for Sophocles' staging, and this arrangement is possible. Dramatically, however, the tension is more effective if Oedipus remains onstage. In this way the horror of the prophet's uncanny knowledge stands in an even more powerful contrast to Oedipus' rationality, as Teiresias' closing two lines suggest: "Go inside and *reckon* these things up; and if you catch me as one who's false, then say that my *intelligence* in prophecy is nil" (461–62).

If Oedipus does hear these lines, as seems more likely, there is also greater dramatic effect in the shift between Teiresias' second-person addresses to him at the beginning and end of his speech (447–50 and 461–62) and the oracular pronouncement itself in the third person (452–60). The contrast emphasizes the contrast between Teiresias' "human" voice of angry old man and his prophetic voice of divine seer. It also sets off Oedipus' lack of comprehension: he does not grasp that the prophet's "you" and "he" are the same. Either way it is staged, the scene is a powerful visual enactment of the clash between human and divine knowledge.

It is characteristic of Sophocles' art that a formal symmetry contains and controls all these heated emotions. Teiresias exits with the same word with which he began, "intelligence" or "understanding" (*phronein,* 462 and 316). He is "the only man in whom *truth* is inborn," the chorus tells Oedipus as the prophet enters (299). "Consider if you find me *false,*" Teiresias says as he leaves (461). The echoes keep the intellectual themes in the foreground.

The scene has still another function in the progression of the action. Oedipus does not entirely forget Teiresias' words; he remembers them at Jocasta's more detailed account of the past. "I am in fearful despair that the prophet might have vision," he cries at that point (747), harking back to the metaphors of sight for knowledge and blindness for ignorance that play about his meeting with Teiresias. Thus the vagueness and horror of Teiresias' statement prepare us for Oedipus' growing anxieties later and help us to feel them, too, as this incredible, nightmarish prophecy by an angry old man turns out to be fact.

FIRST STASIMON (SECOND CHORAL ODE)

The power of Teiresias' prophecy is kept alive in the choral ode (the first stasimon) that immediately follows his exit (463–512). Teiresias' parting words, as we have noted, refer both to the problem of truth and falsehood and the power of prophetic knowledge: "If you find me having spoken *falsehood,* then say that I have no intelligence in my *prophetic art*" (461–62). In contrast to the confused and contested authority of human speech in the exchange between Oedipus and Teiresias, the chorus now offers a vision of the "divinely speaking" rock of Apollo's Delphic oracle (463–64; compare the chorus' "divine prophet," 298–99, above). The striking description of Delphi as the "divinely speaking rock" also raises the question of how this "divine" voice reaches mortals and how valid these intermediaries of the divine truth are. Hence near the end of the ode, as the chorus questions the truth of these oracles, it harks back to the "divinely speaking rock" of their opening, but with less certainty, as it hesitates to accept Teiresias' pronouncements as "a correct speaking," literally "an upright word" or speech (505).[5]

Reacting to Teiresias' pronouncement in this ode, the chorus combines puzzlement about the killer's identity with confidence in the radiant truth of Delphic prophecy. The ode invites us to connect the Delphic oracle given to Creon with what we have just heard from Teiresias, and in this way it opens further speculation on the interconnections among all the oracles in the background, and thereby also deepens the rift between human and divine knowledge. At the same time it shows the city's deep confidence in Oedipus and its belief in his innocence. After all, Teiresias, though a prophet, is a mortal man, while Zeus and Apollo are gods, and so (the elders imply) Teiresias could be wrong (489–506). Remembering again how their king saved the city by defeating the Sphinx, they conclude with their faith in Oedipus unshaken (504–11).

As often is true in Sophocles' plays, however, the ode has multiple points of reference. "Delphi's divinely speaking rock" and the snowy peak of Parnassus (the mountain on which Delphi stands) at the beginning of the first strophe and antistrophe, respectively (463–64, 473–75), form part of a pattern that associates the mountains with the unknown, demonic world beyond human knowledge. Cithaeron was the mountain where Oedipus was exposed to die as an infant. Teiresias had mentioned it ominously (421), and it will recur powerfully later. Delphi, which (as the chorus sings) holds the "mid-navel of the earth" (480), contrasts with the wild landscape above it, where the unknown killer wanders, among "savage woods and caves, [as] the bull of the rocks" (477). At the end of the play these images of remote wilderness will fit Oedipus, the polluted outcast who asks to be expelled to Mount Cithaeron (1451–54; see also 1391–93, 1088). When the chorus declares that "Apollo, son of Zeus, is leaping armed upon" the killer, they take up a metaphor that Oedipus had used of Laius' death (263) and that he will use again of himself when the horrible truth emerges (1311). This "leaping" of a god, like the mountains and the bull, mysteriously combines bestiality and divinity and weaves the thread of divine causation into the human action of investigation and discovery.

SECOND EPISODE (513–862)

After the references to the remote gods in the scene with Teiresias and the choral ode, the play moves back to human behavior and politics with the return of Creon. He enters with an address to Thebes' "citizens," and he calls Oedipus by his full and precise title, "the tyrannos Oedipus," *ton tyrannon Oedipoun* (513–14). This is a very different entrance from Creon's first appearance, for Oedipus has lost no time in making known his suspicions. Dramatically, the scene keeps our attention directed away from Oedipus' own history and prevents the revelation of the truth from coming too soon. Sophocles needs both to delay discovery and to stimulate expectation, and the scene with Creon accomplishes both admirably.

Instead of the mysterious thought–world of the blind prophet and his terrible knowledge, we are on the familiar ground (familiar, at least, to an Athenian audience) of legal debate. This is a courtroom scene, and it unfolds entirely on the level of human motivation and behavior. Oedipus is angry, suspicious, and in control. He is determined to take all the necessary precautions against a conspiracy. His deduction is not unreasonable, given the circumstantial evidence. Creon is a likely successor to Oedipus, he and Teiresias knew one another long before Oedipus' arrival, and the idea of consulting Teiresias originated with Creon (288). The city's crisis would be a natural time for a coup d'état. Perhaps Creon and Teiresias even conspired in the past too, to eliminate Laius and share the power, but were prevented by Oedipus' arrival. In any case, as a ruler from outside, a "tyrant" rather than a "king" (514) Oedipus has reason to feel insecure. Not all of this reasoning is presented overtly in the play, nor is it all absolutely necessary, but this is the kind of reasoning that an Athenian audience, thoroughly steeped in political machinations, might expect Oedipus to be making.

In contrast to Oedipus, with his impetuous energy, Creon is reasonable and even a little pedantic. He is cautious where Oedipus is rash—a contrast to be reenacted in the play's final scene. He has good answers to Oedipus' accusations: Oedipus should verify the response he brought from Delphi and investigate any previous association between Creon and Teiresias. To Oedipus, however, this only sounds incriminating: he assumes that Creon has taken care to cover his tracks and that he is stalling for time. He knows, rightly, that a conspiracy could move quickly, especially at this time of crisis in the city, and that he too "must make [his] counterplot with speed" (619–20). Exile or death had been the cleansing prescribed by Delphi and endorsed by Oedipus, and Creon assumes that Oedipus will ask for the lighter penalty, but Oedipus has decided differently: "Your death, not your exile, is what I want" (623).

This insistence on the death penalty, along with the emphasis on haste, suggests that Oedipus is veering toward the imperiousness of the bad ruler, the tyrant, in the pejorative sense, like Creon in *Antigone*. Indeed, when Oedipus exclaims, "O city, city," Creon replies, "But I too and not you alone have a share in the city" (630), and the line recalls the debate between the autocratic Creon and his son Haemon in that earlier play. "There is no city that belongs to a single man," Haemon had told his father (*Antigone*, 737; see also *Oedipus*, 579).

At this impasse Jocasta enters from the palace. This is the first time since the opening scene that Sophocles stages a three-way exchange (four ways, with the chorus). Jocasta had been mentioned briefly in the previous scene of debate between Oedipus and Creon. "I will not be convicted as the killer," Oedipus says, and Creon replies: "What then, don't you hold my sister in marriage?" (576–77). That apparently fortuitous, though abrupt, transition from Oedipus as "killer" of Laius to Oedipus as having Jocasta "in marriage" seems innocent and natural in its context, but it now takes on a darker meaning when Jocasta enters and soon after describes the oracle that her child was to be "the killer of his father" (721).

Jocasta's opening words show at once her commanding presence and authority. Both Creon and Oedipus treat her with respect, although we may shudder a little at Creon's first line to her (639), which brings together the terms "sister of the same blood" and "Oedipus your husband," reminding us that her husband is also "of the same blood."[6] In any case she and the chorus of elders together persuade Oedipus to accept, reluctantly, Creon's oath of innocence. But the men do not part on good terms. Creon's parting shot, like Teiresias' in the previous scene, holds a warning for Oedipus, although this lies wholly in human terms. People like Oedipus, he says, have "natures" that are "rightly most painful for themselves to bear" (674–75). Oedipus is unforgiving: "Won't you leave me and get yourself away?" (677). This sharp parting will add to Oedipus' shame when Creon returns at the end.

The short scene that follows (679–702) repeats a now familiar pattern: one character tries to elicit answers, and the respondent is reluctant to tell. The questioner is Jocasta, and the one who withholds information is Oedipus, evasive about Teiresias' accusation that he is Laius' killer. It is the reverse of the situation between Oedipus and Teiresias, and the situation will reverse again in the following scene, close to the discovery, when Oedipus presses Jocasta for more details and she begs him to stop (1056–68). She in fact uses the same entreaty, "by the gods," in both cases (698 and 1060).[7]

When Oedipus does finally report Teiresias' words, Jocasta's reassurance that prophets have no skill anyway sets in motion another narrative pattern: the one who tries to bring relief in fact brings anxiety or disaster. This pattern has already been at work in the oracle from Delphi and in the appearance of Teiresias, and it will occur again. Here, to prove that "the prophetic art" is worthless, Jocasta tells how Laius was to have been killed by his own child, whereas (as she believes) he was killed by robbers. This is the first report of this oracle in the play, and to it Jocasta adds the detail of the triple crossroads, which immediately electrifies Oedipus (707–27). In fact, she supplies him with several new facts: the oracle itself, her exposure of a child on the mountain after "yoking together" the child's feet, and Laius' death at the "triple road." She also confirms the earlier tale of "robbers" as the murderers.

Amid all the details of Jocasta's dense narrative Oedipus picks up only one phrase, the "triple roads" (727). The situation resembles Oedipus' dialogue with Teiresias: the prophet's full accusation had little effect, but a single word ("parents") throws him into turmoil. For the first time we see the commanding power of the king falter. He will never again regain the confidence and composure of the opening scenes, although at the end he will find a strength of another kind.

NOTES

1. How many figures were actually onstage in this opening scene is a matter of controversy, but it seems likely that Sophocles would have had enough extras to simulate an actual supplication scene. For discussion and bibliography, see Peter Burian, "The Play Before the Prologue: Initial Tableaux on the Greek Stage," in John H. D'Arms and John W. Eadie, eds., *Ancient and Modern: Essays in Honor of Gerald F. Else* (Ann Arbor: University of Michigan Press, 1977), 79–94, especially 83 and 91–94.

2. Seneca's *Oedipus* (line 278) has Creon mention the crossroads early in the play, but Oedipus takes no notice of the word. His recognition is to come through the ghost of Laius, not his own investigative energy.

3. This interpretation requires the widely accepted emendation of the Greek text at 293, "doer" for the manuscripts' "seer."

4. This is the solution adopted by Fagles in his stage direction after 446 and 456, following the interpretation of Bernard Knox, "Sophocles, *Oedipus Tyrannos* 446: Exit Oedipus?" *Greek, Roman and Byzantine Studies* 21 (1980), 321–32, and his *Essays Ancient and Modern* (Baltimore: Johns Hopkins University Press, 1989), 146–47; see my review of the latter in *Arion*, 3d Series, vol. 1, no. 1 (1990), 221.

5. Cf. *orthon epos*, "upright speech," "correct pronouncement," 505, and *thespepeia*, "divinely speaking," 463–64).

6. Cf. Oedipus' phrase, "blood of the same race," 1406, in his self-accusation after the discovery.

7. This entreaty, "by the gods," also occurs at a number of critical moments in the play: see 326, 646, 1037, 1153.

8

Discovery and Reversal

JOCASTA AND OEDIPUS

The tale of Jocasta comes at approximately the halfway point of the play and is a turning point in the action. It creates an abrupt shift in Oedipus, from power, confidence, and control, to uncertainty and fear. He continues to act rapidly and efficiently, but he is now on the defensive. More important, the direction of his search is completely changed, for he now begins to investigate not just who killed Laius but also who is Oedipus.

Creon's exit at line 677 encourages the one-on-one dialogue between the king and queen, although the chorus, in accordance with the conventions of Greek tragedy, remains on stage and even participates in the discussion (834–35). The scene is long (634–862) and is carefully balanced between the two crucial narratives about the past, first Jocasta's, then Oedipus'. Jocasta's story is the first of her attempts to allay Oedipus' anxiety, which troubles her.

Sophocles, unlike Euripides, is not concerned with domestic realism, and the dialogue between Oedipus and Jocasta remains formal and severe. She speaks with the dignity of her position. She repeatedly addresses him as "lord" (697, 770, 852). Although there is nothing particularly domestic in their talk, this serious, more or less private exchange between husband and wife evokes the marital bond between them and contrasts markedly with the more public, heated exchanges that Oedipus has just had with Teiresias and Creon. This quieter setting also helps refocus the action on Oedipus' recollection of his past.[1]

By using Jocasta as the means to Oedipus' discovery of the truth, Sophocles gains the effect of a double tragedy, for Jocasta's denial and recognition begin to parallel those of Oedipus himself. As we shall see, Sophocles also creates a double climax as the two protagonists come to their respective recognitions at different times. There is a tragic irony in the way in which Jocasta directs the action from human to divine knowledge. She cites Laius' oracle to disprove the validity of prophecy, and her skepticism about oracles continues into the next scene (see 977–83). But her story about the oracle only sharpens the question of divine foreknowledge and the role, therefore, of some external force that governs human lives.

The irony of this reverse effect is conveyed in a verbal play that is difficult to translate into English. Jocasta would disprove the validity of Laius' oracle about his child with the explanation, "As the rumor (*phatis*) is, strangers, robbers, killed Laius at the triple roads" (715–16). Her term for "rumor" here, *phatis*, also means "oracle" and is so used regularly throughout the play. Thus her words can also mean something like, "He died *as the oracle said he would*," which is the exact opposite of what she intended to say. It remains one of the mysterious coincidences working in the play that she chooses just this moment to tell of a past with which she has lived for so many years. Here too the motif of "chance" or "fortune," *tychê*, is important.

Under the impact of Jocasta's revelation, Oedipus, so concerned with Thebes' present crisis, begins to look away to the past, indeed to his own past, not in Thebes but in Corinth, at Delphi, and on the "triple road" between these three cities. He now tells his own story, the foil to Jocasta's. It is a critical narrative, and we must attend to it carefully. Sophocles has withheld it until this crucial point at the center of the play, so that we will listen to it with the suspense and horror that Jocasta's accounts of Laius' death and of her own child have aroused.

Telling the story of his life, Oedipus begins with his parents: "My father was Polybus of Corinth, my mother Merope descended from Dorus" (774–75). It is the most natural of beginnings, but we know how deeply flawed even this innocent-seeming statement is. What Oedipus takes to be the least problematic part of his tale will soon become his most anxious point of inquiry. Indeed, he goes on to tell how he went to Delphi to ask about his parents. Apollo's reply was terrifying, and Oedipus reports it in the first person: "I must have intercourse with my mother and show to men a race unendurable to look upon, and I will be the killer of the father who begot me" (791–93). This is the third and last of the Delphic oracles mentioned in the play, the other two having been Creon's report from Delphi and Jocasta's account of the oracle given to Laius. But this is the first time we hear of an oracle given directly from the god to the person for whom it is intended (788–90). Whereas Jocasta, characteristically, had tried to blunt the force of the address from the god ("not from Apollo himself but from his servants" [711–12]), Oedipus' account makes us feel the awe of encountering the divine voice, and (as he tells us) he at once fled Corinth in terror. Oedipus' recounting of his oracle here is also the first and only time that he mentions incestuously born children as part of the prophecy—a detail that will be important when we see some of these children on stage at the end. Teiresias had alluded briefly to the children, but with all the obscurity of his "riddling" language (425, 457–58). When Oedipus repeats his oracle at the end of his tale, he omits any reference to the children (825–27).

Oedipus still does not see any connection among the three oracles, for neither of the two previously mentioned had said anything about incest. His immediate concern is that he may be Laius' killer and therefore subject to the terrible curse that he pronounced against this person earlier. This concern is uppermost in his mind as he tells of his fatal meeting at the crossroads. It is a story emblematic of Oedipus' destiny as a hero who supplants his father in every way, and it uses the motif of walking as a symbol of a journey through life, a journey marked by tragedy and bloodshed.

A young man on foot is attempting to advance on his path, but his way is blocked by an older man, bearing all the trappings of power and wealth. The "old man" strikes just as he "sees" the younger "trying to pass by his chariot," that is, as the youth tries to make his way beyond this blocking figure on the road of life. It is a cruel blow, with a double-pointed ox-goad, aimed at the head, and Oedipus struck back in anger (800–13).

Oedipus' account stresses the deliberate aggressiveness of the older man: he is the one who "sees," "aims" his blow, and "comes down with it" on the head of Oedipus (807–9). The active verbs of this man's attack are followed by the passive verbs of his fall, as he is "struck" and "rolled out" of the chariot (811–12). Oedipus evokes the scene in only five lines, with a few rapid, specific details. Though it happened some twenty years before, it is as fresh as if it were yesterday, and he tells most of it in the present tense. The five verses of Laius' actions, in the third person, are framed by Oedipus' two simple, direct first-person statements, both in the historical present tense: "I strike in anger" (807) and "I kill them all" (813).[2]

"I killed them all," Oedipus says, quite simply, but Laius struck first, and so to strike back was justifiable homicide. Was it justifiable to kill the others, or was that too in self-defense? Oedipus' concern is not with the legal problems; instead, he worries about the curse that he himself pronounced on the killer, the cause of the plague, and about the added pollution of being married to the wife of the man he killed (813–33). As he views the consequences of his act from his present distance, he shifts abruptly from the vivid narrative style to more abstract language. If that "stranger" whom he killed "has any relation of kinship with Laius," he says, "then who is more wretched, who more hateful to the gods than I?" (813–16). Still holding to a shred of hope, he is careful to describe the "stranger" in a noncommittal, cautious way; but his word "kinship" evokes his still hidden family connections, which here contrast ironically with "stranger" and can refer to both Oedipus and Laius, who are of course not "strangers" but son and father.

If Oedipus is Laius' killer, he must go into exile to free Thebes from the plague and fulfill his own curse. But because of his oracle he cannot go back to Corinth either, for the oracle had foretold that he would commit incest and parricide (825–27). The levels of Oedipus' ignorance compound the ironies, for of course he has already committed the crimes foretold in the oracle. When he says that he will not be permitted to "see my people" (824), he ironically foreshadows his future blindness. When he speaks of Polybus as "the father who *nur-*

tured and *begot* me," his reversal of the normal biological order contains the hidden truth that Polybus *only* nurtured him. We also recall the terms of the oracle as Oedipus first gave it, that he "will be the killer of the father *who begot me*" (792). Sophocles makes the oracle prove to be true with a bitter literalness: Oedipus has two fathers, Laius and Polybus, and he kills the one who "begot him." This is also the father who, because of his own oracle, deliberately did *not* "nurture" him.

The clustering of the oracles at this point works closely with the gradual emergence of powers beyond human control. When Oedipus refers to the "cruel divinity" (*daimon*, 828) that has guided his life and its luck, he harks back to his statement just before (816) that he had a "hostile daimon" over his life. The man who had seemed so much in control now looks increasingly toward strange, supernatural forces that seem to surround him. *Daimon*, his word in 816 and 828, is the most general term for "divinity," and Oedipus will use it again after the discovery and self-blinding: "O daimon, where you leapt forth" (1311). At that point he will have learned how "cruel" that daimon has been and how closely it is connected with the role of Apollo (see 1329–30).

Everything now turns on the question of one killer or many, and Oedipus presents this as a problem of calculation: if the Old Herdsman, the sole witness, "still declares the same *number*, then I didn't kill him, for one would not be equal to many" (843–45). Oedipus is still the man of reason and reckoning. But his logic of noncontradiction, "one would not equal many," will not work in the strange world opening before him, where he himself is the most tragic paradox of all, the figure who in fact is one and many simultaneously. The play rings many changes on the ironies of counting, particularly in Teiresias' prophetic vision of the coexisting opposites in Oedipus, which he ended with the taunt, "Go inside and *calculate* these things" (460–61).

Oedipus, though fearful, is still logical, but Jocasta becomes more desperate. She relies not so much on logic as on the irrelevant argument that the witness cannot take back what he once declared before the whole city (849–50). Then she falls back on the oracle to Laius that initially provoked all the terror. Even if the Herdsman should change his story, she says, there is still the oracle that Laius "must die at the hands of my child; and yet that unfortunate child didn't kill him but himself perished first" (854–57). She has almost stumbled on the truth, but she immediately veers away to the wrong conclusion.

As Oedipus clings to rational calculation and the logic of noncontradiction ("one cannot be equal to many"), Jocasta clings to the denial of oracles—a denial that only reveals how deeply involved she remains with the oracle of Laius' death and her own "dead" child.[3] Nevertheless, the exposed child still has a kind of life for her as she refers to him as "that ill-starred one" (855), and she will repeat that term as the "last thing" she has to call Oedipus in her horrified recognition of the truth at the end of the next scene. The present scene ends with Oedipus, characteristically, pressing on for more evidence and demanding to see the Herdsman-witness.

THE SECOND STASIMON (THIRD CHORAL ODE)

The ode that follows the scene between Jocasta and Oedipus (863–910) allows time for the Herdsman's arrival, but it has many other functions. It is a complex poem and one of the most controversial in Sophocles' plays. On the surface it is a prayer for piety, justice, and a world of moral clarity, where the evil are punished and the oracles are a valid sign of the gods' presence in human affairs. More profoundly, it shows the attitudes toward the oracles, and therefore toward the gods and the divine order generally, polarized between a belief in divine governance (see especially 898–910) and a belief that everything in life is random, that it all happens by chance. This is the position that Jocasta will enunciate at the beginning of the next scene. Thus the ode is to be seen not simply as a statement of pious belief by a serene Sophocles demonstrating divine justice, but rather as a meeting point of opposite ways of trying to make sense of random suffering. Jocasta will die in her anguished vision of a random or irrational world order that has doomed her and those she loves to terrible suffering. The elders of the chorus here provide a counterstatement: they want to believe in a moral order emanating from the gods, but they speak in general terms that do not fit the present circumstances at every point.

The first strophe invokes the laws in the heavens, a timeless, ageless order, fathered by the gods, not born from mortal nature (866–72). This incorruptible law of the gods, however, seems remote from humankind. Eternal, celestial, and elusive, it is at the furthest possible remove from the mortal processes of generation and the tangled, impure, incestuous origins of Oedipus that are so much involved with "fathers," "birth," and "begetting," all prominent words in this passage. The adjective "high-footed" that describes the Olympian laws (in the sense of "lofty" or "on high") suggests a tragic contrast in this distance, for it reminds us of the recurrent image of feet in the play and especially of "Oedipous," whose feet keep him very much on earth and among the mortal woes of birth and generation.

The antistrophe warns, "Violence (*hybris*) begets the tyrant," and it continues with warnings about the man of excess who is lifted too high and then cast down to earth "with useless foot" (878)—that is, injured and impotent. Does "tyrant" here mean only "ruler," as it usually does in the play, or does it mean "tyrant" in the pejorative sense, which is certainly possible in this period? And is the chorus referring to Oedipus or to evil men in general and especially to the still unknown killer? The problem is difficult, but we should not jump to the conclusion that the ode is just an attack on Oedipus for his "tragic flaw." Oedipus has shown anger but not really *hybris* (a violent disregard of others' rights) or injustice, and the chorus' attitude toward him has been consistently favorable. At most, this section of the ode reflects the discrepancy between the terrible fate that the oracles seem to be accumulating for Oedipus and the basic decency and just behavior of his life and rule.

What the ode brings out most poignantly is the gap between the timeless laws of remote Olympus and the struggles of men on earth to understand the ways of the gods and to make moral sense of their lives. And yet the chorus, as a voice of civic concern and ordinary morality, desperately wants the world to make sense and wants to believe in the established religious institutions, the worship of the gods in rituals like choral dance and the oracles.

The opening of the ode, with its reference to Olympus and the divine laws "in the celestial ether," recalls the high summit of "snowy Parnassus" in the previous ode, from which the first oracle "flashed forth" to point the way to healing Thebes' plague (473–76). These two high mountains, Parnassus and Olympus, are places of truth, light, and purity, indicators of the remoteness and inscrutability of the divine will. In contrast to them are the earth of Thebes and the local Theban mountain, Cithaeron, connected with Oedipus' dark past and painful future (1451–54) and with mortal generation, birth, impurity, and suffering. Now that more oracles have emerged, that divine will is far less clear; as the end of the ode implies, the chorus is caught between wanting to see the authority of the gods maintained and not wanting to see the suffering that the truth of those oracles now implies. In the previous ode too, after Teiresias' terrible prophecies, the elders were torn between the apparent "truth" (501) of the oracles and their confidence in Oedipus (498–511). That ode, however, celebrated the brilliant flash of Apollo's oracular truth (473–82); now, that truth is far less certain, and the chorus ends with a remarkable statement of doubt about the validity of oracles and indeed about the worship of the gods in general (906–11): "For already the oracles of Laius are fading and are being expunged, and nowhere is Apollo manifest in honor; but the power of the gods is perishing" (Lloyd-Jones' translation). The chorus' closing words here raise the threat of the collapse of the entire divine order and with it everything that makes the world intelligible to humankind.[4]

The ode's opening image of divine laws engendered outside of time also reminds us that the oracles, in the timeless perspective of the gods, have already been fulfilled. The gods have seen them as both going to happen and having already happened. The next scene shows the protagonists caught in mortal time, trying to unravel the mysteries of their past to understand what they are in the present. To be free of time, like the gods, is also to be free of its tragic patterns of birth, change, generation, memory and forgetting (see 870 and 904), and death.

THIRD EPISODE

The ode's broad perspectives on the distance between men and gods contrast with the immediate anxieties of the two following scenes (911–1085, 1110–1185), which are the climax of the play as the horrifying truth of Oedipus' past emerges into the light. Here, as Aristotle observed, the discovery or recognition (*anagnorisis*) brings about the reversal (peripety, *peripeteia*), and this coincidence, in Aristotle's view, makes for the best kind of tragedy (*Poetics* 11. 1452a 32).

In keeping with Sophocles' sense of form, the two scenes are symmetrical. In each a new character enters: first the Messenger from Corinth, then the Herdsman. Each ends in a powerful discovery: the first with Jocasta's cry at her recognition of the truth (1072–73), the second with Oedipus' similar discovery and outcry (1182; see also 1071). The previous scene had ended with Oedipus' energetic summoning of the Herdsman (859–62), and it is his arrival that we expect. Instead, a new and hitherto unmentioned figure from Corinth delays the recognition for Oedipus, but gives Jocasta enough information for her to piece together that part of the truth that has most concerned her, the identity of the child she and Laius exposed at its birth.

The choral ode of hope and confidence that separates the two scenes (1086–1109) not only heightens the suspense but also creates what is perhaps the play's most powerful dramatic irony, the last and greatest contrast between illusion and truth. The contrast is also enacted visually in the staging. Jocasta exits in full, tragic knowledge; Oedipus continues on the stage in his misguided optimism. Their roles are also the reverse of that of the previous scene, in which he had been the fearful one and she had maintained optimism and hope.

Just before the Corinthian Messenger's entrance, as we have noted, the chorus sang of the honor due to Apollo and his oracles. Jocasta's entrance with wreaths and incense suggests a frightened change from her previous skepticism and also harks back to the play's opening rituals of supplication. Her entrance marks a kind of second beginning, but its echo of the play's first scene also provides a measure of the change of mood. Instead of being confidently in control, Oedipus is fearful and despondent; instead of being the one to be supplicated, supplication is offered on his behalf. Fear dominates the passage. "Oedipus excites his spirit to excess with griefs of every sort," Jocasta says, "nor, like a man of sound sense, does he infer the new (events) by means of the old ones, but he is at the mercy of every speaker if one speaks of fears" (914–17). The king's strengths—analysis, decisiveness, energy—are not only useless, but in this sudden, irrational set of coincidences they become liabilities. He is too quick, too frantic, to handle evidence properly and so foregoes the careful sifting of facts that he had practised at the beginning. Instead, what he hears and whom he listens to are both distorted by "fears." Yet it will finally be Oedipus, not Jocasta, who does push through to the logical end and does draw the terrible inferences from "old" and "new," whereas Jocasta would prefer to "live at random," that is, just take things as they come (979).

There are multiple ironies in the language of these lines (914–17) that subtly anticipate the reversals about to occur. First, the alternation of "old" and "new," the same collocation as in the very first line of the play, points to the disastrous coming together of the parts of Oedipus' past.[5] Then the phrase "excites his spirit to excess," literally "lifts up his spirit too high," introduces an image of height at just the point when Oedipus is about to lose that elevated position that he gained through his intellectual prowess and confidence.

"Height" now points to his failure and confusion. If we recall the "high-footed laws" of the previous ode (866), the image may also evoke the mysterious divine powers in the background of this reversal, the *daimones* (divinities, 912) to whom Jocasta now offers her futile prayers.

"We are all in fear," Jocasta continues in this passage, "seeing him panic-stricken, as one would fear for the pilot of a ship" (922–23). The familiar metaphor of the ship of state harks back to the nautical metaphors of earlier scenes, in which Oedipus' rule is compared to piloting a sea-tossed vessel (23–24, 694–96); but now not the ship but the pilot himself is in trouble. In the first ode the chorus had described itself, collectively, as "trembling with fear" (155); in this scene Oedipus in his anxiety about the oracles is twice described as "trembling" (947, 1014).

With the heightened mood of anxiety in Jocasta, we might expect a messenger's speech that will reveal all. The end of the previous scene, as we have noted, led us to expect the Old Herdsman, who would, of course, bring the investigation to its horrible conclusion. Instead, the Corinthian Messenger's entrance, unannounced and totally unexpected, is the prelude to two scenes of intense question-and-answer dialogue. Sophocles probably invented the figure of the Corinthian Messenger. This figure differs from the usual messenger of tragedy in a number of ways. Unlike the Second Messenger later (1223–96), he is not merely an unmarked bearer of news but has a distinctive personality and point of view and a life story that bears directly on the lives of Oedipus and Jocasta. He does not just report his news but engages in extensive question-and-answer dialogue. We shall follow the convention of referring to him as "Messenger" or "Corinthian Messenger," keeping in mind, however, his special role and characterization.

With this figure, Sophocles achieves a brilliant stroke. He delays the final discovery and at the same time juxtaposes the innocent and peaceful death of Polybus with the violent death of Laius. In addition to creating suspense, the dialogue with the Corinthian Messenger also makes the recognition emerge from Oedipus' own determination to find the truth. The author of a recent commentary on the play writes, "With the possible exception of some scenes in Homer, the next three hundred lines constitute the finest achievement in Greek poetic technique to have survived to our era."[6]

The scene carries double meanings and verbal ironies to a new pitch. The Corinthian Messenger begins with a play on Oedipus' name and on the Greek phrase "know where" (*oida pou*), and the chorus in reply points out Jocasta as "Oedipus' wife and mother—of his children" (924–26, 928). There is a further irony of situation: the Corinthian seems to be savoring Oedipus' happiness and success, in part because (as we learn later) he rescued Oedipus from death and in part because he expects to increase that happiness by bringing what he assumes to be good news from Corinth and thus win a handsome reward (1006). Instead, every piece of news, every propitious word, will turn into its exact opposite.

95

If the preceding ode suggested that the human situation is tragic because it is caught in time, this scene reveals the tragic situation of being caught in language. The ambiguities of speech both result from and in turn feed the illusions in which these lives are enmeshed. The power of speech that Sophocles' contemporaries regarded as one of man's unique gifts, the basis of the legal and political system of the Athenian democracy, is here shown to be a source of the deepest error. Teiresias, as we have seen, has "truth" as an inborn gift, but when he puts it into human language he is accused of lies (see 461). In the present scene the Corinthian Messenger also asserts his claim to truth ("If I do not speak the truth I deserve death," 944), but this truth is dreadfully entangled with the errors surrounding basic kinship terms like *father* and *mother* and even the name of the king of the land.

The Corinthian Messenger announces the death of King Polybus, and Jocasta, ever solicitous of Oedipus' moods, seizes upon the words as she had seized on the "one robber" in the Herdsman's original story. The oracles are worthless, she cries joyfully, since Polybus died "by chance" and not at his son Oedipus' hand (946–49). But chance, as always in the play, proves far from helpful. In the euphoria of this prayed-for "release" (see 921), she seems to see confirmed her plea to Oedipus, at her first appearance in the play, to disregard the oracles (707–9). Now, as in that previous scene, the oracle in question is about a son killing his father (713–14). It was such an oracle, about parricide, Jocasta remarks later, that sent Oedipus into exile, "trembling in fear lest he kill that man," his father (947–48). But Oedipus, in the ensuing scene, will quickly remind Jocasta of the other part of his oracle, the incest, and Jocasta will have to take another tack to soothe this fear as well (976–83).

Oedipus arrives onstage with the "speed" that Jocasta had recommended (945) and shares Jocasta's joy at the death of his "father"; like her, he is relieved that the oracle of his parricide and incest now cannot come true (950–87). That joy, however, is ironically compromised by a hidden meaning in Jocasta's apparently happy news. She reports the Corinthian Messenger as "announcing that your father Polybus is no longer, but is dead" (954–55); but the last part of her sentence can also mean, "Polybus is no longer your father, but your father is a man who is dead." The last word of this line, "dead," also coincides with the two earlier references to "Laius dead," first by Creon in describing the circumstances of Laius' death (126), and then by Jocasta in describing the Old Herdman's return to Thebes when he found "Laius dead" and Oedipus on the throne (759). This verbal echo is the kind of small detail that the audience might not notice, but it is a mark of the tragic poet's awareness of the interlocking pattern now emerging in these tales about "a father dead."

There is a still further irony in Oedipus' joy at having escaped the oracle, for he also echoes the words of Teiresias who foretold its fulfillment. Oedipus says:

Why should one look
to the birds screaming overhead? They prophesied

that I should kill my father! But he's *dead,*
and hidden deep in earth.

(Grene's translation, 965–68, my italics)

Teiresias had said, "Do you know who your parents are? Unknowing / you are
an enemy to kith and kin / *in death, beneath the earth and in this life*" (414–17,
Grene's translation; my italics). In his conflict with Teiresias, Oedipus had scorn-
fully dismissed prophecy and the reading of bird-signs (398); here he repeats
that confidence in dismissing oracles, only to demonstrate how ill-founded is
such confidence.

When Oedipus expresses continuing anxiety about the other part of the oracle, incest with his mother, Jocasta reassures him by generalizing enthusiasti-
cally on the principle of "randomness" or chance in human life:

Why should man fear since chance rules everything
for him, and he can clearly foreknow nothing?
Best to live randomly, as one can, unthinkingly.
As to your mother's marriage bed,—don't fear it.
Before this, in dreams too, as well as oracles,
many a man has lain with his own mother.
But he to whom such things are nothing bears
his life most easily.

(Grene's translation [slightly modified], 977–83)

She is urging that we live our days one at a time, without concern for a divine
plan, supernatural direction, or meaning for our life. Jocasta is not necessarily
being impious here but, in her release from the catastrophe hanging over her
and Oedipus, she pulls back gladly to a nontragic attitude of enjoying life. Why
should one's life, after all, have some awful shape behind it? Why is it that decent people cannot live out happy, ordinary lives, taking each day as it comes?
But this eagerness to deny the power of oracles also comes from a woman who
saw her newly born son sacrificed to the fear of an oracle. If she believed in the
inexorable fulfillment of oracles, the whole fabric of her life would be destroyed.
Yet her most vehement denial comes at just the point when that is about to
happen.

Oedipus mentions his continuing fear of the other part of his oracle, incest
with his mother, and this alerts the Corinthian Messenger. Jocasta had referred
to Polybus as Oedipus' father in line 955, as she repeats the Messenger's news
of the old king's death, and the Messenger had let this identification go by in
silence, but he now becomes interested in Oedipus' supposed "fear of his
mother" (988–89), and this in turn leads him to announce that Polybus and his
wife are not really Oedipus' parents. The effect of this statement is analogous
to the first scene of revelation, in which Jocasta's account of her oracle led to the
chance mention of the triple road.

Oedipus now resumes his earlier role as the keen investigator, but his curiosity about himself, which had flashed into his mind briefly at Teiresias' reference to his parents (437), now obliterates his search for Laius' killer. The intertwining of eagerness to know, the oracles, human blindness, and the deceptiveness of language reaches another peak of excitement and tragic irony here as Oedipus again reveals his oracle (994–96): "Loxias [Apollo] said that I must at some time mingle with my own mother and must take my father's blood with my hands." This is the third repetition of his oracle (the previous occasions were in the scene with Jocasta, 791–93 and 825–27), but he omits what will prove to be the crucial word at this moment, "the father who *begot* you." The Messenger at once promises to "release" Oedipus from his fear (1003) but instead elicits from him the question, "But didn't Polybus *beget* me?" (*exephuse*, 1017). This is the same verb that Oedipus had used in his two earlier accounts of the oracle about killing the father who "begot" him (*phuteusantos patros*, 793; *exephuse*, 827).[7] With what seems like a diabolical twist of language, Oedipus is pronouncing the terms of his curse at just the moment when he is supposedly escaping it.

The Messenger's negative fact ("Polybus is no kin to you" [1016]) leads to the next electrifying piece of positive information, "I found you in Cithaeron's glades" (1026).[8] The name of the mountain had been pronounced only once before in the play, in Teiresias' prophecy, "What [part of] Cithaeron will not echo with your cries" (421), and we now see a pattern crystallizing the origins of Oedipus' life into its tragic shape.

When the Messenger calls himself Oedipus' "savior," having "released" him from the bonds that "pierced his feet" (1030–34), he repeats the pattern of reversals in which "saving" and "release" produce the opposite effect (see 921, 1003). This is the first specific mention of "piercing" the feet; Jocasta had called them "yoked" in her story (718)—a vaguer and gentler description, but she is standing by in silence, hearing everything and fitting it all together. Because the actors wear masks, there can be no change of facial expression to indicate that she has recognized the truth, but the actor could have signalled this with a gesture like a start of horror or an upraised arm.

The Messenger's mention of the pierced feet, however, does force from Oedipus the unexpected cry *oimoi*, "alas"; and he asks, "Why do you mention that old suffering?" (1033). The abrupt exclamation creates another moment of suspense. Has Oedipus in fact seen the truth? If he pieces the fragments of information together now, the recognition would be upon us. Once more Sophocles has pushed the dramatic tension to the furthest possible point.

The Messenger, however, has more to tell, and Oedipus is eager for the details. He takes Oedipus back to that buried childhood:

OEDIPUS: Terrible the insult that I received from my swaddling clothes.

MESSENGER: So that you were named who you are from that chance.

OEDIPUS: Oh, in the gods' name, was it from my mother or father? Tell me!

MESSENGER: I don't know. The giver knows this better than I.

OEDIPUS: Did you then take me from someone else and find me by chance?

MESSENGER: No; another, a herdsman, gave you to me. (1035–40)

Trying to pierce the darkness of that mysterious time of his birth, Oedipus seems to be drawing on old, buried memories: the "old hurt" to his feet, the curiosity about his name, and the "insult" from his "swaddling clothes" that recalls the "insult" about his birth with which he was taunted at Thebes long ago (1035 and 784). In place of the normal care of a baby's "swaddling clothes" he received only the pierced feet that gave him his name, "swollen foot" (*oidein*, "to swell," and *pous*, "foot"). By refusing him a name, his parents also refused him a normal human identity; they condemned him to a social as well as a biological death. In the untranslatable pun of line 1038, only "the-giver-knows" (*oid' ho dous*) names *Oidipous*.[9]

So far, the scene has concentrated on the two male interlocutors. Now, as the tension relaxes slightly, the chorus contributes another piece of the puzzle. Turning to the chorus, Oedipus asks for information about the Old Herdsman. "Tell me," he says, "since it is the *right moment* (*kairos*) for these things to be found out." In this line he says more than he realizes, as we recognize when the chorus, after the discovery, sings, "All-seeing time *found you out*" (1213). Here, however, the chorus merely confirms that the "giver" of Oedipus to the Messenger is the same Herdsman/escort/witness who has already been summoned (1047–53).

This last bit of information leads Oedipus back to Jocasta, who has been standing by in silence during the whole interrogation. When he first entered in line 950, Oedipus had addressed her by name (the only time in the play) and with a mixture of dignity and affection: "My dearest wife, Jocasta." Now he is clipped and colloquial: "Wife, do you recall that man—the one we just sent after? Is he the one whom this man here means?" (1054–55). Jocasta stalls for time, repeats the question, and tries to distract him: "What about that man he spoke of? Pay no attention! Don't even wish to make mention of these things that have been spoken all in vain" (1056–57). Her language is elliptical and cryptic, as it must be, for we see that she has recognized the truth. Her only hope is to persuade Oedipus to stop. Her advice, especially the phrase "spoken all in vain" or "all to no purpose," recalls her earlier statement about "living at random." In fact her word "make mention" (1057) also means "remember," so that there are implications of old memories—old oracles, old actions—coming fearfully alive, as they will come alive for her in the last words she utters in life, as reported by the Second Messenger later, where she again speaks of "mentioning/ memory" (1246).

Oedipus removes all hope and dooms himself, and her too, with his predictable refusal: "This cannot be; there is no way for me to take such tokens and not show forth my birth" (1058–59). His word "tokens" or "signs" (*semeia*), like the "clues" or "tokens" (*symbola*) of 221, belongs to the myth of the foundling (see above, Chapter 6). An abandoned baby frequently has such tokens left with him, as in Euripides' *Ion* and a number of folklore versions of the Oedipus myth. In fairy tales of this type such tokens prove the child to be of princely or divine birth and joyfully confirm his right to the kingdom. In Oedipus' case the tokens are the scars on his feet that in one way prove his royal birth but in another way undo his kingship.

The next moments are among the most anguished of the play. Oedipus and Jocasta have hitherto been subject to the same errors and illusions, and Jocasta has supported Oedipus in his fears and impatience and in the ups and downs of hope or worry. Now their paths diverge, and Oedipus will face the rest of his suffering alone. He, the hunter and searcher, cannot be stopped by her pleas. Her last words to him are those of a mother and wife both. She knows his nature and knows too that her pleas will have no effect, but still, as she begs him four times not to go on with his search, she makes this last desperate attempt to save him.

"If you care for your own life," she begs him, "don't search this out. My disease is enough" (1060–61). This is almost her last utterance onstage, and her metaphor of "disease" contains a full recognition of what their life together now means. It not only takes up the literal disease of the plague but also reveals its source in the diseaselike pollution that spreads out like an infection from the house of Oedipus—the "house" to which the Messenger at his entrance promised "good things" (934). "I well know that you are diseased," Oedipus had said to the suppliants compassionately in the opening scene of the play, "but there is none of you who bears this disease equally with me" (59–61). The full truth of Oedipus' unique place in this "disease" is now becoming clear.

The whole of this discovery scene has taken us closer than ever to the mystery of Oedipus' name. "Named who you are from that chance" (1036), the Messenger had said. "May you never know who you are" (1068), Jocasta now cries. And her last words of the scene are also a final naming: "Ill-starred—this is the last address I have for you—nothing else ever again" (1071–72). The mother who gave him no name at his birth now renames him in his terrible maturity, "Ill-starred." It is the same term that she used for her doomed infant in the previous scene, in her attempt to show that oracles do not come true (855).

The chorus is alarmed at her distraught, silent exit (1073–75), which, like that of Deianeira in *Trachinian Women* and Eurydice in *Antigone*, forebodes suicide. Oedipus, however, is blinded by his hope of discovering his parents. Once more he is the eager quester for truth. Let her go, he says, to "rejoice in her rich birth" (1070). He means that she can still take pleasure in her royal ancestry, whatever his birth may be, but the phrase also means "rich kinship" and so alludes to the over-rich kinship of the incestuous union. Calling himself a "child of chance" (1080), Oedipus is sure that he "will not be dishonored" by being proved the child of a slave. The choral ode that follows takes up his confident mood with speculations in the opposite direction, that he may be the child of a god. But, in fact, chance and time, which Oedipus regards as his allies ("the months my kindred," 1082), have worked together to produce a life of to-tal "dishonor."

Third Stasimon (Fourth Choral Ode, 1086–1109)

Carried along by Oedipus' mood of elation, the chorus sings an ode (the third stasimon) that depicts a mountain world of nymphs and Pan, Hermes, and Dionysus. It is the only moment of sustained joy in the play, but the happiness will be short-lived. In this setting of god-inhabited mountains, the chorus cele-brates Cithaeron as Oedipus' "fatherland and nurse and mother" (1092). "Nurse" and "mother" are in the reverse of the biological order, as were the analogous terms on the father's side when Oedipus first spoke of Polybus who "nurtured and begot me" (827). This error about his "mother," who is now very much in our minds after Jocasta's sudden departure, parallels the mistake about his fa-ther. The truth about both parents will soon make Oedipus curse Cithaeron (1451–54), which the chorus here addresses with such hope and joy.

The parodos, the first ode of the play, also ended with a joyous Dionysus, the "wine-faced" god leading his maenads (ecstatic women devotees) in their nocturnal processions on the mountain (209–15). In both passages the chorus in-vokes Thebes' major divinity as their last hope. But the joy of this ode contrasts with the bleakness of the parodos—a contrast that will not last for long. Recall-ing the desperation of the plague-stricken city of that first ode, the third stasi-mon also points up the massive shift from the Thebans' suffering to the king's.

Both in mood and content the third stasimon is also almost the reverse of the second. The previous ode emphasized the gap between god and mortal and the remoteness of the gods on Olympus (867). The present ode also names Olym-pus (1088) but in its almost hysterical joy brings the gods close to men and gives semidivine status to a doomed mortal. The god of the previous ode was an un-named power (872, 881), pure and remote, the defender of timeless laws in an ageless world free of procreation and birth. The gods of this ode are jolly, play-ful beings who cavort with mountain nymphs (1099–1100), "join in their sport" (1109), and beget mortal children, one of whom is supposedly Oedipus.[10] In turning away from the tragic realities of Oedipus' birth, the chorus also turns away from that austere vision of "god" in the previous ode to the playful mul-tiplicity of specific, named gods in their fully anthropomorphic, sensual aspects. By mythicizing both the gods and Oedipus' birth, they distort the truth of both.

Fifth Episode (1110–1185)

With this joyful song still in our ears, we see the long-awaited Herdsman enter the orchestra. Herdsmen are rude and rustic workers and slaves, and this old man, come from the hills and the company of his beasts, forms a sharp contrast to the nymphs and playful gods of the ode. He brings us back to reality in more ways than one. The chorus quickly identifies him as "Laius' trusty herdsman," and the Corinthian Messenger also names him as the man of whom he has been speaking (1117–20). The Herdsman at first says little, only a line at a time, but the Messenger, ever eager to volunteer details in what he thinks is a helpful and profitable course, reminds him of that remote time when the two of them tended sheep together on Cithaeron (1132–40).

This is the only departure from line-by-line repartee in the scene, and it depicts an almost bucolic serenity in the herdsmen's seasonal rhythms, "from spring to winter, six-month seasons," as they make their regular shift from summer to winter pasture (1136–39). The scene's workaday routine is a pendant to the mythically colored mountain landscape of the previous ode, and it offers a momentary respite from the looming horror. Its quiet, untragic view of time in the dull life of shepherds also sets off, by contrast, Oedipus' measuring and calculating of critical dates and the moment-by-moment tension of the present scene.

"You speak the truth, although from a long time ago," the Herdsman says, as he acknowledges the Messenger's recollection of the events (1141). "Truth from a long time ago" seems an ordinary statement, but it crystallizes what is happening onstage: the process whereby truth—the truth that Teiresias had by inborn nature—is gradually forced out of its covering of time. The scattered bits of the past now fit into the pattern that had been shrouded in falsehood for so long.

The Messenger, happy to do his new king a service, as he thinks, emphatically identifies the Herdsman, but the latter tries to shut him up: "Go to perdition, won't you! Won't you keep silent?" (1146). The outcry in the first half of the line holds one of those small ironies in Sophocles' use of colloquial speech, for it exactly echoes Oedipus' cry when Teiresias pronounced him the killer of Laius and the source of the pollution: "Is it endurable to hear such things from this man here? *Go to perdition, won't you!* Won't you quickly turn around and get yourself out of these halls?" (429–31). Now, however, Oedipus is intensely eager to hear (see 1170), and this scene enacts the Teiresias scene in reverse. Yet it parallels the first half of the Teiresias scene too in that Oedipus overrides someone's reluctance to speak, as he also did just before with Jocasta (1056–57).

Oedipus keeps narrowing the range of his questioning. Is he the Herdsman's own child? No. The child of a citizen of Thebes? The Herdsman balks, and Oedipus, unrelenting, perhaps even calm, forces him: "You are a dead man if I ask you this again" (1166). And so the Herdsman answers, but he still takes refuge in ambiguity, for his answer can mean either "a child of Laius" or "a child of someone in the household of Laius" (1167). Oedipus must then ask again, "A slave, or begotten by him, of his own race?" (1168).

The suspense does not let up, for Oedipus has a last, though faint, hope. To be proved to be a slave would be bitter and humiliating; it would deflate all the exuberance in the previous ode about being the child of a god. But the alternative is more bitter still, for Oedipus must remember Jocasta's account of the oracle given Laius, that he would "be killed by a child born from myself and him." This is indeed the "terrible point of speaking," as the Herdsman says; it is the moment he has dreaded all the years that he has lived with his secret, and Oedipus echoes his words :

HERDSMAN: I am at the uttermost terrible point of speaking.
OEDIPUS: And I of hearing, but hear I must. (1169–70)

Oedipus' echo of the Herdsman's words verbally marks the strange kinship that has thus drawn together these two lives, the slave's and the king's.

"The woman inside would best tell how these things are" (1171–72), the Herdsman says, and the answer shifts perspective. Oedipus' thoughts at once go back to the mother. "She gave him to you?" Yes, my lord." "For what purpose?" "To kill him." "The mother, poor woman?" "Yes, in fear of evil prophecies." "What?" "The tale was that he would kill his parents." With these words the Herdsman brings us back to Jocasta's oracle about Laius (712–14) and draws it together with the oracle given to Oedipus.

And so the truth comes out, but with an unexpected show of feeling in Oedipus. In the previous scene he had cried out in surprise, almost pain, at the mention of his feet (1033) and asked whether that wound came "from the mother or the father" (1037). The scene before showed a slight flutter of Oedipus' emotion toward family members when he reflected that his "father," Polybus, might have died out of longing for him (969–70). And at the end we shall see his deep concern for his children. Now, learning the truth, he thinks about the mother, perhaps in pity, perhaps in horror, anger, or revulsion, perhaps all the above, for his phrase in 1175, "the mother, poor woman," can imply all of these feelings, and the word for "mother" here is not *mêtêr*, but *tekousa*, literally "she who gave birth."

It is worthwhile to pause over this moment a little longer. Oedipus' phrase in 1175, "the mother, poor woman," which is actually only two words in Greek, *tlêmôn tekousa*, shows how difficult it is to translate Sophocles' density and richness of meaning. A translator must usually choose one meaning where the original implies two or more. Thus R. C. Jebb translates the phrase as, "Her own child, the wretch?" David Grene renders it, "She was so hard—its mother?" Hugh Lloyd-Jones has "Poor thing, was she its mother?" Robert Fagles perhaps comes closest to the ambiguity with, "Her own child? How could she?" R. D. Dawe's paraphrase, in his commentary, catches both the particular nuance of *tekousa* and the ambiguity of *tlêmôn*: "After giving birth she must have been *unhappy* to *venture* on such a step."[11]

Consider too what Oedipus does *not* ask the Old Herdsman. This man was introduced in the first scene of the play as the sole surviving witness to Laius' death (118–25), and his evidence on that point was the primary motive for Oedipus' intense eagerness to search him out later (755–66, 836–50, 859–61). Yet now, face to face with this witness, Oedipus does not ask about the scene at the cross-roads, only about the exposure of the infant; to such an extent has his investigation shifted from the plague and Laius to his own identity. He would push back his knowledge of himself to his earliest origins, the mother who exposed him on the third day after his birth. "Was it the mother or the father—by the gods, tell me," he passionately demanded of the Corinthian Messenger (1037). Later, after the blinding, he will again name both parents as the agents of his intended death in infancy on Mount Cithaeron (1452–54).

Having moved beyond his "terrible point of speaking," the Herdsman for the first time utters more than a line or two at a time. Pity was his motive for saving the baby, he says, as he explains how he gave the exposed infant to the Corinthian Messenger (1177–81). There seems to be pity for the grown Oedipus too, as he tells him, "If you are the one whom this man says you are, then know that you have been born as an ill-starred man." Unknowingly, he echoes Jocasta's penultimate words to Oedipus, just before she ran inside the palace: "Ill-starred man, may you never know who you are" (1068).

Like Teiresias, the Herdsman knew a secret and was forced to tell it, but this simple, fearful man is at the opposite remove from the haughty, powerful prophet. Ironically, the deep truths that Teiresias pronounced were ignored, while this slave's little piece of truth brings Oedipus' whole world crashing down around him. Whereas Teiresias spoke his revelation in the pride and anger of an offended prophet, the Herdsman, simple as he is, speaks with pity. The Herdsman had spoken only of the one oracle that he knew about, namely that the child he saved would kill its parents (1176). Oedipus, now knowing all three oracles and having lived with the horror of his own oracle since adolescence, cries out in horror that "everything now has come out clearly" (1182). At this moment of awful clarity, as illusion turns into truth, vision turns into blindness. Calling on the light that he would see for the last time, he rushes into the palace with a string of short words, untranslatable in their sound and syntax, that conveys the interwoven curses of parricide and incest.

FOURTH STASIMON (FIFTH CHORAL ODE)

The ode that follows (1186–1222) releases the almost unbearable tension of Oedipus' discovery. Like many of the odes, it also serves to mark the passage of time, here the time during which Oedipus has entered the palace for his last great act. In contrast to the previous ode of hope and joyful anticipation that Oedipus will prove to be the son of a god, this fifth ode reflects on his fall from honor to utter misery and places his tragedy in the wider context of the uncertainty of all human happiness: "O generations of men, how I count you as equal to nothing while you live" (1186–88). This cry takes up the theme of counting when all of Oedipus' calculations have failed miserably. In contrast to the ageless laws of the gods invoked in the second stasimon (863–72), mortal life appears in its fullest subjection to time, change, and the terrible entanglements of its begetting. In the previous scene, Oedipus exulted in the news of Polybus' death because it made the oracles "worth nothing" (971–72). Now his own birth has made him the chief example of the "nothingness" of all humankind.

The ode virtually passes in review all of Oedipus' great achievements now that they have come to "nothing": his conquest of the Sphinx, his protection of the city as its "tower," his great honor as ruler of Thebes (1198–1204). The "happiness" and "good fortune" on which the Corinthian Messenger had congratulated his house (929) are now empty (1198). "Famous Oedipus," the chorus says, and the phrase ironically echoes his own confident term for himself in the opening scene (see 1208 and 8). Born from the "furrows" that he plowed, he finds all the relationships of his time-bound mortality to be filled with horror (1211–16). Time itself, which Oedipus had in a sense mastered in answering the Sphinx's riddle, has now "found him out" in the terrible riddle of his own life, his "marriage that is no marriage" (1213–15).

The ode completes a pattern of images and motifs that have been building throughout the play and turns them from strength to weakness: counting, equality, harbor, agriculture, vision, silence. It is important for the rest of the play, however, that Oedipus' achievements are not wiped out. The chorus reflects on what Oedipus meant to them when he was strong: "To use straight speech, I breathed in relief thanks to you and closed my eyes in sleep" (1220–22).[12] These closing lines hark back to the chorus' continuing confidence in Oedipus in the first stasimon, despite Teiresias' accusations (505–11); now Teiresias has been proven right after all, but the chorus has not completely abandoned Oedipus.

NOTES

1. Interpreters sometimes find traces of maternal solicitude for Oedipus in Jocasta—an effect developed by modern dramatists like Jean Cocteau in *The Infernal Machine*.

2. The word for "all" in Oedipus' phrase, "I killed them all," is an emphatic collective form, *sympantes*, "all together," less common than the simple term for "all," *pantes*. We have heard this word just some sixty lines before, when Jocasta gave her account of this event: "There were five in all" (*sympantes*, 752).

3. Cocteau will develop this aspect of Jocasta with a characteristically modern psychology in *The Infernal Machine*. See below, Chapter 12.

4. It is hard to convey the threat of total disorder in the chorus' clipped closing phrase of 910, literally "things divine are gone." See Albert Henrichs, "'Why Should I Dance?': Choral Self-Referentiality in Greek Tragedy," *Arion*, 3rd Series, vol. 3, no. 1 (1994/95), 66: "The laconic locution *ta theia* [things divine] epitomizes the sum total of polytheism, including the entire range of divine and human interaction and reciprocity: the divine world order, the observance of ritual, down to the consultation of oracles and to the very dance performed by the *khoreutai* [chorus members] in the orchestra as they sing." The chorus' fear in 908, that "Apollo may be nowhere

clear in honor," is soon to be disproven when Oedipus, getting closer to the awful truth, fears that "Phoebus (Apollo) may come out (proven) clear" (1011). Cf. also 735, 1182.

5. On the ironies of "new" and "old" see also 666–67, and in general see my *Tragedy and Civilization* (Cambridge, MA: Harvard University Press, 1981), 231.

6. R. D. Dawe, ed., *Sophocles, Oedipus Rex* (Cambridge: Cambridge University Press, 1982), 190 (on lines 922–23).

7. The significance of the verb "beget" is underlined in the repetition a few lines later, 1019–20. Oedipus asks, "And how is the one who begot me (*phusas*) equal to nothing?", and the Corinthian Messenger replies, "But he didn't sire you (*egeinato*), neither he nor I." There is a chiastic play here of the two words of paternity, *genei* (kin) and *exephuse* (begot) in 1016–17 and *phusas* and *egeinato* in 1019–20. In other references to Polybus in this scene he is referred to only as "father" (955, 967), or just as "that man" (948).

8. The ironies of Oedipus' ignorance are reflected in a number of plays on the name "Oedipus" that are not easily translated into English, e.g. *ouk eidôs*, "not knowing," in 1008, and *ouk oid'; ho dous*, "I do not know; the man who gave (the child) [knows]," in 1038.

9. *Oid(a)*, "I know," here in 1038 is, of course, first person, and there is a strong syntactical pause after it; nevertheless, the pun would be heard by an audience sensitized to the ubiquitous play on Oedipus' name, and a number of recent interpreters have pointed it out, although they do not all interpret it in the same way.

10. The combination of Nymphs, "play," and the upland pastures at the end of the ode (1101–1109) may evoke the very different atmosphere of a famous passage in Homer's *Odyssey*, Odysseus' meeting with Nausicaa (*Odyssey* 6.105–6), where the castaway hero compares the fresh, young princess to the Nymphs of Artemis who "play in the wild-pasturing uplands" (*Numphai . . . agronomoi paizousi*; cf. *plakes agronomoi . . . Numphân sumpaizei* in *Oedipus* 1103, 1108 ["wild-pasturing uplands . . . one of the Nymphs joins in play"]). If Sophocles is recalling this famous Homeric scene, it may be to contrast the two situations. For Odysseus the evocation of the playful mountain nymphs foreshadows his escape from the sea-world of his trials and its vengeful deity, Poseidon, whereas for Oedipus the ostensible escape is in fact the prelude to disaster. As commentators note, the ode also echoes the invocation to Dionysus by the sixth-century lyric poet Anacreon (fragment 357 in David A. Campbell, ed., *Greek Lyric*, vol. 2, Loeb Classical Library [Cambridge, Mass.: Harvard University Press, 1988], 54–57): "Lord with whom Love the subduer and the blue-eyed Nymphs and radiant Aphrodite play, as you haunt the lofty mountain peaks . . ." (*Numphai . . . sumpaizousin*; and cf. *Oedipus* 1109, *sumpaizei* "join in play"). Here too the evocation of the happy and playful eroticism of the famous love-poet sets off the tragic reversal soon to come here. For other aspects of this ode see my *Sophocles' Tragic World* (Cambridge, MA: Harvard University Press, 1995), 190–94; for ironical undertones in the language of the ode that hint at the disaster in the background, see David Sansone, "The Third Stasimon of the *Oedipus Tyrannos*,"*Classical Philology* 70 (1975), 110–17.

11. Dawe, *Sophocles, Oedipus Rex*, 214 (commentary on line 1175). See also Nicole Loraux, "L'empreinte de Jocaste," *L'Écrit du temps* 12 (1986), 40–41.

12. The translation of the last clause (1222) is not entirely certain, and commentators are divided. The sequence of particles seems to me to favor the translation I have given in the text, and so too Dawe in his commentary. Fagles translates, "And now you bring down night upon my eyes," following R. C. Jebb, *Sophocles: The Plays and Fragments*, Part 1, *The Oedipus Tyrannus*, 3d ed. (Cambridge: Cambridge University Press, 1893), 161. Hugh Lloyd–Jones, ed. and trans., *Sophocles, Ajax, Electra, Oedipus Tyrannus*, Loeb Classical Library (Cambridge, MA: Harvard University Press, 1994), translates, "To tell the truth, you restored me to life and you lulled my eyes in death."

9

Resolution: Tragic Suffering,
Heroic Endurance

EXODOS (CLOSING MOVEMENT)

After the great crisis of the recognition scene, the chorus' generalizations restore an atmosphere of calm and solemn expectation. Its concern also assures an attentive hearing for the Second Messenger, who now enters. His long speech holds a succession of horrors: first Jocasta's suicide, then Oedipus' frenzied entrance to her chamber to find the body, and finally his self-blinding.

The Second Messenger's introduction, though perhaps a little tendentious, raises two points important for Oedipus' appearance in the final scenes: purification and the distinction between involuntary and self-chosen suffering:

> I tell you neither the waters of the Danube
> nor the Nile can wash this palace clean.
> Such things it hides, it soon will bring to light—
> terrible things, and none done blindly now,
> all done with a will. The pains
> we inflict upon ourselves hurt most of all.
>
> (Fagles' translation, 1227–31)

Greek tragedies tend to luxuriate in such accounts of physical suffering, generally narrated and rarely shown onstage—a tendency that they passed on to the Roman tragedian Seneca and thence to Elizabethan dramatists like Shakespeare and Webster.

The Messenger's abrupt-seeming announcement of Jocasta's death immediately after these lines contains a pathos and an extraordinary mixture of conversational dialogue and poetic phrasing typical of Sophocles' style. What the Messenger says in line 1235 is literally, "The divine head of Jocasta is dead." This is fairly common Greek poetic idiom, however stilted it sounds in English, and it casts an aura of epic dignity, grandeur, and sorrow around the queen's death. But this idiom had an earlier occurrence in the play, namely at line 950, when Oedipus enters to hear the ostensibly good news of Polybus' death. "O dearest head of my wife, Jocasta," he says at that moment, and this is the only time in the play that Oedipus addresses Jocasta by name and uses the superlative, "dearest." The echo of that loving address in the Messenger's stark words now marks the reversal of all happiness in the house of Oedipus.

In a play so much concerned with the revelation and recovery of a deeply buried past, the climactic acts of both characters face backward. Jocasta, whose last words the Messenger quotes, recalls Laius and the ill-starred begetting of their child (1246–51). Oedipus reenacts symbolically both the incest and the parricide by "striking into" the palace and "striking" his eyes (*epaisen, eisepaisen*, 1252, 1270), using the same verb that he used of "striking Laius" (807). His breaking through the closed double doors of Jocasta's chamber symbolically reenacts the incest, entering places that should have remained closed to him, especially as the "double doors" recall the "double bedding" and "double field" that describe the incest just before (1249, 1257). The word for the "sockets" of his eyes (*arthra*, 1270) in his self-blinding is the word used for the "joints" of his ankles in both Jocasta's and the Corinthian Messenger's accounts of the exposure (718, 1032). On a Freudian reading the eyes are a symbolic substitution for the male genitals, so that the self-blinding is also a symbolic act of self-castration, and in many societies castration is the punishment for incest.[1] Be that as it may, the coincidence of feet and eyes also suggests the completion of a tragic life-pattern that has been awaiting Oedipus all these years, as if the pierced "sockets" of the king's eyes were already implicit in the pierced "joints" of the infant's feet.

Oedipus' frenzied shouting, which the Messenger reports, is the climax of the panic that arose in him when Jocasta first mentioned the triple roads. His emotional violence here contrasts with her quiet suffering. Whereas she left the stage stifling her despair in a last brief cry, Oedipus shouts. Whereas she withdrew to her chamber for a moment of bitter memory and reflection just before her suicide (1240–50), Oedipus rushes about the palace and asks for a sword, whether to kill himself or Jocasta, or both, we do not know (1252–55).

Like Eurydice, Creon's wife, in *Antigone*, Jocasta takes her suffering inside, to the hidden, private enclosures of the house. Oedipus, in the next scene, will cry out to be shown "to all the Thebans" (1288), making a public and civic display of his crime and his punishment. A woman's grief, like her life, must be hidden away from the public world of the city. Despite Jocasta's earlier adroitness in resolving the quarrel between Creon and Oedipus and in receiving the Corinthian Messenger, her place, at the last crisis in her life, is in the interior space that defines a woman's identity in classical Athens.[2]

The narrated but unseen events are overwhelming in their specific details and sensory impressions: the sound of Oedipus' cries and the sight of the hanging woman inside her chamber, the golden pins, the dark red flow of blood on Oedipus' beard. But these surface details of human suffering also belong to a larger pattern of divine action, suggested, for example, in the presence of some "divinity" (*daimon*), as the Messenger says, that showed Oedipus the way to Jocasta's chamber (1258–59). The wider implications of Oedipus' pollution are also evoked in the metaphor of "black storm and bloody hail" for the wounds to Oedipus' eyes and in the repeated agricultural images of "seeds" and "plow-fields" (1246, 1257). These metaphors suggest the catastrophic disharmony between man and nature caused by the pollution in the royal house. They remind us specifically of Apollo's warning of a "storm of blood" upon the city if the pollution is not expelled (100–101) and also of the plague's effect of sterility in the fields (25–27, 171–73).

The language that describes the blinding also has sexual associations, which deepen the meaning of the scene both as a fatal reenactment of the wedding night and as a destructive perversion of the "sacred marriage" between king and queen that should insure abundance and fertility for the land. The Messenger's "mingled woes for man and woman" in 1281 can also suggest the sexual "mingling" in intercourse between "husband and wife" (*andri kai gunaiki summigê kaka*).[3] The "shower of blood" that falls from Oedipus' wounded eyes in the lines just preceding (1276–79) evokes the fertilizing rain that the personified sky-god Ouranos sends down into the lap of Gaia, the personified earth, in the archetypal "sacred marriage," the union that makes all life possible. A famous passage in a lost play by Aeschylus, imitated by a number of later authors, described this mythical marriage as follows: "The holy sky loves to wound the earth, and desire seizes the earth to have this marriage; and the rain, falling from the sky as he has union with earth impregnates her."[4] For Thebes, however, there is blood instead of rain and plague instead of fecundity.

The Messenger's speech ends with the motifs of sight and spectacle as he prepares us for the entrance of Oedipus. The actor playing Oedipus now wears a mask that shows his bloodied eyes, and he returns to the stage through the palace doors into which he had rushed in horror at the moment of discovery in the previous scene. The chorus is the first to respond to that horrible sight (1297–1300): "O deed of woe terrible for humankind to look upon, o most terrible of all that I have ever come upon." Its song of horror (1296–1306) parallels the bitter ode on the nothingness of human life at the end of the previous scene (1186–1222). But now the chorus immediately rejects its role of detached generalization to express direct engagement with Oedipus in their intense cries, "Alas, alas, ill-starred man" (1301). These words are then echoed by Oedipus' "alas, alas" (*aiai, aiai*) in 1308. Initially, the chorus members regard the blinding as either madness (*mania*, 1300) or as the attack of some powerful *daimôn*, and they shudder with a horror that makes it hard for them to look at him. But they do not shrink from him and are eager to learn more of his motives (1297–1306). As Oedipus gradually becomes calmer and more articulate, the gulf between them closes. Almost at once the chorus enters into a shared lyrical dialogue with him (1312–66).

This is the first time in the play that Oedipus joins the chorus in a lyrical exchange, a kind of duet, that begins with his outcries of pain and suffering. Hitherto he has spoken only in the dialogue or recitative meter of the iambic trimeter. By joining the chorus in the song meters, he expresses both a new level of emotion, in contrast to his previous control, and a new bond of sympathy and humanity, in contrast to his previous commanding distance.

If the Messenger's speech contains the climax of the action, the appearance of Oedipus immediately after is the climax of the drama as a visual spectacle. Instead of the proud king of the prologue, we see the anguished, blinded sufferer. Instead of confident speech and clear reasoning, we hear a series of monosyllabic cries and scarcely coherent exclamations:

> Where am I going? where on earth?
> where does all this agony hurl me?
> where's my voice?—
> winging, swept away on a dark tide—
> O dark power of the god, what a leap you made!
>
> (Fagles' translation [slightly modified], 1309–11)

Like Teiresias, Oedipus now needs a guide (1292–93), but with his weakness he also takes on something of Teiresias' vision of truth. Sophocles has frequently played on "Oedipus" as meaning "know where" (*oida pou*, "I know where").[5] The man who, as Teiresias said, did not know "where he was" in suffering or in his place among his closest kin (367, 413–15) now, in his physical blindness, literally does not "know where"; and at this point he begins to shed the figurative blindness of illusion for a truer vision of his life.

The maxim of the oracular god, Apollo, at Delphi is "Know thyself," and this Oedipus has begun to do. This phrase, however, means not just to know one's idiosyncratic, individual personality, in the sense in which a contemporary North American or European would speak of "finding yourself" or "expressing yourself." Rather, it refers to grasping the nature of mortal life and, in particular, the limitations that surround human life: the accidents of birth and unpredictable suffering or illness. In this sense Oedipus, as the previous ode suggested (1193–96), has begun to know himself as a mortal being, the example par excellence of human suffering and the precariousness of human fortunes. It is in this light that we can now understand the Priest's address to Oedipus in the opening scene as "first of men in the circumstances of life and in the meetings with divinities" (33–34). As he says a little later, Oedipus now considers himself "of mortals the most hateful to the gods" (1345–46). Echoing the chorus, he calls himself "ill-starred" (1303, 1308), using the epithet that Jocasta had given him as her "last address" (1071). Oedipus has, in a sense, discovered his true name and his true mortal identity.

Whatever the events in his past that lay beyond his control, Oedipus has pushed through the errors and lies surrounding his life to reach this moment of dreadful clarity. Having recognized that his life hitherto has been founded on a horrible illusion, he makes the decision, based on full knowledge, to change its course radically. He insists on the distinction between the suffering that came from Apollo and his own self-chosen and self-inflicted punishment:

Apollo, friends, Apollo—
he ordained my agonies—these, my pains on pains!
But the hand that struck my eyes was mine,
mine alone—no one else—
    I did it all myself!
What good were eyes to me?
Nothing I could see could bring me joy.

                    (Fagles' translation, 1328–35)[6]

Choice is important, and it marks Oedipus' strength, decisiveness, and moral clarity even in the midst of his sufferings.

When he returns from lyrical meter to iambic trimeter, he speaks more calmly. The chorus wonders if Oedipus would not have been better off if he simply commited suicide, as Jocasta did (1367–68). This statement impels Oedipus to his strongest and clearest defense of his resolve to remain alive (1369–90), now in trimeters and in a sustained logical argument and no longer in the brief lyrical outcry of some forty lines earlier (1336–46). He reveals this growing strength in the impatient sharpness of his opening line (1369–70): "That these things were not done for the best don't teach or counsel me." What pleasure could he take in looking on his parents in the underworld or on his incestuously begotten children in this world (1369–90)? There is a cruel reversal in these lines because Oedipus, before the discovery, explained to the Corinthian Messenger his regret at exiling himself from his supposedly native city and added, "And yet to look upon the eyes of parents is most sweet" (999). Now, after the oracles are fulfilled, he shuns looking on those parents even in the underworld (1371–73).

Although Oedipus realizes that Apollo, not chance, has "leaped upon" him to cause his sufferings (compare 1311 with 263 and 469), he does not blame the god. He merely accepts the divine will as the mysterious source of the tragic pattern that life held for him. He knows, factually, that he has touched the deepest suffering possible for a human being (1365–66). He recognizes the cruel irony that the man who "saved" him from death in infancy has in fact been the source of disaster rather than comfort, and he curses his rescuer (1349–55). But, having survived, he now has the understanding to see his life as a whole and the strength to bear its terrible suffering.

THE HERO IN HIS SUFFERING

The last two hundred lines, after the emergence of the blinded Oedipus from the palace, are an indispensable part of Sophocles' interpretation of the myth of Oedipus, and need to be studied carefully. They express Sophocles' view of the tragic heroism of this great sufferer. Three aspects of Oedipus' situation are especially important.

First, Oedipus has decided to survive his horrifying discovery, to punish himself with blindness rather than death. In this he is the model for the heroic endurance of Euripides' Heracles in *Heracles Mad*, who makes the conscious decision to "resist misfortunes" and "endure life" after the madness in which he killed his wife and children (1347–51). Sophocles does not intellectualize the issue of suicide as Euripides does. When we see Oedipus returning, blinded, to the stage, we know that he has passed through this dark moment and survived the worst that life can hold.[7] His is a heroic pattern that embraces the course of a whole lifetime. He follows neither the epic pattern of the semi-divine hero, like Achilles, who chooses death in the flower of his strength and beauty and wins "imperishable glory," nor the older tragic pattern of figures like Ajax, who prefer death to shame and dishonor.[8] For this reason too, perhaps, we see Oedipus' life still open before him at the end.

Second, although Oedipus wants to be led away and expelled from Thebes as his curse requires, he is not alone. The elders of the chorus do not abandon him. Though they find his presence hideous, they do not turn away. They are full of pity, and he addresses them as "dear friends" for the first time in the play (*philoi*, 1321, 1329, 1339). He is moved and grateful to find them so concerned:

> My friends, you still attend me, steadfast, for still you have the endurance to care for me in my blindness. O woe, O woe. Yet you are not hidden from me. In darkness though I am, I yet recognize your voice; I know it clearly (1321–25).[9]

Despite Oedipus' momentary wish to cut off all his channels of perception of the outside world (1386–90), he does not break his bond of closeness with his Theban citizens, nor does he hide himself away in shame and debasement.[10] Earlier he had asked to be "shown to all the Thebans" as the criminal that he is (1287–96), an act of moral courage worthy of a great ruler. Even in his despair he shows himself to be a king. It is tempting to draw a comparison with King Lear's equally tragic, though perhaps more pathetic, "Ay, every inch a king" (*King Lear*, 4.6.106).

Third, weak as he is, Oedipus has an inner strength, and this becomes surer and clearer as the scene goes on. The chorus says compassionately, "It is no wonder that amid such sufferings you have a double grief and endure double woes" (1319–20). Oedipus will soon take up the chorus' word "endure" as he himself comes to reflect on his growing strength (1415).

These three qualities of Oedipus—his ability to survive the torment both from the gods and from his own self-punishing remorse, his continuing bonds with his citizens and his family, and his inner strength in the midst of physical weakness—do not appear as a moralizing "message" or in a simple linear progression. Rather, Sophocles shows us, in concrete, emotional terms, a human being possessed of deep resources of spirit who is afflicted with an overwhelming disaster of unpredictable, irrational suffering but is not totally annihilated by it. His dialogue with the chorus in lyrical meter (1307–66), as we have noted, expresses this new intensity of feeling.

113

Even after this lyrical passage, however, Oedipus continues to swing between bitterness and acceptance, despair and courage, especially in his two long speeches in lines 1369–1415 and 1446–75. We watch him groping his way toward what and who he now is. When the chorus, meaning well, agrees that he would have been better off dead, he snaps back, "Do not try to teach or counsel me that what I did was not done for the best" (1369–70). He still has the afterglow of the strength in his terrible decision, and although he values the chorus' concern for him, he also feels a fierce justice in accepting the punishments that he had called down upon the killer when he was king. He has gone beyond where other men go and has little patience with banal condolences.

Oedipus is still struggling to come to terms with his new identity, and part of his struggle is a search for self-understanding through reviewing his life. He names the crucial places of his past—Cithaeron, Corinth, the triple road—and imputes to them a demonic quality (1391–1402). He personifies the triple road as a gigantic beast that drinks his and Laius' blood (1399–1401), and he rails bitterly against Cithaeron as the place destined by his parents to be his tomb, the place that buried the normal human existence from which he was cast out (1449–54).

Polybus and Corinth "nurtured" him, he says, as "something handsome with evils festering beneath the sore" (1394–96). He sees his life in a new way, as a delusive surface that has now been stripped away, but he also takes up the play's pervasive imagery of disease. Oedipus' very body is now revealed as the city's hidden disease. His word *nurtured* here also suggests that he is finally obeying Apollo's command, "Drive out the land's pollution as being nurtured in this earth" (96–97). At the height of his energy and power, Oedipus ferociously accused Creon of trying to "do harm to my body" (i.e., my person, 642–43). But now that regal person/body of the king has become the "wretched form" (1388) of the blind beggar whose hearing he would also block up if he could, since his physical being in the world can now give him no joy (1386–90). Indeed, Oedipus' body has become increasingly a source of suffering as he moves from the discovery that his "form" resembled Laius' (740–43) to the "terrible insult" of his pierced feet (1034–35), the torn eyes and bloodied beard of his self-punishment (1275–79), and finally the "wretched form" here in 1388.

It is among the paradoxical reversals of illusion and reality, vision and blindness, that Oedipus, by bringing surface and depth together, is becoming more whole. The last statement of his long speech is remarkably calm:

It's all right. Touch the man of grief.
Do. Don't be afraid. My troubles are mine
and I am the only man alive who can sustain them.

(Fagles' translation, 1413–15)

In his growing strength, Oedipus begins to act out, though he will not complete, the ritual pattern of the scapegoat, the *pharmakos*, the figure who is laden with all the evils and impurities of the community and then expelled to purify it.[11] Thus the Thebans need not fear pollution from his touch any longer. Oedipus has separated himself from the monstrous, polluted self that has been hidden within him for so long.

Creon's entrance at this point is brilliantly timed. Officially, he has replaced Oedipus as the king whose sacred function it is to assure the harmonious relation between the human world and the forces of nature on which the city's life depends (1418). And yet that sacred office still essentially resides in Oedipus. Oedipus reiterates to Creon what he had asked of the chorus, namely that he be cast out of the land or killed, thereby fulfilling his own curse and what he took to be Apollo's command (1410–12, 1436–37).

Where Oedipus is passionate and eager for the expulsion to take place with all possible speed (1436), Creon is cautious and unsure. He hesitates to act on his own authority, and he once more sends to Delphi to inquire of Apollo (1438–43). The short exchange brings the play back to the opening situation, but with Creon now in the role of king Oedipus, sending an emissary to Delphi to ask what to do about the pollution. The contrast between the two men sets into relief that energy, efficiency, and confidence that brought Oedipus his success— and his ruin.

Oedipus continues to fight down waves of bitterness and despair. Though he asks to be thrown forth to dwell on the wild Mt. Cithaeron, which his parents destined for his death (1449–54), he abruptly turns away from thoughts of dying. His very survival of the death intended for him in infancy points toward the life of suffering for which he has been singled out (1456–58). Taking back his wish, a hundred lines earlier, not to have survived that death by his fettered feet (1349–55), he now sees his "portion" (*moira*) as extending from that infancy to the "terrible sufferings" of the present, and he can extrapolate from these to a future whose course he does not yet know:

> And yet I know this much: no disease or anything else would have destroyed me, for I would not have been saved from dying except for something terrible. Let my life's portion go wherever it will go (1455–58).

It is a remarkable and important statement, a broad vision of a whole life, from earliest childhood to the present. His was a life dominated by rejection, suffering, and death from the very first, and with no clear reason for the suffering. This acceptance of a life of suffering in his cry, "Let my life's portion go wherever it will go," is at the opposite pole from his wild optimism at the first inklings of the truth earlier, when he confidently saw himself as the child of a beneficent good fortune and shouted, "Let whatever will break forth" (1076). And yet, with a very different view of his life's pattern, Oedipus affirms the inner strength equal to the suffering. In the scene just before, speaking to the chorus of Theban elders, Oedipus called for his death or expulsion as the land's pollution but then saw himself as touchable again, since "no one of mortals except myself can bear my woes" (1414–15). Now, speaking to Creon, he repeats and exceeds that spirit of endurance and accepts the tragic shape or "portion" of his life as a whole.

Sophocles has chosen this moment of courage for another surprise. Addressing Creon by name for the first time in the scene (1459), Oedipus asks him to look after his children—not the boys, who are already "men," but his "wretched, piteous two daughters," Antigone and Ismene, who always shared his table (1460–65). The detail illustrates Oedipus' capacity for affection and sense of his responsibility for his family as well as for his city. He has also moved beyond self-pity. Here he begins to free himself from the past's dark burden and to think of the future; he asks for the burial of Jocasta and for the care of his children. For the first time we see Oedipus speaking as a father, not to his city but to his own offspring, the two daughters now onstage.

When Oedipus asks Creon not to make his daughters "equal to his own sufferings" (1507), we can see Sophocles reshaping the Aeschylean treatment of the legend. Instead of cursing his sons, Oedipus invokes the responsibility of fatherhood and asks for Creon's help, "since you are left as the only father to these two girls" (1503–4). The chorus, shortly before, introduced Creon to Oedipus as "left as the only ruler of the land instead of you" (1418). Oedipus thus resigns to Creon his place as the father of his family, but in both cases he continues to be concerned for those whom his curse demands that he leave behind.

It is a further surprise that the girls appear onstage, another bold stroke on Sophocles' part. Oedipus, who, as he said, had no use for vision, is eager for touch. He thanks Creon for his pity and welcomes his daughters into his arms (1480–88). In the first line of the play Oedipus, as king, had addressed his citizens as "children." He now addresses his actual children with the same word (1480), but with the horrible resonances of the pollutions of incest and parricide, for "children" is here coupled with "sisters" in the next line (1481).

In contrast to the concealment of the incestuous relation in the past and his horror when it came to light, Oedipus now faces his crime squarely, in grimly familiar, agricultural imagery. Born where the "sowing" in the "double field" was wrongly fertile, his daughters will be left unmarried, as "barren soil" (1497–1502). Acknowledging his helplessness, Oedipus again asks for pity (1507), calls Creon "noble"—a far cry from his insults of their last meeting—and asks for the touch of his hand (1510). Throughout the scene it is important for Oedipus to establish the human contact of touch with those close to him, despite the terrible pollution that he knows he bears (see 1413, 1469, 1481ff.).

Creon's matter-of-fact authority checks the outpouring of emotion. He calls for an end of weeping and separates Oedipus from his daughters, to which Oedipus reluctantly agrees. Despite the reversal of roles, however, something fundamental in the two men remains unchanged. When Creon, close to the end, tells Oedipus, "I am not accustomed to speak vainly about what I do not understand" (1520), he is repeating almost verbatim what he had said about Teiresias when Oedipus had accused him of conspiring with the prophet (569). And he still admonishes Oedipus about his exercise of power (1522–23). With these lines, marking the formal end of that role as king of Thebes with which he began, Oedipus is slowly led back into the palace, while Creon's attendants lead his daughters offstage.

Sophocles may have ended his play here. The extant manuscripts have seven additional verses, in which the chorus addresses the citizens of Thebes and moralizes on Oedipus' fall and the uncertainty of human fortunes (1524–30). Scholars are divided as to whether Sophocles himself wrote these lines; many hold that they were added later, for use by acting companies. Aside from a number of grammatical problems, these lines bear a suspiciously close resemblance to the ending of Euripides' *Phoenician Women*, written some twenty years after *Oedipus*. On the other hand, all of Sophocles' extant plays end with a statement by the chorus. The banal moralizing achieves closure, to be sure, but might not Sophocles have wanted the more austere ending? Such would be the effect of closing with Creon's words in lines 1522–23, "Do not wish to exercise power in everything, for even those things over which you were powerful did not follow along with you in life."[12]

THE CLOSING SCENE

It is hard for a modern audience to gauge the tone of the final scene. A modern audience may balk at the presence of the young girls beside a bloodstained father who speaks frankly of their incestuous birth. But the ancient audience was far less squeamish about children's feelings. In Euripides' *Alcestis* and *Suppliant Women*, small children are present at their mother's death and lament over her body.

The visual spectacle reinforces the range and power of emotions. There are contrasts of pollution and loving touch, isolation and the bonds of family, Oedipus' helplessness and his growing inner clarity, his dependence and his continuing sense of authority. In a play whose chief effect is reversal, the closing scene forms the antithesis to the opening. Now Creon is in command, and Oedipus is the subordinate. Instead of being the receiver of supplication, Oedipus is the suppliant and asks for pity. Oedipus began as a proud king, "called famous by all," as he says of himself in the first scene (8), surrounded by a throng of admiring, respectful subjects; he is now set apart from all men as the disease of the city.

Modern directors are sometimes tempted to make the last scene turbulent and gory, emphasizing the contrast between the bloodstained king/criminal and the still-innocent young daughters.[13] But what is perhaps most striking about the ending is its calm and its emphasis on pity and the power of human ties in the midst of all the horror. One must not sentimentalize. There is still deep bitterness in Oedipus; still an imperious will. But he also has the simplicity of his greatness. He can ask for pity and try to shelter those he loves from the hard life that he knows awaits them. Despite his isolation and the sufferings of his house and his city, he helps reknit the bonds of family and society. Although he is no longer king, his appeals to the elders and to Creon help the curse-driven city to regain its health as a human community.

In the last movement Sophocles scales the action down from politics and the world order to the personal ties within the family. Even Creon, for all his hesitation, shows pity and understanding. Oedipus would give his daughters fatherly advice and hope for a better life than his, and seeks to enlist Creon as a kind of surrogate father (1503ff.). But he cannot cease being Oedipus the king, and Creon, the lesser man, senses his lingering will to power, and so admonishes Oedipus to take a more submissive attitude. Oedipus' resistance is consonant with his heroic strength in the play's closing movement. Yet even in this new stage of his life, he seems to be reenacting the confidence and the second-guessing of the gods that contributed to his tragedy. It would be mistaken to see the hero as merely exhibiting the pride that caused his fall, for, as we have seen, such a reading is inadequate to the play's presentation of his tragedy. Sophocles chooses to leave us with some questions rather than final answers.[14]

So it is that the actual fate of Oedipus is left suspended. We do not know whether he will be exiled or will remain in Thebes. Both stories were current in the fifth century. In one sense it does not matter, for the inner drama of Oedipus is completed when he brings his doomed infancy on Cithaeron together with his present life in Thebes and rejects the death that the former moment held.

Oedipus' concern for his children at the end completes another pattern in his life. He cannot, of course, cancel out the incest, but he can transform its monstrosity into something humanly bearable. When his father had struck him at the crossroads, Oedipus made him "pay back no equal share" in turning the blow back fatally upon the attacker (810). Now he asks Creon not to make his daughters "equal to my evil sufferings" (1506). He does not perpetuate in his own life his father's aggression against his child. Reading backwards from this final scene, one perhaps recalls Oedipus' sudden bursts of anxious curiosity about whether his mother or his father exposed him for death on the mountain (1037, 1173–76). In regarding his daughters with compassion rather than with abhorrence, violence, or rejection, and in trying to provide for their future, he has drastically reversed the treatment that he received from Laius and Jocasta.

Finding the proper ending must have been one of the great challenges of Sophocles' dramatic artistry. Having watched Oedipus' struggles and suffering, we the audience cannot emotionally assent to his request and send him into the wilderness to die. The appearance of the daughters is part of the reaffirmation of Oedipus' right to human community, polluted as he is. And yet simply to send this polluted, blinded, bleeding sufferer into his house would be to diminish the enormity of his situation and to lessen the fact that what he has done sets him apart from all other human beings. The present ending, with Creon's hesitation and appeal to the Delphic oracle, implicitly recognizes the uniqueness and the numinous power that have played around the life of Oedipus from the moment of his birth. It gives his polluted state its full impact but also keeps him in touch with the citizens whom he has loved and served and with us, the spectators, who have seen him fall from power to misery. He will reenter his house not as a secure member of city and family, but as a polluted outcast, still human and still endowed with all the feelings that have made him a tragic figure. Further, an unknown future still hangs over him, a future that, like his past, has something to do with the gods and especially with Apollo.[15]

The ending, while full of the horror of great suffering, is not cast in a mood of hopelessness or despair. Oedipus' fear for himself made him rather callous about his supposed father's death (a gentler replay of his killing of his real father, Laius), but after his passage through the anguish of discovery and self-punishment he has pity for his daughters' future and concern for the decent burial of Jocasta. He has become the paradigm not only of the fragile, uncertain condition of mortality, but also of the courage and spiritual strength of humanity. With his self-inflicted punishment for his past and his responsibility for those ties of blood and family in the present, Oedipus overcomes in himself the animal brutishness of incest and parricide.

After his frenzied rush into the palace at the moment of discovery, Oedipus' calm at the end is neither Stoic resignation nor Christian remorse. He sees himself as still "hated by the gods" (1519) but does not rant against them or immerse himself in guilt. He belongs to a culture in which the mere fact of having performed the acts of parricide and incest leaves an indelible stain or pollution, regardless of the motivations or intentions. He accepts the objective fact of being horribly polluted, and he can live with the inner torment of knowing these crimes. This continuing torment is expressed in his decision to live the rest of his life in blindness. In his long speeches to the chorus and to Creon he struggles with accepting his life's pattern, his "portion," in the fearful form that it has come to have (see 1413–15, 1455–58).

"Most hateful to the gods," Oedipus calls himself in what is nearly his final utterance onstage (1519). In the last scene Creon is sending to Delphi to ask a question of one of these gods, just as Oedipus did in the first scene. Sophocles does not tell us what answer Apollo will give. By concluding the play in this manner, Sophocles is not just showing us Creon's prudence or marking a circularity of structure; he is leaving us with a question. Oedipus has, in a sense, already received his answer in the events that followed his own inquiry, but it is an answer that only leads us to ask deeper questions about the gods and their role in human life.

Oedipus' tragic success in discovering himself as Laius' killer and thus as the source of the pollution may or may not end the plague of Thebes. The play has gradually shifted away from the suffering of the city, with which it began, to the suffering of Oedipus. He requests exile, but is still left in an uncertain, suspended state. The silence about the plague at the end of the play also indicates the new course Oedipus' life has taken. He is no longer merely a hero of external victories and rewards. Along with his change of focus comes his shift from weeping over the city's woes in the first scene to his weeping over the sufferings within his family at the play's end (66 and 1486). He has become a hero of inner vision and personal suffering. Indeed, it is precisely by showing Oedipus' life against its earlier success and power that Sophocles defines it as tragic and thus creates the form of the "tragic hero" in Western literature: a figure whose force of personality and integrity set him (or her) apart for a special destiny of pain and struggle and enable him to confront that destiny with clarity and courage after a difficult journey to self-knowledge.[16]

NOTES

1. See George Devereux, "The Self-Blinding of Oidipous in Sophokles: *Oidipous Tyrannos," Journal of Hellenic Studies* 93 (1973), 36–49.

2. In his famous Funeral Speech, probably delivered a few years before *Oedipus*, Pericles commended the common Athenian view, urging the women of Athens to be as inconspicuous among men as possible, whether for praise or blame (Thucydides 2.45.2).

3. Oedipus used the verb of the same root -*mig*-, "mingling," from this phrase "mingled woes for man and woman" here in 1281 (*andri kai gunaiki summigê kaka*) earlier in 791 and 995 when he described the incestuous union foretold in the oracle. *Oedipus* 1281 may also be a reminiscence of Aeschylus, *Seven against Thebes* 741. Aeschylus there describes the curse on the house that results in the blood pollution of the fratricidal deaths of Oedipus' sons (737–41): "Who could bring purifications? Who could wash them? O fresh sufferings of the house *mingled* with the woes of old" (*palaioisi summigeis kakois*). Here too Aeschylus describes the blackness of this blood (*melampages haima*, 736; cf. *melas . . . haimatos, Oedipus* 1279–80); and immediately afterward Sophocles' Messenger speaks of the "old happiness" of the house (*palaios olbos*, 1282). If Sophocles does have this passage in mind, he has transferred the imagery of pollution and the stain of blood in the fratricidal killing to the sexual pollution of Oedipus' incestuous marriage, and, as elsewhere, he has kept the motif of the family curse in the background, leaving only the bare hint in the reference to the "wealth of old" in 1282.

4. Aeschylus, *Danaids*, fragment 35 (44 Nauck) in H. Weir Smyth, ed., *Aeschylus II*, revised by Hugh Lloyd-Jones, Loeb Classical Library (Cambridge, MA: Harvard University Press, 1971), 395–96. For the sexual overtones of the Sophoclean passage see Richard Seaford, "The Tragic Wedding," *Journal of Hellenic Studies* 87 (1987), 120. For a more extravagant perversion of the sacred marriage, see Clytaemnestra's boast over the body of her murdered husband, Agamemnon, in Aeschylus, *Agamemnon* 1384–92.

5. See especially 924–26 and the comment of Knox, *Oedipus at Thebes*, 183–84.

6. Fagles' translation of 1334 ("What good were eyes to me?") is a beautiful touch, suggesting (intentionally?) Shakespeare's Gloucester in *King Lear* 4.1.18: "I have no way, and therefore want no eyes."

7. It is interesting to compare Herodotus' tale of the accidental killing of Croesus' son by Adrastus, which has a number of parallels with the *Oedipus*, especially the motif of trying to evade an oracle that is tragically fulfilled after all. Here the unfortunate Adrastus, who is not legally guilty of homicide, does in fact commit suicide (*Histories* 1.45).

8. On the play's refusal of these earlier heroic patterns, see Thomas Van Nortwick, *Oedipus: The Meaning of a Masculine Life* (Norman: University of Oklahoma Press, 1998), 25–27, 90–92.

9. In 1325, Oedipus addresses the chorus, "You do not escape my knowledge, but I know you clearly." R.C. Jebb, ed., , *Oedipus Tyrannus* (Cambridge: Cambridge University Press, 1893), commenting on this verse, suggests that there is "a distinct echo" of *Iliad* 24.563 here, the speech of Achilles about to ransom Hector's body, to King Priam: "I recognize you, Priam, in my heart, nor are you hidden from me." The Homeric resonance of this magnanimity between a Greek chief and his helpless suppliant gives Oedipus' lines here an atmosphere of epic grandeur and heroism. By having Oedipus speak Achilles' lines, however, Sophocles reverses the Homeric relation between the strong (Achilles) and the weak (Priam), and thus perhaps suggests the new inner strength emerging in Oedipus.

10. This is what Pope Gregory does in the medieval and Christian version of his Oedipus-like life: see above, Chapter 4.

11. See J. C. Kamerbeek, *The Plays of Sophocles*, Part 4, *The Oedipus Tyrannus* (Leiden: Brill, 1967) on 1411–12 (p. 256). For a more sceptical view of the scapegoat pattern see Oliver Taplin, "Sophocles in his Theatre," in *Entretiens sur l'antiquité classique*, vol. 29, *Sophocle* (Vandoeuvres-Geneva: Fondation Hardt, 1993), 170–71. The scapegoat pattern has fallen into disfavor with recent critics (and indeed seems to have become something of a litmus test for interpreters of the play). I am unrepentant in believing in its relevance, though I hasten to call attention to the qualification noted above, that the pattern is not actually completed at the end. For a balanced recent discussion, noting both the importance of the scapegoat pattern and its modification in the play, see Walter Burkert, *Oedipus, Oracles, and Meaning*, Samuel James Stubbs Lecture Series (Toronto: University College, 1991), 19–21.

12. For the arguments against the authenticity of the closing lines, see R. D. Dawe, ed., *Sophocles, Oedipus Rex* (Cambridge: Cambridge University Press, 1982), p. 247. In favor of the lines are Hugh Lloyd-Jones and Nigel Wilson, *Sophoclea: Studies on the Text of Sophocles* (Oxford: Oxford University Press, 1990), 113–14, who also retain the lines in their Oxford Classical Text; see also Brian Arkins, "The Final Lines of Sophocles, King Oedipus," *Classical Quarterly* 38 (1988), 555–58. I incline to regard the lines as spurious. If these final verses did replace a closing choral song, it was probably a short generalizing reflection on the sadness of the events.

13. A performance of the play at the Odéon Theater in Paris in the summer of 1985, for example, staged the last scene with a naked Oedipus, splashed with blood, standing before his daughters.

14. On these issues, see below, Chapter 11.

15. With this kind of divided solution, we may compare the ending of Sophocles' *Electra*, in which Orestes, who wants to draw out the pain of Aegisthus' punishment, enters the house of Atreus to kill him, whereas, Electra, now eager to get the whole thing over with, remains outside, standing before the uncovered body of her mother, Clytaemnestra, whom she has helped Orestes kill. The end of the *Trachinian Women* also offers close analogies.

16. See Bernard Knox, *The Heroic Temper* (Berkeley and Los Angeles: University of California Press, 1964), chapter 1, especially pp. 7ff.

10

Inner Vision and Theatrical Spectacle

SEEN AND UNSEEN

The theatrical spectacle of *Oedipus Tyrannus* works as much by what is not said and not shown as by the spoken and visible elements of the performance. Certain things are more powerful for being left unsaid and unseen. Such is the case with the events in the two long narratives, one by Oedipus and one by the Second Messenger. The first describes the death of the father, Laius, at the blow of the son's *skeptron*, the staff or scepter that Oedipus carries; the second describes the death of the mother, Jocasta, and the self-blinding of the son. Both scenes are left hidden, without visual enactment, so that they may be played out all the more effectively in the interior theater of our imaginations. In this way Sophocles gives us a glimpse of what psychoanalytic critics have called the "other scene," the imaginary place where the repressed fears and wishes of the unconscious are played out.[1]

These two narratives of crucial past events in *Oedipus Tyrannus* are complementary scenes of horrible violence involving the death of parents. In their presentation of a son's aggression against a father and the death of a mother, they resemble Freud's primal scenes: traumatic experiences that disturb emotional development because they stir up deep fears or anxieties about one's basic identity or view of the self—like a young child's witnessing of parental intercourse. Both scenes in the play are enacted in the nonvisual medium of a buried memory.

The second narrative, the tale of Jocasta's death, begins with the Messenger's qualification, "Of what was done the most painful things are absent, for vision was not present" (1238–39). The "absence" of the "painful things" is symmetrical with the nonpresence of the "vision." The most acute pain would result from actually seeing these acts; hence the difference between the representation of violence in Greek drama and the modern cinema. The Second Messenger will tell "the suffering of that unhappy woman," he goes on, in so far as his memory permits (1239). The collocation of presence and absence in his first line is appropriate to the indirect mode of narration used here (as opposed to the direct mode of dramatic enactment onstage) and to the necessarily partial recovery of lost events through memory.

Sophocles takes pains to show us how we *know* what we *see* in this crucial scene. The Messenger's "memory" leads us verbally into the interior chamber of Jocasta's marriage bed (1241–42). He tells how Jocasta "dashed closed the doors" behind her "when she went inside" (1244). The narrative relies on the medium of sound to reveal what occurred in the chamber. Those left *outside* heard a voice from *within*. But the account includes also something more than the voice, namely memory (the Greek word *mnêmê* here [1246] includes both "memory" and "mention"). This "remembering" by Jocasta is deeper and more painful than the Messenger's "memory" eight lines before (1239), and it takes us into the remoter past:

> When she went *inside* the doors, she dashed them closed *inside* and calls on Laius now *long since* a corpse, having *memory* [making mention] of the sowing [seeds] of *long ago*, by which he himself died, but left behind the mother of a child for ill-starred childmaking with his own (1244–48).[2]

The repetition "Laius *long since* a corpse" and the "sowing of *long ago*," combined with the emphasis on memory (1239, 1246), reinforces the movement back to the past. Jocasta brings to her mind (and ours) the night when Laius made her pregnant with Oedipus ("the sowing of long ago"). Her reported gesture of closing the doors behind her as she calls up this "memory" from her first marriage, prepares the way for the symbolic reenactment of her second, incestuous marriage in the ensuing narrative, with the son now replacing the father.[3] She, recalling her union with Laius, her last "memory" in life, closes the gates. Oedipus bursts into the palace and asks for a sword, searching for Jocasta (1252–57).

The following action of the narrative recalls the crimes of Oedipus' past as well. The weapon that he seeks now, however, is one of penetration (1255), different from the staff/scepter, the weapon he used to club Laius at the crossroads (811). He then forcibly "drives into the double gates," "pushes inward the hollow bolts," and "falls into the chamber" (1261–62). He thus forces his way into the mother's closed, "hollow" (1262), interior space, the private chamber that she had barred behind her as she remembered those "seeds" of Laius in the past (1246).

Here, in this place of terror, the events are envisioned through memory rather than in the immediacy of present event: "There was no vision," said the Messenger, "but yet, as far as lies in my *memory*, you will learn her sufferings" (1238–39). The emphasis on memory is striking when one considers how much memory has distorted the recollection of the past in the play. Jocasta, Oedipus, and the Herdsman have all been shown to have highly selective memories (1057, 1131; see also 870–71). Memory is here correlative with vision, a kind of nonvisual seeing. It is also an interiorized seeing, and we may recall here the metaphor, common in tragedy, of writing on the mind's tablets.

The Messenger's tale not only presents the visual contents of memory but is also an emblematic account of memory's inner vision, for it consists in gradual penetration into increasingly interior and hidden spaces (1239–96). This memory of the Messenger conducts us inside the gates of the palace, where Oedipus rushes around in wild despair. Then it shows us the interior space of Jocasta's marriage chamber, the scene of her suicide and Oedipus' self-blinding. These most important events are forbidden to open vision and are accessible only in fragments, by significant absence rather than through the full presence of the actors or the enacted events. By calling attention to the fact that he is withholding the visual appearance of his chief protagonists in favor of a purely verbal narration, the poet also reveals his own consciousness of the theatrical spectacle as a special form of narrative, mediating between external and interior vision, between visible, physical acts and the emotional world they reveal.

Oedipus' very act of forcible entry creates another blockage of vision and thus deprives the Messenger of certain, visual knowledge of the details. "How after this she perished," the Messenger goes on, "I know no further, for Oedipus, shouting, broke his way in, and by his act it was no longer possible to behold, as in a spectacle, her woe. But rather we turned our gaze toward him as he roamed around" (1251–54). Vision again becomes blurred in the vagueness of the Messenger's report that some unnamed divinity (*daimôn*) "showed" Oedipus the way (1258), "not any one of us men who were present nearby" (1259). The "men" are concrete forms, "nearby," visible, and familiar; the unknown daimon (the vaguest possible term for a god or supernatural agent) is invisible, mysterious, undefined.

Sophocles makes our vision of the narrated events deliberately elusive. Vision was blocked first by the closing of doors (1241–44), then by the violent acts and shouts of Oedipus in the palace (1252–53), and finally by his presence over the body of Jocasta (1264–69). After Oedipus has broken down the doors, we onlookers are allowed to "see into" the firmly shut chamber (1263). The further penetration of the eye inward, into increasingly interior and hidden space, culminates in Oedipus' "seeing" of Jocasta (1265), the goal and result of his forced entry into the locked, forbidden place. From that point, vision is again permitted, although still through the indirect mode of third-person narration. It is now a vision characterized by that quality of the "terrible" that broods over the play from the beginning and reaches its climax in the spectacle of "things terrible to look upon" (1267; see also 1297, 1306, 1312).

This last object of sight, "the things terrible to look upon," is the physical act of putting an end to vision: Oedipus' tearing the pins from Jocasta's robes and striking his eyes. It is reported not as the result of an active verb of seeing, as in the lines immediately preceding—"we saw within," "he sees her" (1263 and 1265)—but in an impersonal way: "From that point there were things terrible to see." It is as if this seeing is already formed into a tableau, a final memorable sight, fixed self-consciously as the result of a narrative of unforgettable power but not in fact shown on the stage. When the pervasive "terror" is fulfilled, "no spectacle is present" (1238). Such are "the terrible things" that the un-staged spectacle has finally to "show."

The horror of the sight is now matched by the horror of the sound. This too comes to us indirectly, by report. Jocasta's "call" to the dead Laius (1245) and her "lament" over her marriage bed (1249) fade into the silence of her still-mysterious death ("how after this she perished I do not know" [1251]). The sounds we now hear come from Oedipus: he "shouts" (1252) as he breaks his way into the palace, "cries terrible things" as he forces his way into Jocasta's chamber (1260), "roars terribly" at what he sees there (1265), and "shouts" again as he strikes his eyes (1271). The crescendo of horror reached in this last cry re-capitulates the horror in the scene as a whole, for it repeats the "terrible shout-ing" as he forced the doors open ten lines before [1260].

Oedipus' last shout is itself closely linked to vision, for he cries out that "his eyes will never see the things that he has suffered or the things that he has done" (1271–72). Fewer than twenty lines later, the Messenger describes how Oedipus, still offstage," shouts out to open the enclosing gates" (1287–88). This shouting no longer concerns the doors of private, interior chambers but the public gates of the palace that will "reveal to all the Thebans" the fearful spectacle that their king has become.

This anticipation of Oedipus' entrance heightens the tension between what is described verbally through narration and what is shown visually as theatri-cal spectacle. The doors of the palace open, and the Messenger describes this scenic action: "These enclosures of the gates are opening" (1294–95). But he is also echoing, now in his own words, the words of Oedipus that he had just quoted, "Open the enclosures and reveal to all the Thebans . . ." (1287–88).[4] "Soon you will see a spectacle," the Messenger continues to the chorus, "such that even the one who loathes it will feel pity" (1295–96). It is as if the play-wright/director were telling his audience how he is utilizing the visual effects of his medium. The chorus, like the audience that now beholds the palace doors opening, gives voice to the proper theatrical response, again in visual terms: "O suffering terrible for men to *look upon*" (1297). The obverse of the present spectacle—the blinded king with his bloodied eyes—is the unseen spectacle of the closed interior chamber where Jocasta died: "It was not possible to behold as in a spectacle her [Jocasta's] suffering" (1258).

The relation between text and action stresses both the parallelism and the contrast between verbally describing the unseen events behind the palace and bedchamber doors and theatrically displaying the spectacle of Oedipus onstage. He now emerges through the palace doors as the center of all attention and the object of pitiable *sight* to all. "O suffering fearful for men to *see*" is the immedi-ate response of the chorus (1297). The terms for vision, spectacle, and the open-ing of gates shift between the narrator and the events he describes, the hideous violence that takes place behind closed doors.[5] Sophocles thus calls attention to the double mode of narration going on before us, the visual enactment and the verbal telling. The Messenger's tale, in the purely verbal medium in which "there is no vision present" (1238), parallels the spectacle on the stage and before our eyes: it too is a way of "opening doors" to the hidden events that arouse our terror and our pity.

DRAMA AND THE INTERIOR VISION

This withholding of vision and partial access to vision in a story that culminates in the destruction of eyes are among the means by which Sophocles stamps the narration with its characteristic feature, a reluctance to emerge into the light, a tale of horror that wants to remain hidden in the darkness of the unseen. Teiresias' blind seeing, reluctant speech, and uncomprehended utterances in the meeting with Oedipus early in the play formed the first explicit model onstage for a story that refused to be told and a knowledge that refused to be known. Now, at the most intense point of the action, the suppression of vision and speech moves to the center of the narrative. Not only does the refusal to see and to say everywhere pervade this telling, but it is through this powerful "won't tell" that the story in fact gets itself told.

This climactic scene is recovered (as we have noted) only by a series of gradual movements backwards into the past and by a steady progression of looking into a closed interior in the present. The discontinuous rhythm of exposure and concealment, vision and nonvision, closing off perception and removing blocking objects, is a symbolical condensation of Oedipus' past. The narrative that unfolds before us contains the climax of a tragic life and is simultaneously a microcosm of that pattern of events that gives such a life its tragic form. It is also a microcosm of the play's dramatic form.

When Oedipus has broken down the doors and does at last "see" Jocasta's body in her chamber, the first thing he does after "releasing" her from the noose is to "pull off the gold-beaten pins [*peronai*] from her garments, [the pins] with which she was dressed" (1268–69). This is the first of "the things terrible to see" (1267) to be described. *Peronai* are not merely decorative brooches, as the word is frequently translated, but the long pins that hold together the loose folds of a woman's dress in ancient Greece. Their removal suggests the act of undressing the queen in her "marriage chamber" (1242) as she "lies there" (1267). This gesture, then, is a grotesque and horrible reenactment of the first night of their union. This is the act for which he "strikes the sockets of his eyes" in the next line, immediately cancelling out in himself the vision that his violation of her chamber has opened up to the audience. If the body of the king becomes that through which the invisible truth is made reality, the body of Jocasta points to something that remains inaccessible to vision and must remain hidden.

In an essay that has only recently become available to the English-speaking world, Vladimir Propp has analyzed numerous folktales of the Oedipus type. Generally, he finds, the identity of the incestuous husband/son is discovered in the marriage bed by a scar or other mark, sometimes on the wedding night itself.[6] (Jean Cocteau brilliantly plays with this age-old motif of discovery on the wedding night in his *Infernal Machine* [see Chapter 12]). Sophocles, however, withholds that recognition until it can bring only the tragic revelation of indelible pollution. But he retains the sexual component of the knowledge by implying the physical union in a series of symbolic equivalents: the forced penetration of the queen's closed chambers, the removal of the pins from the robes on her recumbent body, and the metaphors of "mingling" and the "rain" of blood (1276–81).[7]

There is a suggestive parallel to this scene in another Sophoclean play, *Trachinian Women*. Deianeira, having discovered that what she thought was a love-charm is in fact a poison that is killing Heracles, goes to her bedchamber inside the house. After addressing her marriage bed for the last time, she stabs herself:

> She says nothing more, but with a violent sweep
> of her arm unfastens her gown where a pin
> of beaten gold lies above her breast. She had
> uncovered the whole side of her left arm. (923–26)[8]

Deianeira's unusually masculine form of death (women in Greek tragedy, like Jocasta or Phaedra, generally commit suicide by hanging) continues the instability of male and female roles that runs throughout the play; but it also marks a symbolic *Liebestod* (death-in-love) that takes the place of the union of husband and wife in the house. Both scenes make use of the sexual symbolism involved in loosening a woman's robe in her interior chambers, in close proximity to the conjugal bed. Horrible as the implications of such a scene are for Jocasta in *Oedipus Tyrannus*, they are none the less strongly present. We are accustomed to speak of Sophocles in the same breath as the Parthenon; but he does not always show us things that are nice: we may recall Philoctetes' pus-soaked rags in *Philoctetes* or Ajax's corpse still blowing dark blood from the nostrils in *Ajax*.

There is, in fact, a further ugliness in this scene, for Jocasta, in her last moments, as she recollects the union that produced Oedipus, calls to "Laius long since a corpse" (1245). The husband of her distant past, whose "ancient seed" she received to bear his child, appears in her memory as a dead body. The physical detail of that night with Laius parallels the ugliness of the present scene with Oedipus, in which the removal of the pins from Jocasta's robes also evokes the undressing of the "bride"; that act, as we have noted, is the prelude not to a fertilizing "rain" in a sacred marriage but to a "rain" or "storm" of blood in a self-punishment that has overtones of castration.[9]

The symbolic reenactment of the incest in Oedipus and Jocasta's final union-in-death is part of the temporal enlargement and complication of the action that Sophocles exercises on the myth through the device of superimposing present acts on the remote past. Actions in the present both recall and reenact actions in the past, and the past seems always to be pulling the protagonists back, no matter how hard they try to escape it. This pull of the past contributes to the play's atmosphere of tragic necessity: something surrounding the lives of the chief characters that they cannot escape.

By deepening the temporal perspective through the motif of discovering and remembering a long-forgotten past, Sophocles also calls attention to the representational power of drama, by which a single action unfolding before us on-stage can contain, symbolically, the meaning of an entire lifetime. In the condensed temporal frame of Oedipus' life the tragedian finds also a mirror image of his manipulation of time in the artistic construction of his play.

Greek tragedy has no word for "the self." As John Jones, arguing from Aristotle's *Poetics*, maintains, tragedy concentrates on exterior forms and events, on plot (*mythos*) as a concatenation of actions (*pragmata*).[10] Yet the sense of a self, of a complex inner life of motives, desires, and fears, is everywhere implicit. How does the tragedian make the inner life of the self visible? Where does it appear? Obviously in the interaction between characters, but elsewhere as well: not onstage, but in the action that occurs in the imagined space behind the stage implied by the invisible text; something *there* but not representable, or representable only as a tension between the seen and the unseen. This interplay between interior and exterior space parallels the increasing awareness of the interior realm of the individual personality, and we see it also in Euripides' psychological exploration of motives in works like *Medea* and *Hippolytus*, and in Socrates' emphasis on knowledge and the soul. Greek drama has no general theory about what personality is, but, rather, it poses the self as problem. As so often, the Greeks raise fundamental questions with exceptional clarity, in this case the questions involved in representing "reality" in art.

In the conventions of Greek drama, the interior space of house or palace is not represented on the stage but is often implicit behind the action. The poet composes for a stage that shows only the outside, but that exterior face of the represented world has a depth of meaning derived in part from its hidden interior. That hidden, inner scene corresponds both to the emotional life of the characters and, at some level, to the personal, imaginative vision of the poet, whose act of composition takes place before and apart from the public performance in the theater, where his words are given full realization.

Manipulating real bodies in real space on the stage, the dramatist is intensely concerned with the effect of live performance on an audience who sees these events acted out before them; but he is also a poet/writer who fashions myths into stories about passions with the freedom of his plastic medium of words. Sophocles worked with the visible, public space of the open-air theater of Dionysus to reveal truths about hidden or invisible areas of existence that his poetry could call up in the imagination. Although the publicly enacted dimension of this art form was the most important to its original audience, who responded to it primarily as theater, and indeed political theater, its more private, psychological dimension remains rich with insights for the modern reader, who is more likely to approach these works as written texts.[11]

Oedipus is above all a great drama, but it also contains hints of the poet's awareness of the problem of representing reality, and especially the inner reality of the emotional life. This concern is particularly present in Sophocles' attention to what is shown and what is seen in the climactic scene of Oedipus' discovery of the buried truth, followed by his public display of himself from the hitherto hidden interior of the palace. Revealing to an audience what is concealed behind doors and gates—the gates of the palace, of the mouth, or of the body—is not only a matter of practical dramaturgy. It is also the poet's reflection on the way that his art probes the dark side of life and the hidden depths of the soul, and on the way that our fascination with the spectacle makes us, like Oedipus, see what we would rather not see and know what we would prefer not to know.

NOTES

1. For Lacan's "other scene" ("anderer Schauplatz"), see J. Lacan, *Ecrits, A Selection*, trans. A. Sheridan (New York: Hill and Wang, 1977), 193, 264, 284–85.

2. This translation attempts to bring out the force of the repetition *tiktousan . . . dusteknon* in 1247–48; the repeated root *tek-* ("give birth to") hammers in the horror of the doubled "mothering." Note the triple repetition of the root *tek-* in 1250.

3. On the symbolic reenactment of the union, though with a very different interpretation, see John Hay, *Lame Knowledge and the Homosporic Womb* (Washington, D.C.: University of America Press, 1978), 103ff. and 133–34.

4. Cf. the Messenger's description, earlier in 1262, of Oedipus' bursting through the "enclosures" (i.e., the doors) to Jocasta's chamber. The repetition of the same word in all three of these passages (*klêithra*) emphasizes this opening up of an enclosed, invisible space to theatrical vision.

5. E.g., 1238, 1253, 1261, 1265, 1271, 1287, 1294.

6. Propp, "Oedipus in the Light of Folklore," in L. Edmunds and A. Dundes, eds., *Oedipus: A Folklore Casebook* (New York: Garland, 1983), 76–121, especially 113–14.

7. On the metaphor of "mingling" and the tragic pattern of the "tragic wedding" here, see above, Chapter 9, with notes 3 and 4.

8. Translation by Michael Jameson in David Grene and Richmond Lattimore, eds., *Complete Greek Tragedies*, vol. 2, *Sophocles* (Chicago: University of Chicago Press, 1959).

9. For the inversions of marriage in this scene see above, note 7.

10. Aristotle, *Poetics* 6. 1450a 2ff. See John Jones, *On Aristotle and Greek Tragedy* (London: Chatto and Windus, 1962), especially 24ff., 35ff., 41ff.

11. This self-consciousness about drama's special mode of revealing the self through the narration of what is hidden in interior space may owe something to the transitional moment of tragedy between an oral and a literate culture. For further discussion see my *Interpreting Greek Tragedy: Myth, Poetry, Text* (Ithaca, N.Y.: Cornell University Press, 1986), 75--109; see also P. E. Easterling, ed., *The Cambridge Companion to Greek Tragedy* (Cambridge: Cambridge University Press, 1997), 51–52.

11

"To Look upon the Light for the Last Time": The Place of *Oedipus Tyrannus* in Sophocles' Work

Among Sophoclean protagonists, Oedipus has a special place. If the generally accepted chronology of Sophocles' early and middle plays is correct—that is, *Ajax* (460–450 B.C.E.), *Antigone* (442–441), *Trachiniae* (440–430), and *Oedipus Tyrannus* (429–425)—the *Tyrannus* is the first extant play at whose end the protagonist is not dead or about to die. Correspondingly, it is the first nondiptych play in the extant corpus, that is, the first play that is not bisected by the protagonist's death about two-thirds of the way through, and so it is the first of the extant plays in which the central protagonist holds and dominates his stage from the first scene to the last. With the exception of the first ode (the parodos) on the ravages of the plague, Oedipus is also the subject of every ode in the play.[1] These facts have to be taken with a grain of salt given the small percentage of the surviving plays, but they do tell us something.

Of the three extant plays written after *Oedipus Tyrannus*, only *Oedipus at Colonus* has a protagonist who appears in the prologue and carries through to the end. The *Electra* (419–410 B.C.E.) comes closest, but Electra, like Philoctetes in the other late play (*Philoctetes* of 409 B.C.E.), is the victim of a plot and is cast into the role of one who has to react to and suffer from the deception practiced on her by other mortals. In the *Tyrannus*, however, the "plotting" against the hero (so to speak) comes directly from the gods rather than from mortals. In fact, a plot allegedly by a mortal (Creon) turns out to be a plot from the gods, mysterious though this is.

In the role of the gods in the plot, *Oedipus Tyrannus* resembles the two plays that were probably written in the previous decade, *Antigone* and *Trachiniae*. In *Antigone* the vindication of Antigone against Creon comes from the omens and oracles announced by Teiresias, and these force Creon to reverse his decision to leave Polyneices unburied and to punish Antigone with death. But the news comes too late, and disaster envelops his house. In *Trachiniae* the life of the wandering hero, Heracles, is surrounded by several oracles, given at different periods of his life. These finally come together in a moment of illumination in which Heracles recognizes the divine pattern in his existence and also sees that his death is imminent.[2] Like Oedipus, he remains a heroic figure to the end, but the

131

quality of his heroism is very different. Whereas Oedipus moves from confidence and a certain self-centeredness to tender concern for his daughters, Heracles callously dismisses the suicide of his wife, Deianeira, insists harshly on his patriarchal authority, and forces his son, Hyllus, to marry Iole, the young woman whom he has brought back with him as his concubine and whom Hyllus regards as a source of the ruin of their house.

In *Antigone* Creon's responses to his disasters are just the opposite of Oedipus'. Whereas Oedipus finds the strength to endure, Creon is totally shattered. Some formal details of their language are instructive. Both Creon (in *Antigone*) and Oedipus break into lyric meters for the first time when their worlds collapse and their previous power changes to weakness and misery. For Oedipus this takes places in his long lyrical dialogue with the chorus after he emerges, blinded, from the palace (*Oedipus*, 1307–68). Creon, however, continues almost to the end in lyric meters, primarily excited dochmiac rhythms, that express his confusion and collapse (*Antigone*, 1261–1346). Oedipus, on the other hand, moves from his intense lyrical exchange at the nadir of his power to a renewed sense of authority at the end, as he defends his self-blinding in his long iambic speech just before Creon's entrance (*Oedipus*, 1369–1415). From here to the end of the play, Oedipus speaks in iambic trimeters, with the exception of his closing exchange with Creon in trochaic tetrameters. Both Creon and Oedipus at the end of their respective plays ask to be led away to suffer their doom: "Lead me off as quickly as possible, lead me out of the way, me who am nothing more than nothing" (*Antigone*, 1324–25; also 1339–40); "Lead me off from here then" (*Oedipus*, 1518). Yet there is a world of difference between them. Oedipus, despite his terrible suffering, has a still defiant strength, for which Creon in fact reproaches him in this scene (1518–23):

OEDIPUS: You will then send me forth from the house.

CREON: You ask what is a gift of the god.

OEDIPUS: But to the gods I am most hated.

CREON: Then will you soon win (this gift).

OEDIPUS: Lead me off from here then.

CREON: Go then, but let go of your children.

OEDIPUS: Do not in any way take them from me.

CREON: Do not seek to have mastery in everything, For those things in which you had mastery did not follow along with you in your life.

In *Antigone*, on the other hand, Creon is a broken man who wants only to die (*Antig.*, 1321–25, 1339–46).[3]

A scene in the *Tyrannus* does closely correspond to this closing scene of the *Antigone*, namely Oedipus' moments of disorientation and despair just after the self-blinding:

Aiee, aiee, miserable that I am. Where on the earth am I carried in my misery? Where does my voice fly about aloft? Alas, divine power (*daimôn*), where you leapt . . . Lead me away from the place as quickly as possible, lead me away, my friend, me, fully destroyed, most deeply accursed, and to the gods most hated of mortals. (1307–11, 1341–45)

We may compare Creon's disorientation and his metaphor of a supernatural power that has "leapt" upon him in *Antigone* 1341–46:

Please lead me out of the way, useless man that I am, I who killed you, my child, not intentionally, and killed you here too [my wife, Eurydice], miserable that I am. I do not know which of you to look upon, which way to lean; for everything in my hands is askew, and on the other side an unendurable destiny has leapt down upon my head.

But Oedipus' play does not end with these lyrics; he gradually gains a new strength and a new understanding.

When Oedipus finally leaves the stage at the very end, he harks back to that lyrical passage of 1340–46, repeating the command, "Lead me away." He states his conviction that he is "to the gods most hated" (1519–21), repeating the phrase from his lyrical cry in that earlier passage ("fully destroyed, most deeply accursed, and to the gods most hated of mortals," 1341–45).[4] But the verbal echo only shows us how far Oedipus has moved from that first response to his suffering. Sophocles has taken him not only beyond his own zero-point of misery but also beyond the crushed Theban ruler of the *Antigone*. The text invites this double comparison, as if Sophocles is deliberately showing off his new kind of tragic hero against his earlier models, one in the earlier play and one in Oedipus himself previously in this play.

THE MEANING OF OEDIPUS' SURVIVAL

By the end of the *Tyrannus* the meaning or nonmeaning of Oedipus' life in the perspective of the gods' design becomes the principal question and takes the form of a twofold "why?" Why did Oedipus survive the intent of his parents to kill him? And why, when he saw the awful truth of his life, did he not kill himself? The first question—why did he survive infanticide to live out this terrible life?—is the ultimate metaphysical question of the play (1349–55, 1391–92), and Sophocles answers it only fleetingly and indirectly. The second question, why he blinds himself, gets more explicit attention (1369–90).

As we have observed, Sophocles proposes an ending that will not take place, tantalizing us with the possibility that Oedipus will kill himself. At the moment of discovery, Oedipus addresses the light that he will see for the last time, and these words, like the end of Ajax's suicide speech (*Ajax* 856–65), are easily understood as the cry of a man about to die: "O light, for the last time may I look upon you, I who have been revealed as born from those from whom I should not have been born, living with those I should not have lived with, killing those I should not have killed" (*Oedipus*, 1183–85). The choral song immediately afterwards, the third stasimon (1186–1222), feeds this expectation of death, for it sings of the nothingness of mortal generations and in its last lines pronounces what looks like Oedipus' epitaph (1220–22). His frantic request for a sword reported by the Messenger in the next scene (1255) points in the same direction. In *Antigone* too Haemon's possession of a sword is the prelude to suicide (1232–39). Given the variations in the tradition about Oedipus' end—death in battle in the *Iliad*, continuing rule at Thebes in the *Odyssey*—it may even have come as a surprise to the audience to hear from the Messenger that Oedipus is still alive and then to see him emerge with his bloodied eyes (however staged) from the interior of the palace.[5] Only at his entrance do we now understand that his cry to "look upon the light for the last time" as he rushes into the palace in fact heralds "a fate, without the light, that is far worse than death."[6]

Since nearly everything in the *Tyrannus* is also metatheatrical—that is, pervaded by a self-consciousness of the play as theatrical spectacle—these scenes are also an implicit direction to the audience not just to recoil from the ugly spectacle in horror, as the chorus initially wants to do, but to bear with Oedipus, and with the play, to overcome initial repugnance, and to attend to the hero's (and the poet's) reasons for ending not with suicide but with self-blinding. Oedipus' long speech of self-justification is also the poet's implicit defense of his choice of this particular structure of events.

Oedipus' deliberate choice of self-blinding is simultaneously a reply to the Aeschylean *Oedipus*, at least in so far as we can reconstruct it from the one surviving play of his Oedipus trilogy, the *Seven against Thebes* (see above, Chapter 4). In Aeschylus, we recall, Oedipus blinded himself—probably for the first time in the literary tradition—but in the context of the family curse.[7] When Sophocles' hero puts out his eyes, it is an act of deliberate personal choice, not the result of the *atê*, or infatuate madness, sent by the vengeful *daimon* (divinity) of his accursed house, and he gives a detailed defense of his motives (*Oedipus Tyrannus*, 1369–90). Sophocles' chorus acknowledges Oedipus' own "enduring" spirit: "How did you endure so to extinguish your eyes?" (1327–28). When the chorus then goes on to take up the Aeschylean suggestion of a *daimôn*, a divine power, that might have "impelled" him to the blinding (1328), Oedipus makes the first of his declarations of individual choice, distinguishing between the Apollo who brought his sufferings upon him and his own hand that struck out his eyes (1329–35).

Oedipus refrains from suicide not just because he has the strength to endure but also because his future life remains open to the conflict and the question of who or what controls human existence, individual will or some force from outside, whether this is the gods, fate, or chance. This is the issue between him and Creon in the closing lines. For Oedipus it is as important to take control of the manner of his end as it was for him to distinguish between Apollo's agency and his self-chosen means of punishment by his own hand (*autocheir*, 1329–35). When he speaks of these "sufferings of mine, mine" here in 1330, he also harks back to the "sufferings that are willed and not unwilled" and the "self-chosen sufferings" of which the Messenger spoke at the beginning of his long account of the catastrophe (1229–31). The Messenger's speech thus inaugurates the closing phase of Oedipus' tragedy by immediately focusing on the distinction between sufferings that come from outside and those that are chosen by the hero himself.

Oedipus' refusal of suicide is an essential part of this never-to-be-resolved tension between individual choice and the god-determined shape of his life. As he looks back to the beginning of his life, he sees his very existence as a kind of negative space, a contravention of his death as an infant that was willed by the gods and then accepted by his parents who exposed him to avoid the fulfillment of Apollo's oracle. At the end he repeatedly confronts the death that should have ended his life almost before it began (1349–55, 1391–93, 1452–54), and so he becomes aware of the full shape of his *moira*, his portion of life. This awareness, as he says in the last lines of this first long iambic speech, includes recognizing that he alone "has the strength to endure these sufferings" (1414–15). Such endurance in suffering is the mark of the heroic personality. Heracles at the end of *Trachinian Women* and Electra in her play, the *Electra*, show the same spirit, in their own respective ways, and so does the most enduring of all Sophocles' heroes, Philoctetes, who calls himself "courageous," *eukardios*, as he describes his life of suffering in language very similar to that of Oedipus in 1414–15 (*Philoctetes* 535–38): "I do not think that anyone except me could even take the sight of such things in his eyes and endure them; but through necessity I have learned to accept my woes."

The closing dialogue with Creon continues the pull between Oedipus' control of his destiny and the acknowledgment of some divine force from the outside. This conflict now takes the form of Oedipus' determination to go into exile and Creon's intention once more to consult Apollo at Delphi—as if the whole cycle could start all over again. Now, however, the earlier roles of Creon and Oedipus are reversed. Addressing Creon, Oedipus says, "I shall entreat you," using the word of supplication that he had used to describe the entreaties of his subjects in the first scene (1446 and 41).[8]

THE ENDINGS OF THE TWO OEDIPUS PLAYS

If *Oedipus Tyrannus* constantly looks back to the beginnings of the hero's life to suggest the irrationality of the suffering that surrounds it, *Oedipus at Colonus* emphasizes the resolution contained in the ending of that life. This resolution is no less dominated by the divine and so no less mysterious, but it is in a wholly different key. In the *Tyrannus* the hero's understanding of the meaning of his life comes only at the end, in the flickering uncertainties of his struggles with his pain, his blindness, and the successive waves of contradictory emotions. In *Oedipus at Colonus* that understanding is already implicit at the beginning in the hero's knowledge of his final resting place (44–46, 72–74, 287–90) and in his understanding of the oracles that come to him soon after (391–420, 450–60).[9] In the retrospective mood of the later play, Oedipus can also reflect calmly on his turbulence of mind at the moment of the terrible discovery long ago. When his emotions were seething with passion on that day, he says, death by stoning was his sweetest wish (*Oedipus at Colonus*, 433–36). In *Oedipus Tyrannus*, however, it was his own enduring spirit that kept him alive, not constraint from Thebes' rulers. In the *Tyrannus*, Oedipus' spirit remains supremely and grandly human; in the *Oedipus Coloneus* his supernatural understanding is spectacularly confirmed by the divine epiphany at the end, with the full panoply of numinous events: the voice from the heavens, the thunder from Zeus Chthonios (Zeus of the lower world), the new power of vision in the blind man, and the terrible and unbearable light from which Theseus must shield his eyes (1604–55).

Beneath these major differences in the endings of the *Tyrannus* and the *Coloneus*, however, lie certain common features. In both plays the hero's fate in the foreground is set against the unresolved circumstances of a city in the background. These circumstances here, as in other Sophoclean plays, force us to view the hero's life in the context of a larger community whose trials and tribulations continue even though he himself has accomplished the trajectory marked out for him by his mysterious, god-riven life pattern. The end of the *Tyrannus* notoriously says nothing about the plague. Although many readers assume that it ends with the discovery of Oedipus as the source of the pollution, as does Seneca's version, the play itself is silent on this point.

Oedipus at Colonus also leaves important issues open at its end. Athens will presumably have gained the protection of Oedipus' heroized body, but his curse on Polyneices seals the doom of the Theban royal house. Hence the plea of Oedipus' daughters to return to their city sets the stage, retrospectively, for the beginning of the *Antigone*. Here too, as at the end of the *Tyrannus*, the conclusion of the present suffering may only inaugurate a fresh cycle of tragic woe. Even Athens is not entirely exempt from the divisiveness that may destroy a city, for, as Laura Slatkin has suggested, Athens faces the test of piety that Thebes has failed (see especially 258–91). It does grant asylum to the accursed outsider, but only after considerable hesitation.[10] Colonus, as Lowell Edmunds has recently reminded us, is the site of the most serious division that the citizens of Athens have faced in recent years: it was the meeting place of the conservative faction to overthrow the democracy in 411.[11] As a plea for reconciliation after these political conflicts, the play is also a reminder of the murderous discord that might have afflicted Athens, as it will Thebes.

The religious atmosphere of Oedipus' death in the *Oedipus Coloneus* strengthens this unifying spirit. As Richard Seaford has argued, the heroization of Oedipus at the end of the *Coloneus*, like the implicit heroization of Ajax at the end of the earlier play, reenacts on the stage those unifying emotions that the citizens of Athens experienced in the cult of heroes.[12] The citizens are joined together in a communal grief for the great figures of the past and in the sufferings that attended their deaths. Yet the endings of both of these plays also dramatize the problematical qualities of these heroes and surround the closing funerary rituals with ambiguities and contradictions. *Oedipus at Colonus* ends not with the triumph of heroization in Athens, strong as that is, but with the pull back toward the deaths and suffering in Thebes, sufferings that Oedipus' curses have now assured.

Oedipus at Colonus is Sophocles' most Aeschylean play.[13] Its heroization of a polluted sufferer may be compared to the *Oresteia's* acquittal of the matricide, Orestes, and the implicit purification of a polluted past through the replacement of family vengeance by a court of law and the establishment of civic cult. Yet whereas the *Eumenides* closes with a more or less satisfying civic ritual as the Athenians escort the now transformed Furies to their shrine beneath the Areopagus, the *Oedipus Coloneus* has a foreboding coda pointing to the fratricidal killings in Thebes, the result of the terrible curses that we have seen Oedipus pronounce on the stage. These curses will also envelop his beloved Antigone in the future sacrifice of her life.[14]

While the silence about the plague in *Oedipus Tyrannus* contributes to a suspension of closure, the contrast between Thebes and Athens in *Oedipus at Colonus* seems to offer a clearer resolution. Whereas the Thebes to which Antigone is determined to return will be torn apart by the fratricidal strife that Oedipus' curse on Polyneices confirms, Theseus' steadfastness in Oedipus' final instructions will keep Athens "a land forever without the pain of sufferings" (1764–65).

OEDIPUS' DAUGHTERS: CONTINUITY AND RESOLUTION

Both Oedipus plays give a prominent place to Oedipus' daughters. In both cases Sophocles had a great deal of latitude since neither scene is an indispensable or inevitable way of closing the respective play. The presence of the daughters at the end of the *Tyrannus* is particularly surprising, as they are barely mentioned in the course of the play (though, as we shall soon see, when they are alluded to, it is significant). Their presence, among other functions, bears heavily on Sophocles' conception of Oedipus in the *Tyrannus*, for it confirms our earlier impression that he is a person to whom the emotional bonds within the family are important. We have witnessed his concern with the question of which parent ordered his exposure at birth (1037, 1173–75). Later he offers as one of his reasons for blinding himself his repugnance at seeing his mother and father again in Hades (1371–74). Near the end, even in the midst of his own pain and uncertain future, he solemnly adjures Creon to see that Jocasta has proper burial (1446–48).

The way that Oedipus does refer to his daughters (albeit indirectly) earlier in the play is illuminating for the scene at the end. When he first reveals his oracle to Jocasta, he shrinks in horror from the monstrosity of incestuously born children. According to the oracle, he says, "I would show forth to humankind a race unendurable to look upon" (791–92).[15] This is the only time that Oedipus includes the incestuous birth of his children in his report of the oracle, perhaps because it is too ugly to contemplate.[16] Later, after his discovery of the truth, he includes the sight of the children, "born as they were born," among his reasons for blinding himself (1375–77). At the end of the play, however, Oedipus accepts these children as persons, not as an unspeakable abomination to humankind, and he is intensely eager for their presence.[17] He relates to them in terms of his own feelings, not as a vague, generalized "humankind," and as individuals, not as an accursed "race."

The horror attending this incestuous brood becomes even stronger when we recall that his address to them in 1480, "O children," echoes his first words in the play. Now he is no longer the powerful ruler speaking to his subjects as figurative "children" but a blind father, whose next words are "Where are you?" In the opening scene the "children" of Thebes are afflicted by the plague, one of whose effects, as the chorus sings in its first ode, is the exposure of deformed and dying children on the ground (179–81). The abandonment of a child to die dominates Oedipus' own life story. After his discovery of the truth about his childhood he utters the wish that he had not been saved from that death (1349–55). But in his closing scene he reverses this pattern; by his plea to Creon he will vicariously extend his care for his children into their future.

If we stand back from the intense emotions of this scene, we can also view the ending in terms of Athenian social practices, particularly the construction of masculinity. The two princes of Thebes' ruling house establish a kind of male bonding by what is effectively the exchange of women. Oedipus, at one level, acknowledges his defeat and helplessness by handing his daughters over to their uncle for protection and sustenance. Yet in terms of the dynamics of the Greek family he is also fulfilling an approved and expected patriarchal role by engaging in an exchange of the dependent women of his household with the male head of another household. Yet these girls, as the heiresses of their house of origin, will bring to their new house only their inheritance of curses and self-destruction from Laius and Oedipus, and so they prove Oedipus ultimately right in his prognosis of their unmarriageability. In the *Antigone*, the bridegroom, Haemon, will undo the patrilocal marital system by going to his bride's "house of Hades" for a tragic wedding (*Antigone*, 1234–41). Creon's house will then emerge as a doublet of the house of Oedipus, with the suicide of his wife, the death of his two surviving sons, and the father and king's own collapse into debility and disorientation. That, however, lies in the putative future, even though Sophocles had already written it in the *Antigone* a decade or so before. With the *Tyrannus* itself, however, both Oedipus and Creon through this exchange of women recover a traditional basis for relating to one another in their new, irregular situation, totally outside the norms and expectations of normal family life. Despite the radical asymmetry of their respective positions, this traditional mode of patriarchal interaction in the matter of the house confers a certain equality and dignity on both.

When the ninety-year-old Sophocles returned to the figure of Oedipus in his last play, he retained and developed his hero's relationship with his daughters. In the last moments of his life, as described by the Messenger, Oedipus pays tribute to the close ties of family love (*philia*). Addressing his daughters, he says that this love is the only solace of his long suffering (*Oedipus Coloneus*, 1614–19): "No longer will you have the toilsome task of care for me—hard, I know, but one word brings release from all these toils. For from no one more than from myself did you have love (*philein*), and now you will spend the rest of your lives deprived of this." As in the *Tyrannus* (1503–10), his last request of the city's ruler, in this case Theseus, is that he look after the helpless, now orphaned girls (*Oedipus Coloneus*, 1633–35): "My dear friend, give the ancient pledge of your hand to my children, and you, children, to him; and promise never to betray them of your own accord but with kindly concern always to try to do whatever is to their benefit."

Each play handles Oedipus' loving physical contact with his daughters in the appropriate way (*Tyrannus*, 1466–85, *Coloneus*, 1611–19). In the *Tyrannus* Oedipus, the responsible ruler and father of his house, would continue his paternal role by providing for the still young and needy girls as, in the opening scene, he would provide as a father for his Theban subjects ("my children," 1 and 1480). In the *Coloneus*, old and feeble, he has been the recipient of his daughters' aid in the harsh task of providing his "care" or nurture, *trophê*, from which they are now released (*Oedipus Coloneus*, 1613–16). So at the end it is the daughters, now young women, who seek him out and reach toward him in his absence, as the Oedipus of the *Tyrannus* reaches toward them.

In both plays, however, the tension between the present tragic situation and the warmth of human ties works against a full resolution on the side of family love, *philia*. In the *Tyrannus* Oedipus' plea to Creon uses the repeated agricultural metaphor for the girls' incestuous origin. Doomed to "die as barren fields and unmarried" (1502), they will have a life that is the logical opposite of the excessively fertile plowland where Oedipus was both the sown crop and the sower of seed that should never have been planted. In addressing them, Oedipus not only returns to this painful agricultural metaphor at least four times (1481–82, 1485, 1504) but even begins his speech with the reminder that he is both their brother and their father (1481–82). We should not expect Greek sensibilities in such a moment to be the same as ours, particularly as ancient and modern attitudes toward children are so different. Nevertheless, it is striking that a play so aware of the ugliness of the language of incest (see 1288–89) should show the hero so unsparing of his daughters in his explicitness about the incest here.[18] In requesting Jocasta's burial, for instance, Oedipus avoids pronouncing her name or the word "mother" and calls her only "the one inside the house" (1447). But with his daughters it is as if his obsession with his own pollution overrides any consideration of their feelings.

The girls' future, furthermore, remains just as uncertain as their father's. We do not know whether or not Creon will accept Oedipus' plea that he pity them and become their surrogate father (1505). According to *Oedipus at Colonus* (and also Euripides' *Phoenician Women*), Antigone will indeed share that life of begging and wandering that Oedipus would have forestalled (*Oedipus Tyrannus*, 1503–7): "O son of Menoeceus [i. e., Creon], since you are left as the only father to these children—for we, who gave them life are destroyed, both of us—do not, father, look upon them, your own kin, *wandering as beggars, without husbands*, nor make them equal to my own sufferings." It is possible, then, that Oedipus' assertion of his will here, as in his wish for exile, though motivated by the best of intentions, also marks his failure.

Although Sophocles is generally less strident than Euripides in his questioning of the gods and the world order (e.g., *Hippolytus, Trojan Women, Bacchae*), there is little at the end of the *Tyrannus* (or, as I believe, at the end of the other early plays, like *Antigone, Trachiniae*, or even the later *Electra*) that offers much comfort to those who would like to see a "pious" Sophocles trusting in just or even reasonable gods. Even with its powerful depiction of Oedipus' inner strength in the closing scene, the *Tyrannus* does not tell us definitively what happens to Thebes or even what happens to Oedipus. Like the silence about the plague, the silence about Oedipus' exile is surprising and disturbing, particularly because Teiresias had predicted it so vividly in 417–23. Interpretations that emphasize ritual patterns like scapegoating view the ending as a solution that inscribes past suffering into social and political meaning for the community. Yet the play leaves us with the feeling of a life still in process. A man has undergone the determining struggle of his life and is changed and marked by it forever, but what the rest of his life will be is as hidden from him in this moment as it is from us, the audience. This play, so admired for the perfection of its plot, leaves basic details hanging at the end.[19]

The *Oedipus at Colonus*, although it seems to resolve the question of what Oedipus' sufferings mean, does not have an exactly happy ending. Only a few lines after the Messenger declares that Oedipus' passing was free of lamentation (1663), the girls make their presence known, as the Messenger says, by their conspicuous laments (1668–69): "For the clear voices of their laments show them rushing here." Instead of ending, as he might have, with the safe enclosure of Oedipus in the stable, well-governed, and unified city of Athens, Sophocles concludes with the girls' pull back to the divided and doomed city of Thebes. The action of *Oedipus at Colonus* consists in a series of attempts to draw the hero back to his accursed past, and the girls' closing plea to Theseus to allow them to lament over Oedipus in his grave is the final test.[20] Their request would in fact pull Oedipus back into the funereal orbit of the doomed family, and it has all of the suicidal violence of that Theban past (*Oedipus at Colonus*, 1689–93, 1733–34).

Theseus, true to his promise to Oedipus, refuses and so assures the Theban king's safe place in Athens, now as the hero of a *polis* (cf. *empolis*, "within the city," 637) rather than as the subject of a conflict between *oikos* and *polis*.

As the Oedipus of the *Coloneus* detached himself from his self-destructive Theban house, so he is now detached from its convoluted and conflicted "family love," or *philia*. In moving lines, Oedipus reaffirms his *philia* for his daughters, a love which they have had in greater measure from no other man (*Oedipus Coloneus* 1616–19). Yet this statement stands in the shadow of their imminent separation. Read alongside Oedipus' final speech to them in the *Tyrannus*, it seems to assure that they will indeed remain "barren and unmarried" (*Oedipus Tyrannus*, 1502, 1506). A Freudian might argue that the introverted ties of this family continue in a bond between father and daughters that keeps them tied to him rather than to a future husband. That is not, I think, the meaning of either passage. To the Oedipus of the *Tyrannus* the girls' unmarried future is a misfortune for them and for the family, afflicted as it is with an indelible pollution. And in the *Coloneus* the "love" of which Oedipus speaks in 1616–19 is *philia*, not *eros*, the closeness, belonging, and devotion between family members, not lovers. The Oedipus of the *Coloneus* then transfers that *philia* from Thebes to Athens and from house to city as he addresses Theseus as *philon kara*, "dear friend" (1631). The only time that Oedipus calls Creon a *philos* in the *Tyrannus* is with bitter irony as he suspects "the faithful Creon, the friend from the beginning," of plotting with Teiresias (385).[21]

In the *Coloneus*, as in the *Tyrannus*, Oedipus' last words (as reported by the Messenger) are addressed to his daughters. As he touches them with the hands of his blindness, he gently but inexorably enforces their separation. They must leave this place and neither see nor hear "what is not lawful" (*themis*) for them to perceive (1641). Only Theseus, he says, may remain to learn the solemn ritual acts that need to be done (*ta drômena*, 1644). In establishing Theseus here "in full authority" (*kyrios*, 1643), Oedipus anticipates that mysterious "authority" or "stamp of validity" of the chorus' closing words as it asks for an end of lamentation: "But cease and do not further awaken the dirge; for in every way these things have final authority" (*kyros*, 1777–79).

The *Coloneus*' last line, spoken with solemn finality, powerfully asserts closure. Spoken by the chorus of the men of Colonus, it places us firmly within the nontragic, nonlamenting world of Theseus' Athens. But, just as Sophocles shows us both sides of Oedipus—the father who can love and the father who can curse his children, the man bound by family love (*philia*) to his house and the civic hero drawing away from it to his new role in Athens—so he shows us the two sides of his daughters. Reluctantly and gradually they accept Theseus' prohibitions, but, unlike Oedipus, they cannot resist the pull back to their doomed house, where their efforts "to prevent somehow the slaughter coming upon those of kindred blood" will be futile (1770–72). This language of blood and kinship (*phonos, homaimos*), along with the reference to "primordial Thebes" (1768–69), depicts the world that Oedipus has, finally, transcended. And yet,

because this is the family of Oedipus, that transcendence fully displays its
residue of tragic suffering.

NOTES

1. In *Ajax* and *Antigone* the major protagonist is removed at approximately line
900 of a 1500-line play. In *Trachiniae*, Heracles is still alive at the end, but his death
is imminent, and in any case he does not enter the action until around line 975, after the death of the other major protagonist, Deianeira, in the preceding episode
(862–946).

2. For the oracles in the plot of the *Trachiniae*, see my essay, "The Oracles of
Sophocles' *Trachiniae*: Convergence or Confusion?" *Harvard Studies in Classical Philology* 100 (2000), forthcoming.

3. On Creon at the end of *Antigone*, see my *Sophocles' Tragic World* 119–37, especially 128–32.

4. Cf. *Oedipus Tyrannus*, 816, where Oedipus, fearing that he may be the killer
of Laius, exclaims "What man would be more god-hated (*echthrodaimôn*) (than I)?"

5. For the earlier tradition about Oedipus, see above, Chapter 4; also Jennifer
March, *The Creative Poet*, 121–54.

6. Fiona Macintosh, *Dying Acts: Death in Ancient Greek and Modern Irish Drama*
(Cork: Cork University Press, 1994), 101, with the further references there cited.

7. For the Aeschylean version, see above, Chapter 4; also March, *The Creative
Poet*, 139–48.

8. The manuscripts at 1446 are divided between "I shall entreat" (*prostrepsomai*)
and "I shall exhort" (*protrepsomai*), and editors do not agree. Lloyd-Jones and Wilson print the former in their Oxford text, but defend the latter in their *Sophoclea* (Oxford: Clarendon Press, 1990), 112; with Jebb I believe that the sense favors "entreat."

9. See *Oedipus at Colonus*, 44–46, 72–74, 287–90 and also 391–420, 450–60. See
also Bernard Knox, *The Heroic Temper*, 148–49.

10. See Laura Slatkin, "*Oedipus at Colonus*: Exile and Integration," in J. P. Euben,
ed., *Greek Tragedy and Political Theory* (Berkeley and Los Angeles: University of California Press, 1986), 210–21, especially 217–20.

11. Lowell Edmunds, *Theatrical Space and Historical Place in Sophocles' "Oedipus
at Colonus"* (Lanham, MD: Rowman and Littlefield, 1996), chapter 3, especially 88–94.

12. See Richard Seaford, *Reciprocity and Ritual* (Oxford: Clarendon Press, 1994),
Chapter 4, especially 126–43.

13. See my *Tragedy and Civilization*, 405.

14. See my *Tragedy and Civilization*, pp. 401–4.

15. In the characteristic density of Sophoclean syntax, lines 791–92 can also be
translated, "I would show forth a race unendurable for humankind to look upon."

16. The incestuous birth, however, is alluded to briefly and mysteriously by
Teiresias, 425, 457–58; see above, Chapter 7. When Oedipus calls to the daughters to

come "into the *brotherly* hands of mine," the hands which blinded the eyes of "the *father who begot* you" in 1481–82, he is also echoing the collocation of father and brother in Teiresias' prophecy in 458, "the same one as brother and father."

17. Oedipus' word "unendurable" in 792 harks back to the chorus' allusion to the "unspeakable" deeds of the murderer in 464–65 and to the "unspeakable" words of his incestuous relations, in 1289–90.

18. On 1288–89 see Diskin Clay, "Unspeakable Words in Greek Tragedy," *American Journal of Philology* 105 (1982), 277–98, especially 284ff.

19. March, *Creative Poet*, 148 suggests that *Oedipus Tyrannus* did originally end with the hero's exile but was then reworked for posthumous performance together with *Oedipus at Colonus*, perhaps at the time of the latter's production by Oedipus' grandson. Were one to continue even more radically in this direction, one might suggest that the entire meeting between Oedipus and his daughters had also been added to tally with *Oedipus at Colonus*. Yet given the fact that the language of these passages is fully Sophoclean, it seems more likely that Sophocles developed the ending of *Oedipus at Colonus* with the earlier play in mind and is consciously looking back at the earlier play. For the problem of the authenticity of the closing trochaics of *Oedipus Tyrannus*, see above, Chapter 9, n. 12.

20. On the tests of Oedipus by the pull of the past in *Oedipus at Colonus* see my *Tragedy and Civilization* 375, 383–92, 402–4.

21. The chorus, by contrast, does refer to Creon as *philos* in 656–57, when it tries to defend him against Oedipus' charges.

12

〜〜〜〜〜〜

Reception, Influence, and Recent
Literary Criticism

INTRODUCTION; TRANSMISSION OF THE TEXT

Oedipus Tyrannus did not win the first prize when Sophocles presented it in the 420s B.C.E., along with two other tragedies and a satyr play, whose titles are unknown. Sophocles lost to a little known tragedian, a nephew of Aeschylus named Philocles.[1] History, however, has reversed the judgment of the Athenians and compensated Sophocles with a posthumous victory beyond his wildest dreams. Since antiquity *Oedipus* has been the most famous play of Greek drama, and it has remained in the consciousness of the West almost continuously for the past twenty-four centuries. The young Julius Caesar wrote an *Oedipus*, and the Emperor Nero acted in one.[2] Since Aristotle's *Poetics* (around 340–320 B.C.E.), the play has entered into almost every major discussion of the nature of tragedy, and since Freud's *Interpretation of Dreams* (1900), it has entered into almost every major discussion of psychology, as indeed it still does (see above, Chapter 4).

Oedipus and six other plays of Sophocles (out of some 120 that he wrote) have survived because the scholars of late antiquity and Byzantium chose them for teaching in the schools, their way of creating a canon of "great books." Our oldest manuscript, now in the Laurentian Library in Florence, dates from around 950; some two hundred other manuscripts of *Oedipus*, of varying value, are extant, dating from the thirteenth to the fifteenth century. This is an indication of the play's immense prestige in the Byzantine world.

We have only limited knowledge of how the play was transmitted from the time of Sophocles to the surviving medieval manuscripts. We may assume that copies of the play, probably in very limited numbers, circulated in the form of papyrus rolls in Sophocles' day. Such rolls have almost entirely perished in Greece, but since the beginning of the twentieth century, fragments—and very rarely entire rolls—have been discovered in Egypt, whose dry climate has preserved them. Most of these papyrus fragments are from the second century C.E. and later. Small portions of Sophocles' lost plays have been recovered in this way, but so far these discoveries have not been very important for *Oedipus*.

An official copy of the text of the tragedians was made for the state archives of Athens late in the fourth century B.C.E. This probably formed the basis for the texts edited by the scholars of the Hellenistic world, principally at Alexandria in Ptolemaic Egypt, from the third century B.C.E. on. These texts then began to be copied into papyrus books in the third and fourth centuries C.E. Beginning some five hundred years later, in the Byzantine empire of Greece and Asia Minor, they were in turn copied into the parchment manuscripts that we have, and from these Byzantine manuscripts come our modern texts of Sophocles.

Unfortunately, this long process of transmission has introduced numerous errors into the text, partly because the forms of Greek script changed over the centuries and partly because the ancient and poetical language was often misunderstood or miscopied by scribes. Correcting these errors to get closer to what Sophocles actually wrote has been the work of classical philologists over the last four hundred years, and the process still continues. Although the Greek text of *Oedipus* is basically sound, corrupt passages remain, particularly in the intricate and difficult poetry of the choral odes, and in these cases translators and interpreters have to rely on the conjectures of modern scholars. The acting companies that performed these plays from the fourth century B.C.E. on occasionally added some lines, and modern scholars have also been concerned with detecting these interpolations. Many experts, for example, consider the closing six verses pronounced by the chorus of the *Oedipus* to be such an interpolation (1524–30).

Aristotle's *Poetics* and Other Ancient Criticism

We must here retrace our steps and follow the celebrity of *Oedipus* back to its source, in Aristotle, for whom Oedipus is the tragic hero par excellence. Aristotle considers him the protagonist best suited to tragic action because he represents a man "in great repute and good fortune," "not exceptional for excellence and justice, who undergoes a change to misfortune not on account of baseness or villainy but on account of some error" (*Poetics*, 13.1453a8ff.). The word translated as "error" here, *hamartia*, has long been the subject of intense controversy; it is now generally agreed to mean "intellectual mistake," an error of judgment due to ignorance, and not a moral error or "flaw" of character. Aristotle makes it clear that *hamartia* is not a "flaw" of character, for he defines his ideal tragic hero as one who "does not deserve his fate" and "passes to bad fortune *not through vice or wickedness*, but because of some piece of ignorance [*hamartia*]," mentioning Oedipus immediately after. We should note the sharp contrast between "vice or wickedness" and *hamartia*.[3]

The power of the *Oedipus*, according to Aristotle, lies in its characteristic tragic effect of arousing and cleansing (or clarifying) pity and fear, a process he calls catharsis (literally "cleansing" or "purification"); this effect is produced by an action involving family members or loved ones. It is essential for the tragedy,

145

as Aristotle recognizes, that Oedipus has committed his crimes in ignorance. Though stained by the pollutions of these acts, he is both guilty and innocent.

To Aristotle, *Oedipus* also exemplifies the best type of tragic plot. The events are not illogical or unlikely, except perhaps in the case of necessary background material that lies outside the play itself, like Oedipus' not knowing how Laius was killed (*Poetics*, 24.1460a27–31). Aristotle admired the plausibility of the reversal (peripety, or *peripeteia*) and the dramatic irony that the Messenger who came to free Oedipus from his fears has exactly the opposite effect (10.1452a24). The recognition of the truth (*anagnorisis*) in *Oedipus*, Aristotle says, is the finest in tragedy because it coincides with the reversal in Oedipus' fortunes (*Poetics*, 11.1452a32). Aristotle does not explain why this should be so, but he may have thought that the tragic effect of pity and fear, with the resultant catharsis, was enhanced when the audience simultaneously experiences the intellectual process of the recognition and the emotional pathos of the reversal.

Later critics followed Aristotle's judgment. The author of the interesting treatise *On the Sublime*, known as Longinus (probably of the late first century C.E.), remarks that *Oedipus* alone is worth the entire production of Sophocles' rival, Ion of Chios. Elsewhere Longinus praises the power of Oedipus' cry of horror at his incestuous marriage (1403–8). He also praises the finale of *Oedipus at Colonus* for the vivid presentation of Oedipus' mysterious call from the gods (*On the Sublime*, 33.5, 23.3, 15.7, respectively).

SENECA'S *OEDIPUS*

The Stoic philosopher and tutor of Nero, Lucius Annaeus Seneca (ca. 4 B.C.E. to 65 C.E.), composed ten tragedies, of which two deal with Oedipus. Seneca's *Oedipus* influenced many of the later adaptations of the story: it reduces the role of the chorus and curtails both the civic ritual and the public and political setting, all of which had little meaning after the demise of the independent Greek city-state and the weakening of the Olympian religion. Like many of the later adapters, Seneca also shifts the emphasis from the hero's intellectual quest to an atmosphere of terror and helplessness.

Like Sophocles, Seneca opens his *Oedipus* with the plague, but the mood is far more introspective and psychological. Indeed, the plague is more convincing as a symbolic meditation on the infectious nature of evil in the world and in the soul than as a pollution of the natural world arising from the hidden stain of blood. Instead of confronting the citizens of Thebes in a public scene and with bold confidence, Seneca's Oedipus speaks a long, dark monologue full of foreboding and a brooding sense of guilt. The truth is revealed through necromancy, as Teiresias summons Laius' ghost from Hades, with an accompanying atmosphere of evil omens, heavy shadows, chill swamps, bloody altars, and horrid entrails characteristic of Senecan tragedy (*Oedipus* 530–658). Covered with blood from his wounds, the dead Laius arises like an avenging spirit. He is the objectification of the guilt that Oedipus expressed in the prologue, and he utters terrible accusations and threats against his parricidal son. He calls Oedipus, for example, "a monster more involuted than his own Sphinx" (641, *magisque monstrum Sphinge perplexum sua*). This atmosphere of horror and monstrosity tends to overshadow the universality and humanity of the Sophoclean hero as a mortal who faces the irrational suffering of his miserable life. These sensational details of omens and necromancy, along with the related theme of inevitable fate, also constitute a major change from Sophocles' tense rhythm of discovery and gradually unfolding truth.

The recognition in Seneca's *Oedipus*, though superficially resembling the Sophoclean version, also has a very different mood. Oedipus' accusation of Creon provides the occasion for an exchange of cynical epigrams, in Seneca's best manner, on the necessity for fear and hatred in holding royal power (*Oedipus* 699–706). The self-blinding is motivated by guilt rather than by the Sophoclean motifs of religious feeling, the self-pronounced curse, and the horror of pollution. Seneca also makes the tearing out of the eyes particularly gruesome (962–70). Jocasta's recognition follows Oedipus' (rather than preceding it, as in Sophocles), and she kills herself on stage, plunging a sword into her body with the cry, "Seek this womb here, O my right hand, the spacious womb that bore both husband and children" (1038–39).

As Oedipus leaves Thebes for exile, the brighter sky promises an end to the plague (*Oedipus* 1052–61). Here Seneca, much more explicitly than Sophocles, draws on ancient rituals of the expulsion of the scapegoat (see Chapter 4) and the role of the king as the sacred mediator between the human and supernatural worlds. But his combination of psychology, horror, and the subterranean world, though effective on its own terms, dissolves the subtle Sophoclean relations between character, chance, and destiny. Instead he makes Oedipus an innocent victim of a remote, incomprehensible, and malevolent Fate on the one hand and a Stoic hero-king who endures his suffering to save his city on the other.

Seneca's *Phoenician Women* (*Phoenissae*) is a fragmentary work of some 650 lines, the first half of which shows Oedipus in exile, accompanied by his daughter, Antigone, as in *Oedipus at Colonus*. Unlike Sophocles' hero of that play, however, this Oedipus is still tormented by guilt and troubled by visions of Laius' ghost. He feels that he did too little in tearing out his eyes, and he expresses this sentiment in typical Senecan hyperbole: "Now dip your hand into your brain and there complete the death that I began to die" (180–81).

Although the oldest surviving manuscript of Seneca's tragedies dates from around 1100, these plays did not become popular until the Renaissance. Then *Oedipus* in particular served as a model of how to adapt the political, intellectual, and ritual elements of an ancient Greek play to modern situations. Seneca's psychological direction remained influential, and he appealed to the tastes of the sixteenth and seventeenth centuries for long rhetorical descriptions, hyperbole, melodrama, violence, and supernatural effects. Laius' ghost, possibly

Seneca's invention (though with ample precedent, from Aeschylus through Ovid), was to have a long and happy life on the stage. It may have contributed to the ghost of Shakespeare's *Hamlet*.

THE MIDDLE AGES[4]

Because Western Europe had virtually no access to classical Greek language and literature during the Middle Ages, Statius' long epic poem in Latin, the *Thebaid* (written around 90 C.E.), became one of the main vehicles for the influence of *Oedipus*. The poem opens with a long speech by the shade of Oedipus in Hades telling his story and cursing his sons for neglecting him (*Thebaid* 1.46–87). This work, possibly through a medieval Latin adaptation, lies behind the long twelfth-century epic poem, the *Roman de Thèbes* (*Romance of Thebes*). It transforms into the terms of knightly chivalry the struggle between Oedipus' two sons, Polyneices and Eteocles, for the throne of Thebes. The *Roman de Thèbes* expands Statius' prologue into some nine hundred lines, adding some characteristically courtly touches. Sophocles' drunken Corinthian who taunts Oedipus with bastardy is replaced by a group of jealous courtiers. Oedipus not only solves the riddle of the Sphinx but also kills it and cuts it into pieces. Queen Jocasta is not merely given to him as his reward but falls in love with him, in the courtly manner, when she sees him at the celebratory banquet. On the other hand, drawing on a detail in Statius (himself perhaps influenced by Seneca), the *Roman de Thèbes* gives a particularly lurid account of the self-blinding. The sons find his torn out eyeballs on the ground and in their horror at the incest trample on them. Oedipus later undertakes a voluntary penance for his deeds and has himself imprisoned—a variant on the legend that survives in the Oedipus-like story about Pope Gregory the Great (see Chapter 4).

The long and highly popular fourteenth-century poem, the *Ovide Moralisé* [*Ovid Moralized*], draws on and greatly abbreviates the *Roman de Thèbes* (*O. M.* 9.1473–1537.). It includes the trampled eyeballs, Oedipus' penance, and the old folktale motif of the servants' pity for the infant they are ordered to kill: the child laughs, and so instead of killing it they pierced its feet and left it hanging, still alive—a dubious form of mercy, but the child survives. Jocasta recognizes Oedipus as her lost child when she sees the scars on his feet as he is bathing.

Statius' poem probably also lies behind the account of Jocasta's sufferings in Boccaccio's *De Claris Mulieribus* (*On Famous Women*, 1361–62), from which Christine de Pizan borrows for her *Book of the City of Ladies* (1405) in France and Hans Sachs borrows for his *The Unfortunate Queen Jocasta* (1550) in Germany. Pictorial depictions of the story of Oedipus also exist in several late medieval manuscripts. Particularly striking is the pathetic representation of the exposed baby, hung naked and upside down by his pierced ankles in a tree. In a thirteenth-century manuscript Oedipus kills the Sphinx not by answering the riddle but by striking it through the neck with a huge sword.[5]

THE RENAISSANCE

During most of the Middle Ages in the West, as we have observed, *Oedipus* (or, properly speaking, the myth of Oedipus) was known primarily through Latin authors such as Seneca or Statius. At the beginning of the fifteenth century, however, in the great revival of interest in classical culture known as the Renaissance, Italian scholars began acquiring Greek manuscripts from the Byzantine world. By the beginning of the century, there were four known Greek manuscripts of Sophocles in Italy, the earliest bought by the humanist collector Niccolò Niccoli in 1417; by the end of the century there were over thirty.[6] The first Greek text of Sophocles in Western Europe was printed in 1502, by Aldus Manutius (Aldo Manuzio), the Venetian humanist publisher who specialized in classical texts. Translations into Italian began in the second half of the sixteenth century, and at least four were made between about 1560 and 1600.

The French humanist Robert Garnier produced an *Antigone* (1580), of which the first half draws heavily on *Oedipus*, but with a strong emphasis on Oedipus' sense of his predestination and damnation, themes of great importance in the religious thought of the time. Despite the West's steadily increasing knowledge of Greek and familiarity with Sophocles' plays, however, the more violent and sensational version of Seneca—with its melodrama, necromancy, and ghosts—remained popular and (as we shall see) often entered into later adaptations of *Oedipus*.[7]

On 3 March 1585, Sophocles' *Oedipus* made its formal public debut in the theater of the West. The occasion was the opening of the grand neo-classic Teatro Olimpico (Olympic Theater), designed by the sixteenth-century architect Palladio in the north Italian city of Vicenza, under the sponsorship of the city's "Olympian Academy." The play was translated into Italian by Orsatto Giustiniani, with choruses set to music by Angelo Gabrieli. The play was chosen because it was felt to be the most eminent dramatic work of classical antiquity ("one of the most beautiful tragedies that have ever been written," wrote a contemporary) in an age that passionately hoped to re-create and emulate the lost grandeur of the classical world.[8] The theater's elegant interior, however, was in fact more like the enclosed Roman theater than the simple open-air Greek theater, and the audience of select nobles and litterati was far from the citizen audience that would have attended the original performance. Nevertheless, *Oedipus* was launched on its new career and now entered the mainstream of modern Western literature.

SEVENTEENTH AND EIGHTEENTH CENTURIES

From the sixteenth century on, as *Oedipus* becomes established as *the* classical tragedy, the number of translations and adaptations increases. Interest in the play is also stimulated by the so-called "quarrel between the ancients and the moderns," the ongoing debate about whether the ancient or the contemporary authors are superior. Three plays are particularly important in this period, Corneille's *Oedipe* of 1659, Dryden and Lee's *Oedipus* of 1678, and Voltaire's *Oedipe* of 1718.

All three basically follow Sophocles' plot but add touches from Seneca (e.g., the ghost of Laius appears in both Corneille and Dryden). Corneille, however, reverses the emphasis of Seneca's play and returns to a more Sophoclean mood. Instead of Seneca's concern with the crushing force of an immutable destiny, he emphasizes the nobility of Oedipus and the triumph of virtue and strength over a malign fate.[9]

Theater and theatergoing in seventeenth-century London or Paris were of course radically different from what they were in ancient Greece. In his preface Corneille observes that "what had passed for marvelous in their centuries [that is, in Sophocles' and Seneca's times] could seem horrible to ours." The long description of Oedipus' blinding in the ancient versions, he adds, would disturb "the delicacy of our ladies, and their disgust easily brings with it that of the rest of the audience," and so he decided to conceal "such a dangerous spectacle and introduce the happy episode of Theseus and Dirce," that is, a love story as subplot. Dryden and Voltaire adopted this addition, on the assumption that the Sophoclean recognition plot alone would not interest their audiences. On the whole, classical Greek drama, with its severe sense of form, avoids such subplots. In the modern versions, however, with their more explicit erotic themes, these subplots serve as a positive foil to the illicit sexuality in the relations between Oedipus and Jocasta and help relieve the ugliness of the incest. Yet some of these versions, especially in the latter part of the eighteenth century, spin out these subplots with such complexity that the resultant play looks more like a soap opera than a Greek tragedy.[10]

Corneille, Dryden-Lee, and Voltaire all transform Sophocles' civic setting into a royal court of their own times, eliminate the chorus, and greatly reduce the role of supernatural and ritual elements, like Delphi, the oracles, Teiresias, and the gods. They make the action more naturalistic (though still rather stiff, by modern standards) and emphasize the dignity of kingship, the endurance of fate, and duty. Although some sense of the sacred power of kingship and the sacred body of the king remains, especially in Corneille and Voltaire, these works have little of Sophocles' idea of an invisible and mysterious mythic order that is expressed through the choruses.

Dryden and Lee's complicated play is the most Senecan of the three, with its dire omens, Laius' ghost, and numerous dead bodies on stage at the end. In addition to the erotic subplot, there is also an evil villain, the misshapen Creon, borrowed from Shakespeare's *Richard III*, and Oedipus' disturbed sleepwalking in act 2 borrowed from *Macbeth*. Dryden and Lee's greatest innovation is the insistence on the attraction of the mother and son for one another. Act 1, for example, ends with the couple's profession of their deep love. When Jocasta remarks on the resemblance between Laius and Oedipus, Oedipus says, "No pious son e're loved his Mother more / Than I my dear Jocasta." She replies,

> I love you too
> The self same way [. . .].
> For I love Lajus still as wives should love:
> But you more tenderly, as part of me:
> And when I have you in my arms, methinks
> I lull my child asleep.

As we shall see, this exploration of the private, subjective, erotic dimensions of the incestuous union, so foreign to the conventions of Greek drama, becomes one of the most popular innovations of the twentieth-century versions of the myth. Dryden also rivals Seneca in the goriness of the self-blinding (act 5, scene 1), but actually outdoes him in the horror of the ending. Jocasta murders her four children before killing herself, and Oedipus hurls himself to his death from the tower where he was imprisoned.

The Enlightenment rationalist Voltaire wrote a series of *Letters on Oedipus* in connection with his version of the play, in which he criticized Sophocles' plot for its improbabilities. His critique is part of the famous "quarrel of the ancients and the moderns" still going on in his day. The animosity of this "quarrel" sometimes produces an arrogance and condescension toward the ancient dramatists that may leave the modern reader gasping. In his *Fourth Letter*, for example, Voltaire writes, "If they [the Greek dramatists] had been born in our time, they would have perfected the art that they practically invented in their own period. . . . Their works deserve to be read, undoubtedly; if they are too deficient for our approval, they are too full of beautiful touches to be scorned completely."

In his *Oedipe*, then, Voltaire tries to improve on Sophocles (and incidentally on Corneille) by placing Laius' death just four years in the past and by having Oedipus and Jocasta married for only two years. This last device makes the failure to investigate Laius' death less problematic, reduces the age difference between the royal couple, and eliminates the horror of the incestuously born children. This particularly troubling aspect of the myth, we recall, was a concern as early as the sixth or seventh century B.C.E. (see Chapter 4).

Voltaire's ending combines Seneca and Corneille: Oedipus remains a good, dutiful king in control of his emotions and concerned with his people, whom he saves from the plague with the blood of his mutilated eyes. Jocasta closes the play with her suicide, complaining against the cruelty of fate. Voltaire also follows Corneille (and ultimately Seneca) in giving Laius, so shadowy in Sophocles, a more prominent role. In his characterization of Oedipus as a noble king, Corneille had already introduced a scene in which Oedipus recalls killing Laius in combat—a dignified battle in which Oedipus reluctantly kills his opponent (act 4, scene 3). Voltaire adds the pathetic (and unrealistic) detail of Laius' dying recognition of his lost son, to whom he stretches out his arms, tears in his eyes, in his last moments.

Voltaire's *Oedipe* remained highly popular on the Parisian stage, a testimony to the power of the myth but also to the decorum and rationality of Voltaire's treatment. It led to a spate of further imitations. In his *Oedipe* of 1726, Antoine Houdar de la Motte went beyond Voltaire in whitewashing the parricidal act. He has the dying Laius congratulate the victor (whom he has implicitly recognized as his son) on his valor (act 3, scene 6). Houdar also adds a new twist to the old servant's account of Laius' death. Out of cowardice, this companion of Laius' fatal journey tells the lie that the old king is killed by a lion, so that Oedipus is completely thrown off the track and has no reason to suspect that he might be the killer. Oedipus learns the truth from Jocasta, who kills herself after telling her tale. Houdar then ends the play with Oedipus' suicide and thereby pushes to its logical conclusion the Senecan motif of Oedipus as the sacrificial scapegoat.

NINETEENTH AND TWENTIETH CENTURIES

From the sixteenth to the eighteenth century imitators of *Oedipus* emphasize the Senecan motif of Fate rather than the Sophoclean concern with knowledge and self-discovery. Thus they placed more emphasis on Oedipus' ability to accept his suffering with nobility and strength than on his determination to search out truth in a world of illusion. On the other hand, the continuing concern with kingship enabled Corneille, Dryden, and Voltaire to develop the more public aspect of Sophocles' play. They introduced a mob made restless and hostile by the plague, dynastic conflicts and palace intrigue, the themes of authority, lineage, and succession, and the sacrificial act that brings salvation at the end.

The numerous nineteenth- and twentieth-century versions are more concerned with personal and philosophical themes: the meaning of existence, the individual's alienation from the world and himself, the mystery of individual destiny, the incestuous attraction. Freud, whose reading is discussed in Chapter 4, dominates every view of the myth after him, although there are foreshadowings of his interpretation in the combination of incest, madness, and heredity in the Oedipal elements of Ibsen's *Ghosts* (1882) and, as we have noted, even in Dryden and Lee. *Oedipus* is by now famous enough to invite parody, as in Percy Bysshe Shelley's satirical beast-parable, *Oedipus Tyrannus, or Swellfoot the Tyrant*, and August von Platen's *Der romantische Oedipus* (1828). A freer adaptation is Heinrich von Kleist's comedy, *The Broken Jar* (*Der zerbrochene Krug*, performed in 1808), which combines the Oedipal rivalry between an older and younger lover of the same woman with the motifs of judicial investigation, disguise, and reversal from magistrate to criminal. In a darker mood, Friedrich von Schiller's *Bride of Messina* (1803) fuses the deadly rivalry of the two brothers in *Oedipus at Colonus* with a version of *Oedipus Tyrannus* in which the dread oracle about the birth of the king's child concerns a daughter rather than a son.

Each of the two brothers, ignorant of their sister's true identity, falls in love with her, with disastrous results for the royal house. The *Oedipus'* family violence is thus made to take place a generation later and is transformed to brother-sister incest.

The German Romantic writer Friedrich Hölderlin produced a powerful, highly poetic translation of *Oedipus, Oedipus der Tyrann*, along with an *Antigone* in the same period.[11] The translation boldly catches much of the Sophoclean grandeur, stateliness, and poetic imagery. More controversial are his "Notes on the *Oedipus*" ("Anmerkungen zum Oedipus"), appended to the translation, which, along with the similar "Notes on the *Antigone*," attempt to develop a theory of tragedy. Here *Oedipus* is the model for the tragic individual's confrontation with ultimate reality. He is torn from his normal sphere of life, pulled between the extremes of the human and the divine, and led destructively into the merciless light of the absolute. Hölderlin is elliptical and cryptic, and, despite the enthusiasm of Heidegger, critics have been divided about whether the "Notes" were the product of the poet's genius or the signs of the insanity that ended his creative life in 1804. Genius has been the dominant view recently. In any case, Hölderlin helped establish the Romantic view of *Oedipus* that has strongly influenced recent interpretation, namely approaching the play in terms of the metaphysical questions of ultimate reality, the paradoxes of identity, the intersection of human and divine, and the hero's total isolation in a world of mysterious and remote powers.

The Romantic interpretation appears rather more clearly from a letter of the philosopher Schopenhauer to the poet Goethe (November 11, 1815):

> It is the courage to search problems through to the end that makes the philosopher. He must be like Sophocles' Oedipus, who, in seeking to illuminate his terrible destiny, pursues his quest untiringly, even when he realizes that the answer holds only horror and terror for him. But most of us carry in our hearts a Jocasta who begs Oedipus for the love of the gods not to investigate further.

Here the emphasis falls not only on Oedipus' search for the truth but also on the special destiny of this search that sets him apart from ordinary, more complacent people (Jocasta).

At the end of the Romantic tradition stands Hugo von Hofmannsthal's *Oedipus and the Sphinx* (1905), planned as part of a trilogy that was never completed. Hofmannsthal's is a very metaphysical Oedipus, who swings between nothingness and godhead, despair and exaltation. At the opening he is in suicidal desperation, having abandoned his entire past life when he heard Apollo's terrible oracle at Delphi. Hofmannsthal's post-Romantic lyricism combines a mystical with a psychological tone. The god's oracle is delivered through the intermediary of an alluring female figure, a mother/lover, who will awaken Oedipus to his true identity. The voice of the god, or fate, is thus interpreted in highly personal and inward terms: it holds the secret of the alienated hero's still invisible strength and his ultimate purpose in the world. Oedipus defeats the Sphinx in an eerie setting, in which the struggle is with his own self-doubt and despair rather than with knowledge or monstrosity—a direction already adumbrated by Seneca. The play ends in an ecstatic union between the victorious hero, who seems reborn virtually as a god, and the queen, who is fascinated by his god-like power and beauty. The atmosphere is one of foreboding, mystical visions, and confused desires; self-destructive violence alternates with feelings of limit-less power and godlike bliss. We are closer here to Wagner's *Tristan* and *Siegfried* and to Freud than to Sophocles.[12]

The oneiric atmosphere of Hofmannsthal's version has a precursor in the French play of the same name, *Oedipe et le Sphinx*, by Josephin Péladan (1897). This highly classicizing little drama condenses the story into the period between Oedipus' departure from Thebes and the night of his victory over the Sphinx. In his long account of the confrontation between Oedipus and the Sphinx, how-ever, Péladan puts the solving of the riddle into the background and reinter-prets the conflict between the hero and the monster in elusive symbolic terms as a psychological battle of will and confidence wherein Oedipus must struggle against his own fear in a lonely nocturnal setting. The Sphinx then offers the victor a seductive, sensual pleasure that makes her the dark side of Jocasta: "The caress of the Sphinx, if you knew it," the Sphinx promises, "would make every other delight impossible for you. In my embrace you would think that you pos-sess the mystery; an ineffable joy would warm your veins, and under the power of the pleasure you would believe yourself God" (act 3, scene 2). At the end Oedipus confirms this identification between the Sphinx and his royal bride-to-be by seating Jocasta, on the "throne" of the Sphinx's rock.

The *Oedipe* of André Gide (1930) and *The Infernal Machine* of Jean Cocteau (1934) are perhaps the best known adaptations of *Oedipus* in this century. In con-trast to the high lyrical and mystical tone of Hofmannsthal and the philosoph-ical classicizing of Péladan, Gide and Cocteau bring the myth down to earth with an irreverent, tragicomic mixture of the mythical and the everyday and a lot of talk, spiced with Gallic wit. They also take the opposite tack from Corneille and Voltaire: rather than glossing over the horrors (or giving them a symbolic and mystic meaning, as do Péladan and Hofmannsthal), they set them out fully into a harshly ironic light. Gide's Jocasta knows the truth all along and tries to persuade Oedipus to keep it as a secret between them when he learns it.[13] Gide also adds an incestuous attraction between Oedipus' sons and their sister, Is-mene, to parallel the father's incestuous marriage. Cocteau's entire third act takes place on Oedipus and Jocasta's wedding night in the queen's bedroom, where she keeps a cradle at the foot of the bed to remind her of her lost child, and there are many references to the mother-son relation that mysteriously draws the two together in their love.

Gide's Oedipus is a kind of existentialist hero. He exults in being a bastard since that leaves him free to form his own identity. Gide reinterprets the myth, and especially the incest motif, in terms of a debate between absolute freedom and the restraints of law, society, and religion. Oedipus is a seeker after truth and an independent, free-thinking spirit. His authenticity contrasts with Teiresias' self-righteous piety, Creon's self-serving greed, and Jocasta's willingness to compromise for the sake of a comfortable bourgeois happiness.

Gide's play is more black comedy than tragedy, and it often calls attention to its outrageousness by compressing or parodying the original. In the debate between Oedipus and Teiresias in act 1, for example, the chorus intervenes colloquially, "It's no good, Oedipus, it's no good. You know very well that with Tiresias even a king can't have the last word." Gide's Ismene is a precocious teenager, and Antigone wants to be a nun. The self-blinding at the end is not so much an act of horror and remorse as one of desperate courage in refusing the veil of ignorant happiness that Jocasta would live with.

In *The Infernal Machine* Cocteau creates a counterpoint between his light, contemporary mood and the mythic seriousness of the original with the device of "the Voice" that introduces each act and replaces the Sophoclean gods. This Voice opens the play with a synopsis of the story and, directly addressing the spectator, describes the plot as a diabolical construction "by the infernal gods for the mathematical destruction of a mortal."

Taking a hint from Dryden (and indirectly from Seneca), Cocteau begins the action with a *Hamlet*-like scene of Laius' ghost on the castle walls trying to warn Jocasta of the impending danger. Jocasta, a spoiled and fun-loving socialite, visits the battlements, accompanied by her well-meaning, devoted, but somewhat bumbling priest, Teiresias, whom she affectionately calls Zizi. Cocteau draws on both Freud and the Surrealists for his third act, which takes place on the wedding night. Oedipus and Jocasta both dream some aspect of the truth but cannot quite grasp it consciously. Indeed, they have just the conversation that readers of *Oedipus* often wonder about: Jocasta talks of her lost child, and Oedipus gives an account of the scars on his feet.

Cocteau's ending draws on the mood of *Oedipus at Colonus*. Jocasta's ghost, invisible to everyone except Oedipus, reclaims him as her lost child and joins with Antigone to lead him on his journey to truth. Teiresias returns at the end, speaking with the voice of posterity, to free Oedipus from Creon's authority. He declares that he belongs to "the people, to the poets, to the pure in heart." The line is perhaps Cocteau's antidote to his irreverent treatment, suggesting that the great ancient myths have a universal power and, through the modernized form that Cocteau adopts, still have something important to tell us, but they can speak only in a kind of cool, self-deprecating irony, or, as one critic says, "as though through the din of a cocktail party, he were endeavoring in secret asides to tell a fairy story to a child."[14]

Most of the twentieth-century dramatizations give Oedipus and Jocasta a depth of emotional life in keeping with the psychosocial realism of modern drama. Both characters acquire a range of feelings and memories and have an intimate emotional and erotic life that we are allowed to peer into in detail. In Sophocles this sexual dimension of the incest is very much in the background; where it does appear, it is conveyed only indirectly, through subtle suggestions and the imagery of plowing and sowing. Indeed, where Greek tragedy deals with the erotic, it tends to externalize it as an elemental power or an irresistible divine force, like Aphrodite in Euripides' *Hippolytus*, rather than as a realm of private, subjective emotions.

Dryden and Lee had led the way in this eroticization of the incest as a sub-conscious attraction between mother and son. Cocteau, as we have seen, takes us into the royal bedchamber on the wedding night. Gide's Oedipus avows for Jocasta "a love almost filial and conjugal at the same time" (act 1). This psy-chological atmosphere is already anticipated in Péladan's dreamlike version, in which Jocasta, initially reluctant to think of remarriage after the death of Laius, feels strangely moved when she sees Oedipus. Noting the resemblance between him and Laius, she reminisces, "Your appearance—I don't know how—makes me think of a child dead in his cradle" (act 2, scene 10).[15] Oedipus, in turn, just before encountering the Sphinx, anticipates the joy of winning Jocasta as his bride, and reflects, "Scarcely had I seen her than I felt her dear to me. I felt not the desire that her beauty awakens but a deeper and calmer attraction" act 3, scene 1). In the wake of Péladan and Cocteau, Henri Ghéon (*Oedipe ou la cré-puscule des dieux*) and Jean Anouilh (*Oedipe ou le roi boiteux*, 1978) explore the fu-sion of maternal and sexual love with obvious Freudian overtones.

Steven Berkoff's *Greek* (1980) takes the psychological ironizing of the myth far beyond Cocteau's domestic banalization. A working-class Oedipus named Eddy has been separated from his London parents by a disastrous explosion on the Thames. Some twenty years later he discovers that he has accidentally killed his father and unknowingly married his mother. Though he is shocked by the discovery, he decides to continue living with his "Mum." The "plague," in-cessantly in the background, is the philistine meanness and ugliness of British working-class life (Péladan, in a totally different mood and style, had already interpreted the Sphinx as the product of Thebes' spiritual corruption). The end-less obscenities of Berkoff's Joycean stream of consciousness are so insistent as to produce, paradoxically, a kind of mythical distancing. The only bright spot is in fact Eddy's incestuous love for his mother, frankly sensual, but not only that. The play ends on this positive note, both shocking and beautiful (in an in-troductory authorial note Berkoff remarks, "The play is also a love story"), and it explicitly rejects Sophocles' tragic ending. In his closing speech, more mono-logue than dialogue, Eddy reflects, "We only love so it doesn't matter mother, it doesn't matter. Why should I tear my eyes out Greek style, why should you hang yourself . . ."

Even farther from Sophocles is Edward Bond's play *Saved* (1965), which bru-tally demythicizes the story. Like Berkoff, Bond uses the setting of working-class London, but develops an even more sordid mood of social realism. In this vaguely "Oedipal" situation both the incest and the parricide are averted, but the "exposed" infant is killed—a divided solution which doubtless reflects on the deep ironies in the title of this convincing but ugly domestic drama.

Hélène Cixous is one of the few women to write an Oedipus play, a lyrical meditation called *The Name of Oedipus: Song of the Forbidden Body* (*Le nom d'Oedipe: chant du corps interdit,* 1978), set to music by André Boucourechliev for performance at the Avignon Festival. This operatic version explores the subjective side of the incest from the inward perspective of the two lovers, mutually fascinated with one another. The incest, however, is not so much a wild passion, like that of Tristan and Isolde, as a kind of double, all-inclusive narcissism. In this total involvement with one another, each lover feels a loss of self in a timeless fusion with the infinite.[16] Jocasta's maternal instincts, however, make her more capable of this totalizing involvement, whereas Oedipus has a restless and disturbing sense of death as the dark complement to the surrender of self. The dialectic between these two voices constitutes what little true drama there is in this highly lyrical, inward work. Here too the Freudian interplay of Eros and Thanatos, the life and death instincts, is in the background.

Cixous' shifting between lyrical monologue and dialogue recasts the material of Sophocles' play into a dreamlike and allusive mood, reminiscent of Hofmannsthal and Péladan, but, thanks in part to the musical form, Cixous absorbs virtually all of the action into the autonomous, emotional world that the incestuous lovers make for themeselves. Hence the events of the myth appear only as brief, unreal flashbacks amid the lyrical professions of love between Oedipus and Jocasta. Oedipus is haunted by a vague, fearful knowledge of the truth, which gradually spreads to Jocasta. When Oedipus pulls away from her to deal with the plague and so face his mysterious doom, she slips into a peaceful death, watched over by a kindly, androgynous Teiresias. She has no existence apart from Oedipus, but she, rather than Oedipus, emerges as the focus of the play. She appears as his projection of the all-accepting, totally loving wife/mother, who wants only to adore him and protect him from the names of son, father, king. These, in turn, constitute the "name of Oedipus," the identity that he cannot escape. Jocasta's quiet death, cast in a mood very different from that of the Sophoclean scene, reflects her instinctive knowledge and acceptance of this inevitable outcome.

These modern variants not only take a post-Freudian delight in breaking the incest taboo with a union felt as happy or innocent; they also hark back to one of the dynamics of the myth in the earliest periods, that is, a tendency to look beyond the core story of Oedipus and Jocasta and extend the narrative both backward to the past and forward to the following generation, as Sophocles himself does in *Antigone* and *Oedipus at Colonus*, albeit in different plays. Hence the tendency to include Laius (or his ghost) in some way (as Corneille and Voltaire do, following Seneca) or to look ahead (as Gide and Ghéon do, for example) to the coming tragedies of Oedipus' children. We may recall too the backward extension in the life of Gregory the Great (see Chapter 4), in which the "prequel" relates the incestuous union of brother and sister that produces the Gregory/Oedipus of this legend.

Visual and Musical Arts: Recent Adaptations

In addition to its various literary adaptations, *Oedipus* has had a long life in painting and music. The best known paintings are probably the monumental canvases depicting Oedipus and the Sphinx by Jean-Auguste-Dominique Ingres (1808) and Gustave Moreau (1864), now in the Louvre and the Metropolitan Museum in New York, respectively (figures 3 and 4). Ingres's Sphinx stands on a rock above Oedipus, surrounded by the limbs and skeletons of her victims. The narrow defile suggests the hero's passage through a dangerous trial, between death or rebirth. A man in the background looks on with a gesture of amazement or fear. Moreau retains Ingres' ghastly landscape but transforms the meeting into a deadly, quasi-erotic embrace, in which the outcome looks dubious for the hero. The modern Greek poet Constantine Cavafy (1863–1933) wrote a poem called "Oedipus," with an initial note saying that it was "written after reading a description" of this painting. Cavafy here focuses on the distant panorama beyond the Sphinx and, with a view to Sophocles' later Oedipus play, the *Oedipus Coloneus*, interprets the hero's glance as "full of melancholy" for his vision of the long road of life ahead, where "the Sphinx will accost him again / with more difficult and more baffling / enigmas that have no answer."[17] Sophocles' play has inspired many less known paintings, of which the most curious is perhaps Max Ernst's surrealist *Oedipus Rex* (figure 5;1922, now in a private collection in Paris), in which the piercing of Oedipus' ankles and/or his eyes may be suggested by two gigantic fingers that project from a darkened window and are transfixed by a large and shiny metal pin.

There have been musical settings or accompaniments of the myth ever since Gabrieli wrote the music for the choruses of the modern premier of Sophocles' *Oedipus* in 1585. Jean-Baptiste Lully wrote a ballet for Corneille's *Oedipe* in 1664, and Henry Purcell wrote some incidental music to a scene in a revival performance of the Dryden and Lee *Oedipus* in 1692. Rossini, Schubert, Mendelssohn, and Mussorgsky have all written music on the Oedipus theme. In 1852, the German composer Franz Lachner presented an oratorio version of the play, in a fairly literal German translation based on the work of J. J. Donner, with stage music, an overture, and the odes sung by a male chorus. The Italian composer Ruggiero Leoncavallo wrote an opera, *Edipo Re*, which was performed in 1920, the year after his death. More important is George Enescu's large-scale opera, *Oedipe*, first produced in 1936, but composed between 1921 and 1931, with a libretto by Edmond Fleg.[18] The third act in particular follows the rhythm of discovery in Sophocles' play, but the fourth act incorporates the *Oedipus at Colonus*, and this Oedipus too proclaims his moral innocence of the crimes that he has committed.

Around the same time, Igor Stravinsky produced a rather static oratorio version, *Oedipus Rex* (1928), with a Latin text written (originally in French) by Cocteau, a few years before his own dramatic version of 1934. The Stravinsky-Cocteau work has become widely known thanks to its showing on American public television networks in recent years. The somber background, lurid lighting, and larger-than-life puppet-like actors, with their masks and stylized gestures, convey the raw power of Sophocles' plot. The ritual background also gives a sense of the helplessness of the human characters and of the inevitability of the doom hanging over King Oedipus. But the production purchases atmospheric and gestural power at the expense of the subtleties and nuances, both linguistic and dramatic, of Sophocles' play, and the work ultimately owes more to Seneca than Sophocles. Widely known too, but totally antithetical in style and character, is the upbeat mood of the successful Broadway musical, *Gospel at Colonus* by Bob Telson and Lee Breuer (1984), which adapts *Oedipus at Colonus* to a Christian framework and to the music of the African-American spiritual.

The Italian director, Pier Paolo Pasolini, produced a film version, *Edipo Re*, in 1967. Like Cocteau's *Infernal Machine*, it is highly psychological, with a heavy Freudian emphasis on the mother-son incest. Pasolini tries to suggest the universality of the "oedipus complex" by telling the story in three different settings: ancient Thebes (for the dominant part of the film), a vaguely nineteenth-century village in southern Italy, and a contemporary industrial city. Pasolini tells the story biographically, from Oedipus' birth to his blinding and its aftermath, but makes heavy use of the Sophoclean text when he comes to the plague at Thebes. His Oedipus is an impulsive, passionate, sensual man, with little of the searcher after truth about him. Instead, the film (like the versions of Dryden and Hoffmansthal) lingers on the sexual attraction between Oedipus and the queen. It links the crime and the punishment not only by using Jocasta's huge brooch as the instrument of Oedipus' self-blinding, but also by focusing on it earlier in the several scenes of love-making in the marital bed.

The film tries to make up for its lack of philosophical depth by exploiting an anthropological fascination with the primitive. It is Seneca with shamans, one could say. Pasolini's Greece is more like North Africa or Egypt. Neither the Sphinx nor the gods are convincing presences. He shows in graphic detail the horrors that Sophocles removes to narration only. There are imaginative and powerful visual realizations of the Sophoclean material, however, in the exposure of the infant, in Oedipus' consultation of the Delphic oracle, in the questioning of Teiresias, and especially in the sequence in which the young, exhausted, confused Oedipus tries to run away from the encounter with Laius and then, with an access of some demonic energy from a hidden source, turns back to kill the servants and the old king.

The film has a raw, bitter power as a depiction of an unaccountable disaster that overwhelms innocent, puzzled, and helpless people. It reinterprets Sophocles in terms of the meaninglessness and alienation of modern life. This Oedipus at the end is not taught by suffering or heroized by his passage through the limits of human endurance, as is the Oedipus of *Oedipus at Colonus*, but is simply a blind young man lost and adrift in an impersonal modern metropolis.

In modern literature nearly every major modern poet has, at some time or another, drawn on some aspect of the Oedipus legend as a meditation on the

Figure 3 Jean-Auguste-Dominique Ingres, "Oedipus and the Sphinx." 1808. Paris, Louvre. Photograph courtesy of Giraudon/Art Resource, New York.

Figure 4 Gustave Moreau, "Oedipus and the Sphinx." 1864.
The Metropolitan Museum of Art, New York, Bequest of
William H. Herriman, 1921 (21.134.1).

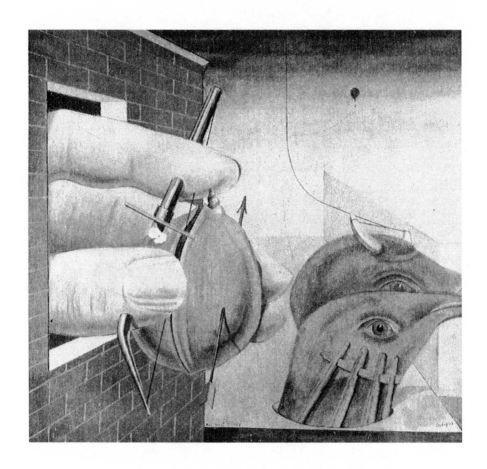

Figure 5 Max Ernst, "Oedipus Rex." 1922. Paris,
private collection.

human condition. Among them are Jorge Luis Borges, Richard Eberhart, William Empson, Randall Jarrell, Stanley Kunitz, Archibald MacLeish, James Merrill, Edwin Muir, Edith Sitwell, Stephen Spender, Alan Tate, and William Butler Yeats. Among novelists, Alain Robbe-Grillet in *The Erasers* and Thomas Pynchon in *The Crying of Lot 49*, with its character Mrs. Oedipa Maas, draw more or less explicitly on the plot structure of *Oedipus*.[19]

Figures like Teiresias have taken on a literary life of their own, from Ovid's account of his tranformation into a woman and back again (*Metamorphoses*, book 3) to T. S. Eliot's *The Waste Land* (1922), in which he is the prophet of a truth more prosaic than that of *Oedipus*: "I, Tiresias, though blind, throbbing between two lives, / Old man with wrinkled female breasts, can see . . ." Eliot also adapted *Oedipus at Colonus* to his late play *The Elder Statesman* (1958), in which the Furies are the old man's guilty memories of unsavory acts in his past, exorcized by confession and love.

Contemporary writers continue to find in the myth symbols and images that speak to a wide range of modern issues. In Alberto Moravia's *Il Dio Kurt* (*The God Kurt*, ca. 1948), a German commander artificially creates an Oedipus drama as part of the barbarity of his concentration camp. Writers in the Arab world, in Africa, and in Bali have adapted the play to local settings.[20] Muriel Rukeyser, in her prose-poem "Myth," finally, has the Sphinx turn the tables on Oedipus, but in a spirit different from Cocteau's use of the same device. Her Sphinx claims that Oedipus' traditional answer is wrong:

> "When you said Man," said Oedipus, "you include women too. Everyone knows that." She said, "That's what you think."[21]

This Sphinx is a female voice demanding to be heard in its own right after centuries of enduring "Man" as the only answer to the riddle.

AFTER FREUD: SOME CONTEMPORARY INTERPRETATIONS OF THE OEDIPUS MYTH

The contradictions surrounding the figure of Oedipus continue to fascinate students of the play and the myth, and I shall discuss here several influential recent interpreters, all French: Claude Lévi-Strauss, the founder of structural anthropology; the classicist Jean-Pierre Vernant; the literary and cultural critic René Girard; the post-Freudian psychoanalyst Jacques Lacan; and the Marxist and psychoanalytic thinkers Gilles Deleuze and Félix Guattari.

Lévi-Strauss views the myth in terms of a mediation of opposites—that is, the mind's attempt to make sense of the world by finding a middle term that reconciles fundamental contradictions, like life and death.[22] The myth consists of all of its versions taken together simultaneously, from Laius to Antigone's death, in *synchronic* order, not just in sequential (diachronic) order. This mode of reading reveals an underlying structure that has to do with the balance between underrating and overrating kin relations. Killing one's father, for example, is an undervaluation of kin ties; Antigone's insistence on burying her brother at the cost of her own life is an overvaluation.

For Lévi-Strauss, incest and parricide are not the real subject of the myth. They are only elements in a larger, signifying system, a "code," which can be understood only in relation to other elements in the system. The extremes of overvaluing or undervaluing kin ties express logical contradictions and their mediation. Tracing the house of Oedipus back to its founder, Cadmus, Lévi-Strauss sees the successive generations as alternating between the overvaluation and undervaluation of kin ties. He finds another constant in the themes of walking and lameness in the family of Oedipus, and he decodes this motif of lameness as pointing to autochthony (being born from the earth). This combination of elements is the clue to the logic or mental "structure" underlying the myth: it provides a model for reconciling the primordial belief that humans are sprung from the earth (i. e., born from only "one") with the knowledge that humans are born from the sexual union of a man and a woman (that is, from "two"). To make sense of our human identity, in other words, we have to reconcile the conflicting propositions, "born from different, born from same"; or, in Freudian terms, we have to understand "how *one* can be born from *two*."

Many critics have rejected Lévi-Strauss's focus on autochthony as arbitrary, and this motif is probably less applicable to Sophocles' version of the myth than to Aeschylus'.[23] Still, his essay is a bold and pioneering attempt to read the myth in terms of its underlying logic of simultaneously coexisting opposites. The logic of "same" versus "other" is certainly relevant to other parts of the myth, although not necessarily in the terms set out by Lévi-Strauss. It may, for example, apply to the ambivalence between the hero's conflict with the father and his reenacting the role of the father—being *other* than the father or being the *same* as the father by repeating his pattern of violence and aggression.

Jean-Pierre Vernant also reads the myth in terms of an underlying logic of paradox, but he grounds this approach in a more historical situation.[24] Oedipus' position as the ruler and the perpetrator of incest belongs to the model of excessive behavior often attributed to "tyrants" in early history, like the sixth-century tyrant Periander.[25] Some fifty or sixty years after Sophocles' play, Plato will combine incest and unrestrained appetite as features of the lawlessness and bestiality that characterize the deformed soul of the tyrant (*Republic*, 9.571c-d). The pattern appears in the mythicized accounts of Roman history's most infamous tyrants, Tarquin's rape of Lucretia (Livy, *Histories*, 1.58–59) and the emperor Nero's alleged incest with his mother Agrippina (Suetonius, *Life of Nero*, chap. 28).

Oedipus' movement from high to low, Vernant suggests, also parallels the ancient Greek institution of the scapegoat or *pharmakos*.[26] In a ceremony that was still performed in Sophocles' day, two scapegoats—people symbolically laden with all the troubles and pollutions of the community—were driven through the town and then ritually expelled (originally they may have been stoned to death). Sophocles' Oedipus is not, of course, literally expelled, but he wants to be, and in any case he gives up his kingship. In Vernant's structure of reversals, the plague creates a situation in which the people are ready to sacrifice their king as a scapegoat. This is in fact almost the situation in Voltaire's adaptation of the play. By bringing king and scapegoat together in a single person, Oedipus reveals the scapegoat as "the king's double, but reversed like the carnival kings crowned for the duration of the festival, when order is turned upside down and the social hierarchies reversed: . . . and in these circumstances the one who sits upon the throne must be the lowest, the most ugly, the most ridiculous, the most criminal" (Vernant 104).

Vernant makes a further connection between the expulsion of the once powerful king and the Athenian democracy's institution of ostracism, begun in the early years of the fifth century. In the system of ostracism the people vote to select a powerful leader to go into exile. The system was devised to avert a political crisis that could result in civil war or the usurpation of power by a tyrant (in the word's original sense, as one who gained power by force rather than by election or inheritance). Oedipus, then, simultaneously the highest and the lowest in the city, is both the leader who accepts ostracism and the scapegoat who bears all that is ugliest and most harmful. Illuminating as this structure is, recent critics, influenced in part by a postmodern esthetic that emphasizes indeterminacy and lack of final closure, find these patterns too symmetrical and too static. They point out the inadequacy of the scapegoat mechanism, for Oedipus is not in fact expelled at the end, and the play leaves both the plague and his future exile in suspension. For the main outlines of Vernant's thesis, however, it may suffice that the pattern is adumbrated, even if it is not completely realized in the action. After the blinding, Oedipus makes a whole series of statements that hint at the scapegoat pattern. Throw me into the sea, he says at 1411–12. He is a pollution that not even the earth or the light can receive, says Creon shortly afterwards (1424–28)—although his response is to close Oedipus up in the house, not send him forth (1429). Throw me out of the land, and let me dwell on the mountains, is Oedipus' continuing request (1436–37, 1449–54).

For René Girard in his *Violence and the Sacred* the central issue is the control of violence.[27] Tragedy forces society to recognize the violence that lies at its center. The Oedipus myth, Girard suggests, shows all masculine relations as "based on reciprocal acts of violence" (48). Laius' violence against his son is perpetuated in the son's violence against the father. The cultural distinction between "father" and "son" is destroyed, and the plague that follows is an expression of this disease of random violence. Order is restored by the unanimous selection and expulsion of a scapegoat, which enables the community to reunite and thus to escape from its endless cycle of revenge and retribution.

According to Girard, the plague parallels the parricide and the incest as the sign of an infectious violence that results from the destruction of differences. The action consists in a desperate hunt for a scapegoat, a sacrificial victim (78).

With the identification of Oedipus as the criminal, the crisis can be resolved and the violence directed toward its proper victim, not randomly against the victims of the plague. By thus giving violence back to the gods, making it sacred and taboo once more, the society can restore its lost sense of differentiation and order.

Girard's stimulating essay is valuable for its recognition of the collapse of differences as the focus of the crisis depicted in the play and the importance in the myth of the equivalence between Laius and Oedipus in their respective aggressive acts. Yet Sophocles' text (unlike the later versions by Corneille and Voltaire) does not place much emphasis on the mechanism of sacrifice and, as we have seen, leaves the actual expulsion of Oedipus at the end up in the air. Girard's theory works less well for this play than for others, such as Euripides' *Bacchae*. His emphasis on the arbitrariness in the selection of the scapegoat and on the victim's submission also dissolves the concern with personal responsibility and justice that are important in both the play and the myth.

Although Girard makes a valid attempt to find a mythic structure concealed by the moral interpretation of the play, one cannot help suspecting that he superimposes his own reading on the mythical material: "From the purely religious point of view, the surrogate victim—or more simply, the final victim— inevitably appears as a being who submits to violence without provoking a reprisal; a supernatural being who sows violence to reap peace; a mysterious savior who visits affliction on mankind in order subsequently to restore it to good health" (86). Girard's savior-victim here is more like Christ in the *Gospels* than Oedipus. His benign view of sacrificial ritual as a "curative process" (83), furthermore, does not take sufficient account of the cruelty and pitiless violence that such rituals can express in tragedy, especially in the perverted form of human sacrifice (as, for instance, in Euripides' *Hecuba* or *Iphigenia in Aulis*). In such cases the ritual sacrifice, far from pointing to release and resolution in "violent unanimity" (101), uses the ritual as a symbolic expression of all the obsessive passions and destructive fixations that cause the tragic situation.

Given the fact that the most influential modern reinterpretation of Oedipus comes from Freud (see Chapter 4), some of the most intense contemporary discussions of the myth take the form of a critique of Freudian theories. I will mention here the two most prominent, those of the psychoanalyst Jacques Lacan and the cultural critics Gilles Deleuze and Félix Guattari.

Lacan closely follows Freud in his concern with the way in which the myth of Oedipus reflects the workings of the unconscious. Rather than seeing in the myth the confirmation of psychoanalytic theory, however, Lacan emphasizes the relevance of the figure of Oedipus, particularly the Oedipus of the *Tyrannus*, for psychoanalytic practice. For Lacan the myth, as dramatized by Sophocles, illustrates the way in which the unconscious finds its way into language, with all the blockages, misunderstandings, and misrecognitions that occur when the subject tries to name his desire. The unconscious is here understood as inseparable from language, but this is an intransitive, noncommunicating language, or as

Lacan puts it, "The unconscious is the Discourse of the Other." In the terms of the Oedipus myth as structured by Sophocles, that "Other" is the oracle of Apollo at Delphi. It is a voice of the Other because its discourse is misunderstood by the ego, the conscious self. For Freud too the oracle is the voice of the unconscious (see Chapter 4), but in a narrower and more deterministic way.

Lacan departs from Freud more radically in his conception of the "oedipus complex" in the development of the personality. He focuses the oedipus complex not on the "family romance," with its incestuous and parricidal impulses, but on the process by which an infant comes to construct himself as a subject with the acquisition of language. At this stage the infant, through the otherness of language, separates himself from an undifferentiated closeness to the mother and passes into the realm of the Law and the Father, which Lacan calls the realm of the "symbolic." The child thus internalizes the prohibitions against incest which form the basis of the Law and are dramatized in the Oedipus myth. Oedipus, then, becomes the archetypal figure for Lacanian psychoanalysis not because he acts out his repressed desires of parricide and incest (as in the Freudian paradigm) but because he becomes able to speak the hidden truth of the oracle with full understanding of its meaning.

Lacan's version of the "oedipus complex," though still based on Sophocles' play, thus has a different emphasis from Freud's. For Lacan the father, as the barrier to the full enjoyment of sexual (and other) pleasure symbolized by incest with the mother, functions not as an actual agent whom the parricidal son must kill, but rather as the Name of the Father, the figure of the Law, associated with the language that the child acquires as he moves from the infant's preverbal and pre-oedipal stage to the "symbolic" realm where he introjects the restraints and prohibitions of society.[28]

Lacan also goes beyond Freud in his interest in the *Oedipus at Colonus* as a work in which Oedipus not only brings his repressed life history into language but fully accepts himself as he is, including the ugliness of what his life has held. In the shadow of his imminent death he faces and acknowledges the potential chaos, meaninglessness, and horror of life.[29] In reading the play as Oedipus' final "tearing apart" or "laceration of himself" in his nothingness, Lacan concentrates on the single verse, "Am I made man in the hour when I cease to be" (line 393, literally, "When I no longer exist, am I then a man"). Lacan interprets the line to mean that life is only a detour on the way to death and has no other meaning than its ending in death. But this nihilistic reading ignores the gods' validation of Oedipus in Sophocles' ending and neglects the ritual dimension of Oedipus' death and the cultic process of heroization that marks his mysterious disappearance in the play.

The *Anti-Oedipus* of Gilles Deleuze and Félix Guattari (1972) is a wide-ranging, post-Nietzschean critique of what they call the "imperialism of Oedipus," which they view as the source of the social and personal ills of Western society.[30] These derive from the modern acceptance of the Freudian oedipal triangle, the insistence on the "family romance" of father-mother-son as the determining influence on emotional life and hence on every area of behavior, from the subjective sense of the body to politics and macro-economic structures. The "oedipalized" family fosters structures of repression and domination, including an obsession with patriarchal power, possessive sexuality, fragmented and neurotic individualism, and ultimately capitalism. The vast, complex, and impassioned global argument of this book is only indirectly concerned with Sophocles' play. It indicates, nevertheless, that Oedipus is not only an inescapable cultural heritage but continues to function as the center of lively debates and discourses. Oedipus remains an intellectual artifact that we seem determined to resist but somehow cannot quite remove from our consciousness.

Recent Trends in Literary Criticism

As this sketch of the reception of the *Oedipus* over some twenty-five centuries illustrates, every age reads its legacy from the past in terms of its own needs, concerns, and experiences. As one would expect, the cataclysms and nuclear and environmental threats of the past fifty years and the consequent weakening of traditional religious and philosophical belief in a beneficent universe have affected the way critics view Greek tragedy. Contemporary interpreters see *Oedipus*, and Greek tragedy in general, as an expression of doubt and anguish rather than of piety, as a questioning of meaning rather than an assertion of meaning. Post-World-War-II critics are thus less inclined to explain Oedipus' suffering by a "tragic flaw" of anger or pride, and relatively few regard the play as the triumph of an equitable divine order.

Interpreters of *Oedipus* and of Sophocles generally over the past four or five decades can be divided into those who emphasize the hero and those who emphasize the gods. These have sometimes been labeled as *humanists* and *theologizers*, respectively, or hero-worshipers and pietists. The humanistic view, eloquently represented by Cedric Whitman in *Sophocles: A Study of Heroic Humanism* (1951), has Oedipus as an individual of heroic grandeur and remarkable energy and courage. Despite the cruel trick that life and the gods play on him, he has an unflinching determination to learn the truth about himself and has the strength to live with that terrible truth even when its horror is revealed.

Bernard Knox in the *Heroic Temper* (1964) and, to a lesser extent, in his earlier *Oedipus at Thebes* (1957), develops a darker version of the humanistic view. The focus is still on the hero, but his integrity and unyielding devotion to ideals of honor and dignity have another side in stubborn self-centeredness, transgressive overreaching, dangerous overconfidence, and vengefulness. Powerful loyalty and commitment can engender powerful hatred and fierce bitterness. Rather than serving as a model of excellence or virtue (*aretê*), the hero is a puzzle and a problem. His independence and greatness of spirit are of the same fabric as his egotism, narrow intransigence, and tendency to excess and violence. Among the heroes of Sophocles' other plays, Ajax, Electra, and Philoctetes are perhaps the clearest examples of this, but we can see some of these traits in Oedipus too.

According to the theological view, the heart of *Oedipus Tyrannus* is not the hero so much as the vision of the gods and the world order that emerges from the action. For moralistic interpreters, of whom the best known is perhaps C. M. Bowra in his *Sophoclean Tragedy* (1944), Oedipus is guilty of terrible crimes, and the gods cause his downfall to illustrate their enforcement of moral laws. Oedipus himself is a model of the fragility of human happiness and the precariousness of human life in general.

A very different theological orientation appears in E. R. Dodds' celebrated essay, "On Misunderstanding the *Oedipus Rex*" (1966) and R. P. Winnington-Ingram's book, *Sophocles: An Interpretation* (1980). Dodds and Winnington-Ingram agree that Oedipus' acts violate the laws of gods and men but stress that he is morally and legally innocent. His downfall illustrates a world order whose workings do not square with human conceptions of justice. The tragic dimension of the play lies precisely in the gap between the remote, incomprehensible gods and any sense of humanly meaningful suffering. Sophocles' traditional "piety" is not to be understood as a complacent acceptance of beneficent gods but rather as a recognition of the inscrutable and mysteriously "other" in divinities who exist in a far off realm untouched by age, change, or time.

Not all of these positions are mutually incompatible. Winnington-Ingram, for instance, makes an interesting synthesis of Knox's darker heroism and a theological interpretation of Sophocles. What makes life tragic in Sophocles' view, he suggests (to simplify a little), is the way human nature and the gods (who are the embodiment of the way the world is constituted) interact to produce suffering for mankind. Tragedy occurs when character and events converge so that men destroy themselves and those closest to them, despite, and sometimes because of, their best qualities.

ATHENS AND THEBES

As we have noted in Chapter 11, *Oedipus Tyrannus* and to a much greater extent *Oedipus at Colonus* fit a pervasive tragic pattern of contrasts between Athens and Thebes, studied by Froma Zeitlin and Pierre Vidal-Naquet.[31] In Athens the polluted past and the aberrant outsider can be integrated into a viable civic order, whereas in Thebes the distinction between insider and outsider becomes a mass of intertwined contradictions whose result is a destructive fusion of opposites and a consequent disintegration of house and city. Particularly illuminating are the parallels that Zeitlin draws between Oedipus in the *Tyrannus* and Dionysus in the *Bacchae*. Both figures are strangers and insiders whose entrance into Thebes and claims to legitimacy in the city veer ambiguously between salvation and destruction for the city. The Athens of the *Oedipus at Colonus*, on the other hand, takes just the opposite approach to the mysterious and numinous

Stranger, whom it can bring across the boundary between wild and civic space and incorporate into the polis as a hero who ultimately assures the city's safety rather than causes its ruin.

Metatragedy

In the last two decades, the study of Greek tragedy has become increasingly focused on the ways in which the plays call attention to their own dramatic processes, to the ways in which the play itself functions as a uniquely theatrical representation of reality.[32] I have touched on some of these issues above, in Chapter 10, particularly in the scene of the blinded Oedipus' emergence from the palace. Here the play not only uses the full dramatic power of a stunning entrance but also reflects on its own use of spectacle as a theatrical device. Indicative of an analogous literary self-consciousness is the chorus' question in the second stasimon, "If such acts are held in honor, why should I dance?" (895–96). The chorus is here agonizing over the wrongdoing in the murder of Laius and trying to reconcile traditional piety with the concealment of such a crime for so long, but the lines also refer to the activity of the chorus itself at that moment (*choros* is itself related to *choreuein*, "to dance"). And so the passage is calling attention to the social and ritual context of its performance and is implicitly reflecting on the meaning of all performances of the tragic chorus at the great civic festivals, that is, their meaning and purpose for the community as a whole.[33]

Critics have gone much farther (perhaps too far) in looking at the action in terms of the play's self-conscious arranging and manipulating dramatic roles and of actors who play, change, or lose roles. There is no question that the Athenians of the late fifth century, now experienced theater-goers, were much interested in the implicit esthetics of these plays and, as Aristophanes' comedies attest, avidly discussed such questions. The danger of this approach, if carried too far, is to intellectualize the works and to turn them into allegories of self-referentiality, which would clearly be a misplacement of effort in the case of *Oedipus*. Nevertheless, the traditional notion that only Euripides' plays engage in this kind of intellectual reflection on his art must clearly be revised.

Gender Issues: Women in Tragedy

The burgeoning of feminist scholarship in the study of Greek tragedy has led to further examination of the ways in which these plays either reaffirm or question the dominant social and political ideology of fifth-century Athens, which includes the secondary position of women and their exclusion from public life. *Oedipus* has hitherto received relatively little attention, but there has been a growing recognition of the parallelism between the tragedy of Jocasta and that of Oedipus. In an interesting and accessible book, the French scholar Nicole

Loraux has pointed out the ways in which Greek tragedy sets the deaths of women apart from male deaths, confines them, ideally, to domestic space, and tends to mark them as unheroic. In this respect Jocasta, unlike Eurydice, wife of Creon in the *Antigone*, supports the dominant model: she effaces herself by a private death inside the house and, as in Homer's *Odyssey*, uses the noose (the approved instrument of female suicide) rather than the sword.[34] When Euripides radically reconceives Jocasta's character in his *Phoenician Women*, however, he has her kill herself with the sword of one of her slain sons on the field of battle (1455–59), not deep within the house.

Although the *Oedipus* is very much Oedipus' play and does not offer the scope for female heroism or for the problematizing of females' roles as do the *Trachiniae* or *Antigone* or contemporary Euripidean plays like *Medea* and *Hippolytus*, it should be recalled that it is Jocasta who realizes and accepts the awful truth, while Oedipus continues to deceive himself with his deluded trust in his life's luck as "a child of Chance" (1054–85). In the clarity and courage of her recognition, it is she who in fact takes on the role of the traditional hero (like Ajax) whose sense of shame and honor compels him or her to suicide. We may recall Cixous' contemporary recasting of the myth to bring out just this superior insight of Jocasta into the tragic situation (see above). Even in the fifth century a skilled actor (male, of course) could bring Jocasta's tragedy closer to the level of Oedipus'. In the scene with the Corinthian Messenger in particular such a peformance, by gesture and intonation, could highlight her growing suspicion of the horror about to break forth upon them and her desperate struggle both to keep her own composure and to shelter Oedipus for as long as she can.

Nevertheless, Jocasta's suicide shows significant differences from the male heroic pattern. Oedipus, ignorant at the moment when she has guessed the truth, mistakenly attributes to her a concern with "shame" and "dishonor" (1078–81); yet in the Messenger's report of her death (1241–50) she says nothing of the honor that is such a high masculine value. Instead, her last words, inside her chamber, are about the bed, marriage, procreation, birth, and children. Her actions here too are the characteristic female gestures of rushing toward the marriage bed and tearing her hair. Oedipus, by contrast, disgraced and disfigured, insists on a public display of himself to "all the Thebans" (1287–91).

In this combination of the language of lamentation and of marriage, her end has the form of what Richard Seaford has called the "tragic wedding." This recurrent pattern in Greek tragedy brings together female mourning, marriage, and death in a narrative that either sacrifices a virgin bride or else places a married woman's death in close proximity to the marital bed. Marriage ritual and funerary ritual, with their accompanying laments, are fused together (as in the death of Sophocles' Antigone or of Jason's bride in Euripides' *Medea*, wearing the poisoned bridal crown).[35] This metaphorical equivalence between marriage and funeral rites may tell us something about women's lives. The satirical sixth-century B.C.E. poet, Hipponax, wrote, "Two days are sweetest for a woman, when one marries her and when one celebrates her funeral at her death."[36]

171

From the point of view of the esthetics of the form, classical tragedy, like classical epic, uses the bloody suicides or sacrificial deaths of women, whether virgins or mothers, as a spectactular feature of its literary effect. Critics differ as to whether this effect is an exploitation of violence against women by a male-centered and sometimes misogynist culture, or whether it reflects a compassionate acknowledgment of the suffering in women's lives. Here, as elsewhere, it would make a difference if we knew for certain whether women were among the spectators of the plays in the fifth century (see above, Chapter 3).

DECONSTRUCTION, INDETERMINACY, AND RESISTANCE TO CLOSURE

The deconstructive and semiotic approaches to literature have emphasized the fact that literary works are constructs of the formal conventions of their signifying systems, not pronouncements of final truths. In this view, literature is the field in which "truth" shows its dependence on the verbal and other filters through which it is formulated and communicated. Such "truth" as literature contains is an elusive construct of our rhetorical forms. Literary texts, then, do not have definitive meanings; they can only point to their own construction of meaning, their own "textuality."

In its extreme form, such an approach reduces literature to sollipsistic vacuity if it insists that literary works are *only* "about" their own communicative methods and signifying systems and nothing else. But the fact that artworks may reveal their creators' interest in exposing their dependency on sign-systems and symbolic forms and conventions to communicate their "reality" does not mean that they can communicate nothing else. Taken in a more limited way, however, this self-consciousness about signification can lead to useful correctives of over-simplified readings and make us aware of the "unnaturalness" of literary discourse, the artifice and constructedness of the work of art. A deconstructive reading of the plot of the *Oedipus*, for example, refuses to accept the surface verisimilitude as a given and necessary condition of the plot's functioning; instead, it calls attention to the arbitrariness of the design that the work has imposed on its audience, an arbitrariness which the play designates as the role of "chance," *tychê*. The deconstructive critic, then, sees his or her task as unmasking the author's tyranny over the discourse and revealing the control and constraint that the work exercises over the "communicative transaction."[37]

This sensitivity to the work's self-conscious artifice leads in another influential direction in recent study of the play, that is, an emphasis not so much on the play's formal perfections as on its tensions, disharmonies, and contradictions, on those problematical features of the plot that may reveal a more open, less certain, less intelligible vision of reality. Here the author appears not so much as the omniscient architect of a totally coherent world order as the designer of sets of possible hypotheses about that order, none of which is necessarily definitive. Even scholars not particularly interested in grounding their interpretations in a theoretical framework have come increasingly to accept the suspended, unresolved endings of Sophocles' plays as a basic feature of his dramatic art, in contrast to earlier idealizations of his work as embodiment of the perfect harmonies and symmetries of "the "classical."[38] These interpretive trends are doubtless influenced, albeit indirectly, by a contemporary sense of the tentative and precarious quality of our judgments about ultimate meanings, particularly at a time when the proliferating researches and theoretical models in astronomy and cosmology, biochemistry, biology, and neuroscience are changing our fundamental ways of viewing the physical world and ourselves.

In the case of the *Oedipus*, recent interpreters have concentrated on the play's areas of uncertainty, nonclosure, and suspension. Some, like Frederick Ahl, have tried to argue that the play offers no final proof that Oedipus killed Laius; Oedipus prematurely convicts himself only by his fallacious acceptance of rhetorical arguments.[39] Although Ahl's view cannot be sustained, Sophocles does leave some important gaps in his story, especially the indefinite interval between the death of Laius, the accession of Oedipus to the throne, and the Old Herdsman's return to Thebes, or the question of whether Laius or Jocasta ordered the exposure of the infant Oedipus. Pietro Pucci, with greater justice, has emphasized the elusiveness of truth in the play's interaction between necessity and chance, embodied, respectively, in the oracles and *tychê*, the questions about the efficacy of the oracles, and particularly the unresolved situation of both Oedipus and Thebes at the end of the play.[40] Not only are we not sure at the end if Oedipus will go into exile, but we cannot be sure whether he has truly gained understanding or is only continuing old patterns of behavior.[41]

Many of these questions have surfaced, inevitably, in earlier chapters, and they are important issues for the interpretation of the play. Whereas previous scholars have tried to resolve these indeterminacies on one side or the other by sifting through the language of the play, the recent tendency has been to accept them as fundamental to the work and in fact as reflective of the nature of literary "meaning" as a process of opening up endlessly ramifying possibilities (or, in the language of Jacques Derrida, "disseminations").

My own view, which is implicit in the interpretation of the play that I have put forth in this book, is that Sophocles holds back from full closure not because he shares a postmodern fondness for open-endedness and indeterminacy, but rather because this ending corresponds to the kind of life pattern that the play seeks to convey. Even though we are changed by and may learn from catastrophic experience, we never fully escape what we are. And so Oedipus and Creon at the end reenact their earlier differences and continue to exemplify deep-seated traits of personality. The forces that initially brought them into conflict are still in place at the end. The two men still exhibit the human passions that will carry the story on to its next phase, and they are still circumscribed by the limited mortal horizons that make them unable to prevent that next phase from repeating the tragic patterns of the past.[42] The end, like the beginning, depicts its hero's life as a series of moments, crises, and uncertainties, in which decision and resolve are required but in which the outcome can never be foreseen. The play shows a life determined by its past, to be sure, but always becoming something new and unexpected as the present merges into its unknown but ever freshly created future.

The fact that the play can invite such diverse interpretive positions, along with their various permutations and combinations, does not mean that Sophocles could not tell us clearly and precisely what he wanted to say. Rather, he has condensed into a single work the problem of the meaning of existence, focused on a single strong, vivid personality, and presented this to us with the balance and complexity that the task requires. If scholars continue to differ over the meaning of the play, it is also because intelligent and sensitive men and women continue to differ over the meanings of art and life.

NOTES

1. This information is given in the prose Argument (Second Hypothesis) prefixed to some of the medieval manuscripts of Sophocles' plays on the authority of the compiler Dicaearchus, (probably) of the late fourth century B.C.E., which adds that Sophocles won second prize. Philocles' victory is elsewhere attested only in a passing remark by the second-century C.E. writer Aelius Aristeides (*Oration* 46, p. 334 Dindorf). See R. C. Jebb, *Sophocles: The Plays and Fragments*. Part 1, *The Oedipus Tyrannus*. 3d ed. (Cambridge: Cambridge University Press, 1893), Introduction, xxx–xxxi. According to the ancient *Life*, Sophocles never won less than second prize. We must remember, of course, that each of three competing tragedians in the dramatic competition of the City Dionysia presented three plays, and considerations other than artistic merit could influence the judges, who were chosen by lot.

2. Suetonius, *Life of Julius Caesar* 56, and *Life of Nero* 21 and 46. Nero was rumored to have had incestuous relations with his mother.

3. Translation here from David Russell and Michael Winterbottom, eds., *Ancient Literary Criticism* (Oxford: Oxford University Press, 1972), 106; my italics. The fullest discussion of the question is Suzanne Saïd, *La faute tragique* (Paris: Maspero, 1978), especially 26–31, 212–16, 452–54 on the *Oedipus*.

4. A full account of the influences of the *Oedipus* on later literature would require a very large volume; what follows is necessarily very selective. For further discussion, see the appropriate works cited in the notes below and in the Bibliography. For a detailed list of works influenced by Sophocles, see Jane Davidson Reid, *The Oxford Guide to Classical Mythology in the Arts, 1300–1990s* (New York: Oxford University Press, 1993), 754–72.

5. Two of these illuminated manuscripts are illustrated in John Boswell, *The Kindness of Strangers: The Abandonment of Children in Western Europe from Late Antiquity to the Renaissance* (New York: Pantheon Books, 1988), plates 2 and 3, after p. 270. The tendency to make Oedipus' conflict with the Sphinx physical rather than intel-

lectual runs throughout the history of the myth, from the fifth century B.C.E. on: see Chapter 5.

6. See R. R. Bolgar, *The Classical Heritage and its Beneficiaries* (Cambridge: Cambridge University Press, 1954), 504.

7. Such, for instance, was the *Edippo* of Giovan Andrea dell' Anguilara (1566), which uses the Senecan motifs of Manto and necromancy but, unlike Seneca, also insists on the fundamental innocence of Oedipus: see Guido Paduano, *Lunga storia di Edipo Re: Freud, Sofocle e il teatro occidentale* (Turin: Einaudi, 1994), 266–70.

8. The quotation is from the contemporary letter of Antonio Riccoboni to the mayor of Vicenza, describing the performance, in R. D. Dawe, ed. and trans., *Sophocles, The Classical Heritage* (New York: Garland, 1996), 3; for details of this performance, see also Pierre Vidal-Naquet, ed., "Oedipus in Vicenza and in Paris," in J.-P. Vernant and P. Vidal-Naquet, *Myth and Tragedy in Ancient Greece*, trans. J. Lloyd (New York: Zone Books, 1990), 361–80; also in Dawe 13–31, with a different translation.

9. See Paduano, *Lunga storia di Edipo Re*, 285.

10. So, for instance, the *Jocaste* of Louis-Léon Félicité de Lauraguais (1781), discussed by Paduano, *Lunga storia di Edipo Re*, 329–332.

11. Hölderlin's translations belong to the period (1797–1804). For discussion, see the essays of Wolfgang Schadewaldt and R. B. Harrison, respectively, in R. D. Dawe, ed., *Sophocles, The Classical Heritage*, 102–110, 111–36; also, on Hölderlin's *Antigone*, see George Steiner, *Antigones* (Oxford: Clarendon Press, 1984), 66–106.

12. On the possible influence of Wagner, see Paduano, *Lunga storia di Edipo Re*, 135–37.

13. A variant of this view, with the figures reversed, is put forth (but as interpretation, not fiction) by Philip Vellacott, *Sophocles and Oedipus* (Ann Arbor: University of Michigan Press, 1971), 104ff. Oedipus, Vellacott argues, knows the truth all along and wants to lead Jocasta to acknowledging it.

14. Francis Fergusson, *The Idea of a Theater* (Garden City, N.Y.: Doubleday Anchor Books, 1955), 212. I have kept Fergusson's translation of Teiresias' remark here.

15. One may wonder of this motif of Péladan's suggested to Cocteau the detail of Jocasta's keeping the cradle of her lost child at the foot of her bed.

16. For the affinities with the all-inclusive love and a "solitude à deux" on the model of Tristan and Isolde, see Paduano, *Lunga storia di Edipo Re*, 234–39.

17. Cavafy, "Oedipus," in Rae Dalven, trans., *The Complete Poems of Cavafy* (New York: Harcourt, Brace and World, 1961), 196.

18. On Enescu's *Oedipe*, see Paduano, *Lunga storia di Edipo Re*, 150–52.

19. For a recent discussion of the relation between Oedipus and Pynchon's novel, see J. Peter Euben, *The Tragedy of Political Theory* (Princeton: Princeton University Press, 1990), 59–63, 281–308.

20. For some of the African and Muslim versions, see Colette Astier, *Le mythe d' Oedipe* (Paris: Armand Colin, 1974), 125–29; Jacques Scherer, *Dramaturgies d' Oedipe* (Paris: Presses Universitaires de France, 1987), 176–79; and also Paduano, *Lunga storia di Edipo Re*, 186–92 on Tawfiq al-Hakim.

21. Muriel Rukeyser, *The Collected Poems* (New York: McGraw-Hill, 1982), 498.

22. C. Lévi-Strauss, "The Structural Study of Myth," in *Structural Anthropology*, trans. C. Jacobson and B. C. Schoepf (Garden City, N.Y.: Doubleday, 1967), 202–28, especially 210–13.

23. For a probing critique of Lévi-Strauss's interpretation within the narrative material of the myth, see Terence S. Turner, "Narrative Structure and Mythopoesis: A Critique and Reformulation of Structuralist Concepts of Myth, Narrative and Poetics," *Arethusa* 10 (1977), 103–63.

24. Jean-Pierre Vernant, "Ambiguity and Reversal. On the Enigmatic Structure of *Oedipus Rex*" (1970), in J.-P. Vernant and Pierre Vidal-Naquet, eds., *Myth and Tragedy in Ancient Greece* (above, n. 8), 113–40; see also Vernant's later discussion, "From Oedipus to Periander: Lameness, Tyranny, Incest in Legend and History" (1982), ibid. 207–26, which views the myth in terms of the contradictions and tensions surrounding the archaic and classical views of the tyrant.

25. On Periander and incest, see above, Chapter 4. Herodotus does not mention incest, but does tell a story of necrophilia, Periander's intercourse with his wife, Melissa, after her death (*Histories* 5.92.2)

26. Vernant, "Ambiguity and Reversal" (above n. 24), especially 131–38.

27. René Girard, *Violence and the Sacred*, trans. P. Gregory (Baltimore: Johns Hopkins University Press, 1979), especially 68–88. For a recent critique of Girard focusing on the *Oedipus Tyrannus*, see R. Drew Griffith, "Oedipus Pharmakos? Alleged Scapegoating in Sophocles' *Oedipus the King*," *Phoenix* 47 (1993), 94–114, especially 96–102.

28. The place of *Oedipus* in contemporary discussions of the oedipus complex continues vigorously, even in the popular media, as one can see from the article by Sarah Boxer, "How Oedipus Is Losing his Complex," *The New York Times*, December 12, 1997, A13, A15.

29. For Lacan's comments on the *Oedipus at Colonus*, see Jacques Lacan, *The Seminar of Jacques Lacan*, ed. Jacques-Alain Miller, *Book II: The Ego in Freud's Theory and the Technique of Psychoanalysis 1954–55*, trans. Sylvana Tomaselli (Cambridge: Cambridge University Press, 1988), 209–10, 229–33. The phrases quoted in the text are on p. 229. For recent accounts of Lacan's approach to the Oedipus myth, with further bibliography, see Shoshana Felman, *Jacques Lacan and the Adventure of Insight: Psychoanalysis in Contemporary Culture* (Cambridge, MA: Harvard University Press, 1987), Chapter 5, especially 128–48, and Pietro Pucci, *Oedipus and the Fabrication of the Father* (Baltimore, MD: Johns Hopkins University Press, 1992), 49–50.

30. Gilles Deleuze and Félix Guattari, *Anti-Oedipus: Capitalism and Schizophrenia* (1972), trans. R. Hurley, M. Seem, H. R. Lane (Minneapolis: University of Minnesota Press, 1983).

31. See above, Chapter 4, end; Pierre Vidal-Naquet, "Oedipus Between Two Cities: An Essay on the *Oedipus at Colonus*," in J.-P. Vernant and Pierre Vidal-Naquet, eds., *Myth and Tragedy in Ancient Greece* (above n. 8), 329–59. See also my remarks in my *Dionysiac Poetics and Euripides' Bacchae*, 2nd ed. (Princeton, N.J.: Princeton University Press, 1997), 367–68 on Zeitlin's work, and my essay, "Frontières, étrangers et éphèbes dans la tragédie grecque: réflexions sur l'oeuvre de Pierre Vi-

dal-Naquet," in F. Hartog, P. Schmitt, and A. Schnapp, eds., *Pierre Vidal-Naquet, un historien dans la cité* (Paris: La Découverte, 1998), 87–109, on Vidal-Naquet. For a survey of recent trends in the literary criticism of tragedy see Simon Goldhill in P. E. Easterling, ed., *Cambridge Companion to Greek Tragedy*, 324–47; also M. S. Silk, ed., *Tragedy and the Tragic*.

32. For a survey of recent work in metatheater, apropos of Euripides' *Bacchae*, see my *Dionysiac Poetics* (preceding note), 369–78; also Peter Burian in P. E. Easterling, ed., *Cambridge Companion to Greek Tragedy*, 193–98.

33. The self-referential meaning of these lines is discussed by Knox, *Oedipus at Thebes* 47. For further discussion, see my *Tragedy and Civilization* 235–36; Albert Henrichs, " 'Why Should I Dance?': Choral Self-Referentiality in Greek Tragedy," *Arion*, 3rd Series, vol. 3, no. 1 (1994/95), 56–111, especially 65–73 on *Oedipus*; Mark Ringer, *Electra and the Empty Urn* (Chapel Hill, NC: University of North Carolina Press, 1998), 88–90.

34. Nicole Loraux, *Tragic Ways of Killing a Woman* (1985), tr. A. Forster (Cambridge, MA: Harvard University Press, 1987), 14–15. See also her remarks on Jocasta and the female body in her "L'empreinte de Jocaste," *L'Écrit du temps* 12 (1986), 35–54, especially 48–54. On the death of Eurydice and the spatial configurations of female death in the *Antigone*, see my *Sophocles' Tragic World*, 133–37, especially 128–32. For some important qualifications, see Patricia E. Easterling, "Women in Tragic Space," *Bulletin of the Institute for Classical Studies, London* 34 (1987), 15–26.

35. Richard Seaford, "The Tragic Wedding," *Journal of Hellenic Studies* 107 (1987), 106–30, especially 119–20. See above, Chapter 9, note 4.

36. Hipponax, fragment 68, in M. L. West, ed., *Iambi et Elegi Graeci*, vol. 1 (Oxford: Oxford University Press), p. 128. I may mention here the chapter on the *Oedipus* by Kirk Ormand, *Exchange and the Maiden: Marriage in Sophoclean Tragedy* (Austin: University of Texas Press, 1999), 124–52, who views the play in terms of the social construction of identity. The identity of both child and wife are unstable, Ormand argues, because of the problems of proving one's identity given the informality of registering marriages and births in fifth–century Athens. On the other hand, as he notes, this play presents the paradoxical situation that biological identity is only too solid and in fact tragically inescapable. Thus the play might seem to vitiate his thesis, but he avoids that conclusion by pointing out that the biological tie that is affirmed is the "unnatural" one of incest. Ormand's further suggestion, that the scene between Creon and Oedipus at the end of the play is a "mock marriage" in which Oedipus plays the role of the virgin bride being led into "her" new home by Creon as the bridegroom (pp. 147–50), will win few adherents.

37. See John Peradotto, "Disauthorizing Prophecy: The Ideological Mapping of *Oedipus Tyrannus*," *Transactions of the American Philological Association* 122 (1992), 1–15, especially 9–10.

38. For changing views of the "classical," see my essay, "Cracks in the Marble of the Classic Form: The Problem of the Classical Today," *Annals of Scholarship* vol. 10, no. 1 (1993), 7–30.

39. Frederick Ahl, *Sophocles' Oedipus: Evidence and Self-Conviction* (Ithaca, N.Y.: Cornell University Press, 1991); for some of the problems with such a reading, see my review of Ahl, *Classical World* 86 (1992), 155.

40. See for example, Pucci (above, note 29), 170–73, on the "endless end" of the play; also, with a very different approach, Oliver Taplin, "Sophocles in his Theatre," *Entretiens sur l'antiquité classique*, vol. 29, *Sophocle* (Vandoeuvres-Geneva: Fondation Hardt, 1993), 155–83, especially 166–84, with the "Discussion," 177–79.

41. See, for example, Deborah H. Roberts, "Sophoclean Endings: Another Story," *Arethusa* 21 (1988), 177–96; also Pucci (above, note 29), 165–68, who finds in Oedipus' speech of "heroic" acceptance at 1455–58 traces of "superb hybris" and "sublime arrogance." Taplin, "Sophocles in his Theatre" (above, note 40), 173 emphasizes Oedipus' powerlessness at the end, whereas George Gellie, "The Last Scene of the Oedipus Tyrannus," *Ramus* 15 (1986), 35–42, especially 38–41 stresses the upward movement from the "bottom of the abyss" in the moment of horrible discovery to the hero's grandeur at the end (39) and a "display of spirit" that is "the compensating pleasure that tragedy stands in need of" (40).

42. For a view along these lines, see Roberts (preceding note), 192–93.

SELECTED BIBLIOGRAPHY

Note: Some works cited in connection with specific problems in the notes are not repeated here. I have concentrated on works in English. For works in other lan-
guages, see the Bibliographies cited below and also the references in my *Tragedy
and Civilization* and *Sophocles' Tragic World* (below).

I. PRIMARY WORKS

Editions and Commentaries

Bollack, Jean. *L'Oedipe Roi de Sophocle*. Lille: Presses Universitaires de Lille, 1990, 4
    volumes. Facing Greek text and French translation, with detailed, line-by-line
    commentary, introduction on the manuscripts and metrical analysis. Particular
    attention to the history of the text and interpretation.
Dawe, R. D. *Sophocles: Oedipus Tyrannus*. Cambridge: Cambridge University Press,
    1982. Greek text, with helpful commentary.
Gould, Thomas. *Oedipus the King*, by Sophocles. Englewood Cliffs, N.J.: Prentice-Hall,
    1970. Prose translation, running commentary, with a heavily Freudian slant.
Jebb, Richard C. *Sophocles: The Plays and Fragments*. Part 1, *The Oedipus Tyrannus*. 3d
    ed. Cambridge: Cambridge University Press, 1893. Extensive introduction, Greek
    text, facing translation into fairly literal prose, and commentary. Still usable and
    valuable all around edition of the play.
Lloyd-Jones, Hugh and N. G. Wilson. *Sophoclis Fabulae*. Oxford Classical Texts. Ox-
    ford: Clarendon Press, 1990. The standard Greek text of Sophocles, though dis-
    agreements on specific textual problems remain.
Sheppard, John T. *The Oedipus Tyrannus of Sophocles*. Cambridge: Cambridge Uni-
    versity Press, 1920. Greek text, facing translation, interpretative essays empha-
    sizing the moral innocence of Oedipus, and commentary.

Translations

Bagg, Robert. *Sophocles, Oedipus Tyrannus*. Amherst: University of Massachusetts
    Press, 1982. A brisk and spirited contemporary verse translation.

Berg, Stephen and Diskin Clay. *Sophocles, Oedipus the King*. New York: Oxford University Press, 1978. Collaboration of a poet and a classicist; an imaginative effort to catch the poetic flavor of Sophocles' language. Brief, helpful introduction. Highly recommended.

Cook, Albert and Edwin Dolin. *An Anthology of Greek Tragedy*. Indianapolis and New York: Bobbs-Merrill, 1972. Contains fairly literal translations of *Oedipus Tyrannus* and *Oedipus at Colonus*; helpful introduction and bibliographies.

Ewans, Michael, ed. *Sophokles. Four Dramas of Maturity*. London: J. M. Dent, 1999. Everyman Library. Spare and vigorous translation, sometimes a bit prosaic, of *Oedipus Tyrannus* (along with *Ajax, Antigone, Trachiniae*) by various hands. Introduction and Notes pay particular attention to staging effects and performance.

Fagles, Robert. *Sophocles, The Three Theban Plays*, Harmondsworth [U.K.] and New York: Penguin Classics, 1984. Combines clarity with the poetic quality and emotional energy of the play; slightly expands the original. Excellent introductory essays by Bernard Knox. Highly recommended.

Fitts, Dudley and Robert Fitzgerald. *The Oedipus Cycle*, New York: Harcourt, Brace, and World, 1948. Elegant and readable verse translation, but freer than Grene, Fagles, or Berg/Clay, especially in the choral odes.

Grene, David. *Oedipus the King and Oedipus at Colonus*, in David Grene and Richmond Lattimore, eds., *The Complete Greek Tragedies*, vol. 2, *Sophocles*. Chicago: University of Chicago Press, 1959; revised 1991. Serviceable free-verse translation, close to the Greek, but sometimes prosaic. Also available in the Everyman Library edition, with Introduction by Charles Segal and notes by James Hogan. New York: Knopf, 1994.

Knox, Bernard. *Sophocles, Oedipus the King*. New York: Washington Square Press, 1959. Straightforward prose version intended for acting.

Lloyd-Jones, Hugh. *Sophocles, Ajax, Electra, Oedipus Tyrannus*, Loeb Classical Library, Cambridge, MA: Harvard University Press, 1994. Smooth, accurate, up-to-date prose translation, with facing Greek text, based on the recent Oxford text. A second volume contains the other plays, including, *Oedipus at Colonus*.

Meineck, Peter, and Paul Woodruff. *Sophocles, Oedipus Tyrannus*. Indianapolis: Hackett, 2000. Clear, readable, and rapid translation, with emphasis on the dramatic movement. The rather colloquial dialogue tends to simplify the density of Sophocles' poetic language. Interesting introduction.

Watling, E. F. *Sophocles, The Theban Plays*. Harmondsworth [U.K.] and New York: Penguin Classics, 1947. Lucid and readable, but dry; follows Sophocles' imagery rather less closely than Grene or Fagles.

Yeats, William Butler. *The Collected Plays*. London: Macmillan, 1953. Contains versions of *Oedipus Tyrannus* and *Oedipus at Colonus*; rhythmic prose intended for the stage. The choruses have many beautiful touches but are much abridged.

Related Primary Texts

Aeschylus, *Seven Against Thebes*. In D. Grene and R. Lattimore, eds. *The Complete Greek Tragedies*, vol. 1, *Aeschylus*.

Aristotle, *Poetics*. Trans. David Russell and Michael Winterbottom, eds. *Ancient Literary Criticism*, Oxford: Oxford University Press, 1972, and many other editions; see Else, below.

Euripides, *Hippolytus, Ion, Phoenician Women*. In Grene and Lattimore, eds. *Complete Greek Tragedies*, Euripides, vols. 3 and 4.

Herodotus, *The Persian Wars*. Trans. George Rawlinson. New York: Modern Library, 1942.

———. *The Histories*. Trans. Robin Waterfield, with introduction and notes by Carolyn Dewald. New York: Oxford University Press, 1998.

Seneca, *Oedipus*, in *Seneca, Four Tragedies and Octavia*, trans. E. F. Watling. Harmondsworth [U.K.] and New York: Penguin Classics, 1966.

Thucydides, *The Peloponnesian War*. Trans. Rex Warner. Harmondsworth [U.K.] and New York: Penguin Classics, 1954.

———. *History of the Peloponnesian War*. Trans. Steven Lattimore. Indianapolis: Hackett, 1998.

Anthologies Containing Oedipus Tyrannus, *Related Primary Works, and Criticism*

Berkowitz, Luci and Theodore F. Brunner, eds. *Oedipus Tyrannus*. New York: Norton, 1970. Contains prose translation of *Oedipus Tyrannus*, selections from *Odyssey*, Thucydides on the plague, Euripides' *Phoenician Women*, and selected anthropological and literary criticism.

Cook, Albert, ed. *Oedipus Rex: A Mirror for Greek Drama*. Belmont, CA: Wadsworth, 1963; reprint, Prospect Heights, IL: Waveland Press, 1982. Contains translations of *Oedipus Tyrannus* and *Poetics* and critical statement and essays from Voltaire to the present.

Kallich, Michael, Andrew MacLeish, and Gertrude Schoenbohm, eds. *Oedipus Myth and Drama*. New York: Odyssey Press, 1968. Contains a modernized version of Jebb's translation of *Oedipus Tyrannus*, *Aristotle's Poetics*, the Oedipus plays of Dryden/Lee and Hofmannsthal, and selected literary, anthropological, and psychoanalytic criticism.

Sanderson, James L. and Everett Zimmerman, eds. *Oedipus. Myth and Dramatic Form*. Boston: Houghton Mifflin, 1968. Contains Watling's translation of *Oedipus Tyrannus*, the *Oedipus* of Seneca, Voltaire, and Gide; Cocteau, *Infernal Machine* (all in translation), selections from Aristotle, Freud, and modern critics.

II. Secondary Works

Bibliographies

Buxton, R. G. A. *Sophocles, Greece & Rome*, Supplement. *New Surveys in the Classics*, No. 16. Oxford: Clarendon Press, 1984.

Johansen, H. Friis, "Sophocles 1939–1959," *Lustrum* 7 (1962): 94–342

Said, Suzanne, "Bibliographie tragique, 1900–88," *Métis* 3 (1988): 409–512, esp. 468–84.

Historical, Cultural, and Archeological Background

Baldry, H. C. *The Greek Tragic Theater*. London: Chatto and Windus, 1971. Useful brief discussion of the Greek theater in its social and historical context.

Bieber, Margarete. *The History of the Greek and Roman Theater.* 2d ed. Princeton: Princeton University Press, 1961. Well-illustrated presentation of the archeological evidence for Greek dramatic performances.

Boardman, John, Jasper Griffin, and Oswyn Murray, eds. *Oxford History of Greece and the Hellenistic World.* Oxford: Oxford University Press, 1991. Well-illustrated cultural history of Greece to 146 B.C.E.

Bowra, C. M. *The Greek Experience.* Cleveland: World, 1957. Attempts to define the character of early Greek civilization by surveying its major cultural achievements.

Burn, A. R. *Pericles and Athens.* New York: Collier, 1962. Readable account of the rise and fall of Periclean Athens.

Cartledge, Paul. *The Cambridge Illustrated History of Ancient Greece.* Cambridge: Cambridge University Press, 1998. Overview of classical Greece, with emphasis on culture and society.

———. *The Greeks.* Oxford: Oxford University Press, 1993. Readable overview of classical Greek culture, emphasizing the specificity of Greek social and cultural forms and their "otherness." Useful bibliography.

Csapo, Eric, and William J. Slater, eds. *The Context of Ancient Drama.* Ann Arbor: University of Michigan Press, 1995. Useful collection of major texts, in translation, and illustrations bearing on the history of the ancient Greek theater,with extensive and valuable interpretive discussion.

Davies, John Kenyon. *Democracy and Classical Greece.* 2nd ed. Cambridge, MA.: Harvard University Press, 1993. A history of fifth-century Greece.

Easterling, P. E., and B. M. W. Knox, eds. *Cambridge History of Classical Literature*, vol. 1. Cambridge: Cambridge University Press, 1985. Standard history of Greek literature, with chapters on the tragedians and dramatic festivals, chronologies, and useful bibliographies.

Guthrie, W. K. C. *A History of Greek Philosophy*, vols. 2 and 3. Cambridge: Cambridge University Press, 1965, 1969. Detailed account of Greek thought in the age of the tragedians.

Hammond, N. G. L. *A History of Greece to 322 B.C.* 2d ed. Oxford: Clarendon Press, 1967. A standard history of Greece.

Kirk, Geoffrey S., J. E. Raven, and Malcolm Scholfield. *The Presocratic Philosophers.* 2d ed. Cambridge: Cambridge University Press, 1983. Texts, translations, commentaries on thinkers contemporary with *Oedipus Tyrannus* and earlier.

Lewis, D. M., John Boardman, J. K. Davies, and Martin Ostwald, eds. *The Cambridge Ancient History*; volume 5. *The Fifth Century B.C.* Cambridge: Cambridge University Press, 1992. A survey of history, politics, the visual arts, and literature in the formative period of Greek tragedy.

Ley, G. K. H. *A Short Introduction to the Ancient Greek Theater.* Chicago: University of Chicago Press, 1991. Concise general introduction to staging and performance.

Pickard-Cambridge, Arthur W. *Dithyramb, Tragedy and Comedy.* 2d ed., revised by T. B. L. Webster. Oxford: Oxford University Press, 1962.

———. *The Dramatic Festivals of Athens.* 2d ed., revised by John Gould and D. M. Lewis. Oxford: Oxford University Press, 1968.

———. *The Theater of Dionysus at Athens.* Oxford: Oxford University Press, 1946. Pickard-Cambridge's three books are still the fullest documentation for the origin, nature, and physical arrangements of the dramatic festivals. Not for beginners.

Pomeroy, Sarah B., S. M. Burstein, Walter Donlan, and J. T. Roberts. *Ancient Greece: A Political, Social, and Cultural History*. New York: Oxford University Press, 1999. Informative history of Greece, from the prehistoric period to the Hellenistic Age.

Rehm, Rush. *Greek Tragic Theatre*. London: Routledge, 1992. Useful account of the conventions of dramatic festivals and conventions, with brief analyses of exemplary plays, including *Oedipus Tyrannus*.

Rodenwaldt, Gerhart and Walter Hege. *The Acropolis*. 2d ed. Oxford: Blackwell, 1957. Brief descriptive account of the major monuments on the Acropolis and Pericles' building program; excellent photographs.

Vernant, Jean-Pierre, ed. *Greek Man*. Chicago: University of Chicago Press, 1994. Essays on major aspects of Greek cultural, political, and economic life, including an essay on "Spectator and Listener" by C. Segal.

Criticism: Books and Parts of Books

Ahl, Frederick. *Sophocles' Oedipus: Evidence and Self-Conviction*. Ithaca, N.Y.: Cornell University Press, 1991. A radical rereading, arguing that Oedipus is mistaken in accepting the evidence that he is Jocasta's son and Laius' killer. Many stimulating and acute observations, but ultimately unconvincing.

Alford, C. Fred. *The Psychoanalytic Theory of Greek Tragedy*. New Haven, CT: Yale University Press, 1992. Emphasizes the directness and intensity of the expressions of the passions in Greek tragedy and the therapeutic value of pity. Discusses both *Oedipus Tyrannus and Oedipus at Colonus*.

Bloom, Harold, ed. *Sophocles' Oedipus Rex*. New York and Philadelphia: Chelsea House Publishers, 1988. Selected recent criticism.

Bowra, C. M. *Sophoclean Tragedy*. Oxford: Oxford University Press, 1944. Focuses on moral and legal issues in the play, with a rather moralistic view.

Bushnell, Rebecca. *Prophesying Tragedy: Sign and Voice in Sophocles' Theban Plays*. Ithaca, N.Y.: Cornell University Press, 1988. A study of the oracular voice in tragedy against the background of Homer, with a chapter on *Oedipus Tyrannus*.

Cameron, Alister. *The Identity of Oedipus the King*. New York: New York University Press, 1965. Somewhat rambling essays, emphasizing theme of self-discovery.

Dawe, R. D., ed. *Sophocles, The Classical Heritage*. New York: Garland, 1996. A collection of essays illustrating changing views of Sophoclean tragedy from the sixteenth to the twentieth century. Several bear directly on the *Oedipus*.

Easterling, Patricia E., ed. *Cambridge Companion to Greek Tragedy*. Cambridge: Cambridge University Press, 1997. Up-to-date overview of the most important aspects of Greek tragedy by leading British and American scholars.

Eden, Kathy. *Poetic and Legal Fiction in the Aristotelian Tradition*. Princeton, N.J.: Princeton University Press, 1986. On the importance of rhetoric, law courts, and legal proof and argument in the ancient view of tragedy.

Edmunds, Lowell, ed. *Oedipus: The Ancient Legend and its Later Analogues*. Baltimore, MD: Johns Hopkins University Press, 1984. Companion volume to Edmunds and Dundes, below. Comparative material for history and diffusion of Oedipus myth.

Edmunds, Lowell and Alan Dundes. *Oedipus: A Folklore Casebook*. New York: Garland, 1983.

Ehrenberg, Victor. *Sophocles and Pericles*. Oxford: Blackwell, 1954. Studies *Oedipus Tyrannus* and *Antigone* in terms of the political currents of the time.

Else, Gerald F. *Aristotle's Poetics: The Argument*. Cambridge, MA: Harvard University Press, 1967. Translation and detailed analysis of crucial sections of *Poetics*, with a fundamental reexamination of "tragic flaw" theory.

Entretiens sur l'antiquité classique, vol. 29, *Sophocle*. Vandoeuvres-Geneva: Fondation Hardt, 1993. Publication of an international conference of expert scholars, with discussions of the papers. Interesting essays by Bernard Knox, George Steiner, Oliver Taplin, R. P. Winnington-Ingram, and others.

Euben, J. Peter, ed. *Greek Tragedy and Political Theory*. Berkeley and Los Angeles: University of California Press, 1986. Essays on the relation of tragedy to social and political thought.

———. *The Tragedy of Political Theory*. Princeton, N.J.: Princeton University Press, 1990. Emphasizes the political and institutional implications of Greek tragedy. Chapter on *Oedipus Tyrannus*.

Freud, Sigmund. *The Interpretation of Dreams*. Trans. and ed. James Strachey. 3d ed. New York: Basic Books, 1955. Contains what is perhaps the most influential view of *Oedipus Tyrannus* in the twentieth century. For discussion, see Chapter 4.

Frick, Werner. *Die mythische Methode*. Tübingen: Niemeyer, 1998. A sensitive and wide-ranging account of twentieth-century adaptations of Greek tragedy, with good observations on style. Extensive discussion of the Oedipus plays of Cocteau and Gide. Excellent bibliography.

Gellie, George. *Sophocles: A Reading*. Melbourne: University of Melbourne Press, 1972. Good study of the dramatic movement of *Oedipus Tyrannus*; helpful general essays on plot, character, gods, poetry in Sophocles as a whole.

Gentili, Bruno, and A. Pretagostini, eds. *Edipo: Il teatro greco e la cultura Europea*. Rome: Edizioni del Ateneo, 1986. Multilingual publication of an international conference on Oedipus; essays on many aspects of the play, myth, later influences.

Girard, René. *The Violence and the Sacred*. Trans. P. Gregory. Baltimore, MD: Johns Hopkins University Press, 1979. For discussion, see Chapter 12.

Goldhill, Simon. *Reading Greek Tragedy*. Cambridge: Cambridge University Press, 1986. Stimulating contemporary criticism of a wide range of Greek plays, including a chapter on *Oedipus Tyrannus*.

Goux, Jean-Joseph. *Oedipus, Philosopher*. Trans. C. Porter. Stanford. CA: Stanford University Press, 1993. Interesting but highly speculative study of the Oedipus myth in terms of initiatory patterns and Dumézil's tripartite functions of the king. Following Nietzsche, Goux views Oedipus' victory over the Sphinx as a break with traditional patterns in an act of man-centered intellectual hybris that leads to the foundation of Western philosophy.

Griffith, R. Drew. *The Theatre of Apollo: Divine Justice and Sophocles' Oedipus the King*. Montreal and Kingston: McGill-Queen's University Press, 1996. An energetic but one-sided, moralistic reading of the play, centered on a supposedly hybristic Oedipus who is justly punished by Apollo for killing Laius. Reductive in its fragmented and selective use of the elements of plot, language, and characterization.

Halter, Thomas. *König Oedipus. Von Sophokles zu Cocteau*. Stuttgart: Franz Steiner Verlag, 1998. Close stylistic comparisons of the language of Sophocles' *Oedipus* with the versions of Seneca, Dryden-Lee, Corneille, Voltaire, and others.

Hogan, James C. *A Commentary on the Plays of Sophocles*. Carbondale: Southern Illinois University Press, 1991. A running commentary on all the plays, based on the translation by David Grene.

Jones, John. *On Aristotle and Greek Tragedy*. London: Chatto and Windus, 1962. Emphasizes the importance of plot and action rather than the depiction of character in Greek tragedy.

Kaufman, Walter. *Tragedy and Philosophy*. New York: Doubleday, 1968; revised reprint, New York: Anchor Books, 1969. A philosophical approach to tragedy in the perspective of Plato, Aristotle, Hegel, Nietzsche, and others. Contains an insightful chapter on *Oedipus Tyrannus* as a tragedy of the human condition, with a useful examination of Freudian and other modern interpretations.

Kirkwood, G. M. *A Study of Sophoclean Drama*. Ithaca, N.Y.: Cornell University Press, 1958. A clear topic-by-topic study of formal elements and dramatic structure in the seven plays.

Kitto, H. D. F. *Poiesis: Structure and Thought*. Berkeley and Los Angeles: University of California Press, 1966. Contains a detailed discussion of *Oedipus Tyrannus*.

———. *Sophocles, Dramatist and Philosopher*. London: Oxford Univerity Press, 1958

Knox, B. M. W. *Oedipus at Thebes*. New Haven, CT: Yale University Press, 1957. A careful study of Sophocles' language and imagery, suggesting that Oedipus is a distillation of Athens in its greatness, power, and danger.

———. *The Heroic Temper: Studies in Sophocles Tragedy*. Berkeley and Los Angeles: University of California Press, 1964. On the darker side of the Sophoclean hero.

———. *Word and Action: Essays on the Ancient Theatre*. Baltimore and London: Johns Hopkins University Press, 1979. Contains several important essays on the historical circumstances of *Oedipus Tyrannus*.

Lattimore, Richmond. *The Poetry of Greek Tragedy*. Baltimore, MD: Johns Hopkins University Press, 1958. Excellent discussion of the foundling theme in *Oedipus Tyrannus*.

Letters, F. J. H. *The Life and Work of Sophocles*. London: Sheed and Ward, 1953. Useful discussion of cultural background, life, personality of Sophocles; sensible criticism of the moralistic view of *Oedipus Tyrannus*.

Mueller, Martin. *The Children of Oedipus*. Toronto: University of Toronto Press, 1980. Studies modern imitations of Greek tragedy from 1550 to 1800, with a valuable chapter on *Oedipus Tyrannus*.

O'Brien, Michael J. *Twentieth Century Interpretations of Oedipus Rex*. Englewood Cliffs, N.J.: Prentice-Hall, 1968. A good selection of critical essays and brief comments about *Oedipus Tyrannus*.

Paduano, Guido. *Lunga storia di Edipo Re: Freud, Sofocle e il teatro occidentale*. Turin: Einaudi, 1994. A critical examination of the Freudian approaches to the *Oedipus Tyrannus*, with a wide-ranging survey of the Oedipus myth in drama from the seventeenth to the twentieth century.

Poole, Adrian. *Tragedy: Shakespeare and the Greek Example*. Oxford: Blackwell, 1987. Attempts to define the qualities of the Greek sense of the tragic (especially the problems of suffering, meaning, and communication) by juxtaposing readings of Greek drama, including *Oedipus Tyrannus*, and Shakespeare.

Propp, Vladimir, "Oedipus in the Light of Folklore," in L. Edmunds and A. Dundes, *Oedipus: A Folklore Casebook* (above), 76–121. Originally published in Russian in 1944, this essay examines narrative motifs in the Oedipus myth in the perspective of both European and other folklore. Despite his limited historical interpretation of the myth as representing a conflict between matrilinear and patrilinear succession to kingship, Propp offers many insights into both *Oedipus Tyrannus* and *Oedipus at Colonus*.

Pucci, Pietro. *Oedipus and the Fabrication of the Father*. Baltimore, MD: Johns Hopkins University Press, 1992. A stimulating poststructuralist reading that emphasizes the connections between the riddles, language, paternity, and textuality. Focuses on the interaction between "chance" and "destination" (or fate and choice) in both asserting and questioning the authority of a father figure (divine and human) as a source of order, authority, and law.

Reinhardt, Karl. *Sophocles*. 3rd ed. Trans. H. and D. Harvey. Oxford: Blackwell, 1979. Full of insights into philosophical and formal aspects of the play; stresses the evolution of Sophocles' drama from play to play and the centrality of illusion and reality in *Oedipus Tyrannus*. Highly recommended.

Ringer, Mark. *Electra and the Empty Urn*. Chapel Hill: University of North Carolina Press, 1998. Detailed study of theatrical self-reference and the performative aspects of the plays in Sophocles. Contains a discussion of *Oedipus Tyrannus*.

Rocco, Christopher. *Tragedy and Enlightenment*. Berkeley and Los Angeles: University of California Press, 1997. Stimulating attempt to incorporate Greek tragedy into contemporary debate between postmodernist and more traditional approaches to political theory, taking Greek tragedy as a reference point for a democratic society's ways of conceptualizing conflict, tension, and "the other." Extensive discussion of *Oedipus Tyrannus* as framing these conflicts, especially in the area of rationality, power, truth, and the sacred.

Rudnytsky, Peter L. *Freud and Oedipus*. New York: Columbia University Press, 1987. A detailed study of the psychoanalytic approach to the Oedipus myth.

Seale, David. *Vision and Stagecraft in Sophocles*. Chicago: University of Chicago Press, 1982. Chapter on *Oedipus Tyrannus* traces the theme of sight, blindness, eyes, and other visual phenomena.

Scodel, Ruth. *Sophocles*. Boston: Twayne World Authors Series, 1984. An introduction to all of Sophocles for the general reader.

Segal, Charles. *Interpreting Greek Tragedy*. Ithaca, N.Y.: Cornell University Press, 1986. Uses a variety of contemporary critical approaches to Greek drama and offers a number of different perspectives on *Oedipus Tyrannus*.

———. "Introduction," *Sophocles: The Theban Plays*. New York: Knopf, Everyman's Library, 1994 xi–xlix. General overview of *Antigone, Oedipus Tyrannus, Oedipus at Colonus*.

———. "Sophocles," *Ancient Writers: Greece and Rome*. Ed. T. J. Luce. New York: Scribners, 1982. I, 179–207. A brief overview of Sophocles' life, times, and dramatic art.

———. *Tragedy and Civilization: An Interpretation of Sophocles*. Cambridge, MA: Harvard University Press, 1981; paperback reprint, Norman: University of Oklahoma Press, 1999. A study of Sophocles against the background of myth, views of nature, man, and society. Contains detailed chapters on *Oedipus Tyrannus* and *Oedipus at Colonus*.

———. *Sophocles' Tragic World: Divinity, Nature, Society*. Cambridge, MA.: Harvard University Press, 1995, paperback reprint, 1998. Offers detailed studies of the chorus in the *Oedipus Tyrannus*, the play's use of the natural world, and the limitations and validity of a Freudian approach.

Segal, Erich. *Oxford Readings in Greek Tragedy.* Oxford: Oxford University Press, 1983. Useful collection of authoritative recent criticism. Includes E. R. Dodds, "On Misinterpreting the *Oedipus Rex.*"

Silk, M. S. ed. *Tragedy and the Tragic.* Oxford: Oxford University Press, 1996. Essays by leading scholars on many important aspects of Greek tragedy; several essays bear directly and indirectly on *Oedipus Tyrannus.*

Steiner, George. *Antigones.* Oxford: Oxford University Press, 1984. A detailed, sensitive study of literary variations on the *Antigone,* with many points of contact with *Oedipus Tyrannus.*

Taplin, Oliver. *Greek Tragic Action.* Berkeley and Los Angeles: University of California Press, 1978. Contains incisive, brief comments on major scenes in the *Oedipus Tyrannus,* from the point of view of visual tableaux, staging, gestures, and dramatic sequences.

Van Nortwick, Thomas. *Oedipus: The Meaning of a Masculine Life.* Norman: University of Oklahoma Press, 1998. Brings together *Oedipus Tyrannus* and *Oedipus at Colonus* in a highly personal reading with Jungian overtones, emphasizing the search for identity in which the destruction of the old self leads to the creation of the new.

Vernant, Jean-Pierre and Pierre Vidal-Naquet. *Myth and Tragedy in Ancient Greece.* Trans. J. Lloyd. New York: Zone Books, 1990. Important and influential essays on Greek tragedy, emphasizing ritual background and political and social meaning. Contains two valuable essays on *Oedipus Tyrannus* and a study of *Oedipus at Colonus;* see Chapter 12. Supersedes 1988 collection of the same title.

Vickers, Brian. *Towards Greek Tragedy.* London: Longmans, 1979. Large-scale study of Greek tragedy, emphasizing the connections between myth, drama, and ritual in an anthropological perspective. Contains a good analysis of the oracles and the chronology of the plot of *Oedipus Tyrannus* (pp. 496–525).

Waldock, A. J. A. *Sophocles the Dramatist.* Cambridge: Cambridge University Press, 1951. Brilliantly but narrowly argues that Sophocles' chief concern is dramatic effect, even at the expense of coherence of plot or meaning. Useful cautionary remarks on the "documentary fallacy," though he falls into his own "theatrical fallacy."

Webster, T. B. L. *An Introduction to Sophocles.* Oxford: Oxford University Press, 1936. Well-focused, detailed discussions of Sophocles' life, thought, characterization, plot, odes.

Whitman, C. H. Sophocles: *A Study of Heroic Humanism.* Cambridge, MA: Harvard University Press, 1951. Elegant refutation of "tragic flaw" approach to *Oedipus Tyrannus;* views the play as a tragedy of irrational suffering.

Wilamowitz, Tycho von. *Die dramatische Technik des Sophokles. Philologische Untersuchungen,* 22. Berlin: Weidmann, 1917. A detailed examination of inconsistencies and illogicalities in the plot structure of Sophocles' plays, including a chapter on *Oedipus Tyrannus* (pp. 69–88). Rejects the excessive psychological reconstruction of characters' motives and instead emphasizes the logic of the events. Argues that Sophocles is more concerned with scene-by-scene effect than with overall dramatic coherence. On the *Oedipus Tyrannus,* especially concerned with the apparent illogicalities in the process by which Oedipus discovers the truth. Useful for acute observations even if the central thesis is reductive and often tendentiously argued.

Williams, Bernard. *Shame and Necessity*. Berkeley and Los Angeles: University of California Press, 1993. Wide-ranging study of the classical moral ideas, especially freedom and responsibility, in the perspective of modern ethical thinking, with considerable attention to tragedy.

Winnington-Ingram, R. P. *Sophocles: An Interpretation*. Cambridge: Cambridge University Press, 1980. Major study of all the plays. Especially helpful on the religious background of *Oedipus Tyrannus* and its roots in archaic thought.

Woodard, Thomas. *Sophocles: A Collection of Critical Essays*. Englewood Cliffs, N.J.: Prentice-Hall, 1966.

Zimmermann, Bernhard. *Greek Tragedy*. Trans. T. Marier (1986). Baltimore, MD: Johns Hopkins University Press, 1991. Rapid survey of the background and conventions of Greek tragedy, with chapters on each of the three extant tragedians. Bibliography is useful, but heavily Germanic.

Criticism: Articles

Note that many articles on *Oedipus Tyrannus*, the myth, and imitations are included in the collections of critical essays cited above.

Buxton, R. G. A., "Blindness and its Limits: Sophocles and the Logic of Myth," *Journal of Hellenic Studies* 100 (1980): 22–37.

de Kock, E. L., "The Sophoklean Oidipous and its Antecedents." *Acta Classica* 4 (1961): 7–28.

Dodds, E. R., "On Misunderstanding the *Oedipus Rex*," *Greece & Rome* 13 (1966): 37–49 (included in anthologies of O'Brien and E. Segal, above).

Edmunds, Lowell, "The Cults and the Legend of Oedipus," *Harvard Studies in Classical Philology*, 85 (1981): 221–38.

———, "Oedipus in the Middle Ages," *Antike und Abendland* 25 (1976): 140–55.

Goldhill, Simon, "Exegesis: Oedipus (R)ex," *Arethusa* 17 (1984): 177–200. Interesting exploration of terms involving the prefix *ex-*, "out of" in the *Oedipus*.

Goodhart, Sandor, "*Lêistas Ephaske*: Oedipus and Laius' Many Murderers," *Diacritics* 8.1 (1978): 55–71. An influential statement of the contradictions and unresolved questions in the plot of the *Oedipus*.

Gould, Thomas, "The Innocence of Oedipus: The Philosophers on *Oedipus the King*." *Arion* 4 (1965): 363–86, 582–611; 5 (1966): 478–525.

Krauskopf, Ingrid, s. v. "Oidipus," in *Lexicon Iconographiae Mythologiae Classicae*. Zurich and Munich, 1994. Vol. 7, part 1, 1–15, and vol. 7, part 2, 6–15 (plates). Brief survery of depictions of the Oedipus myth in Greek and Roman art, with illustrations and bibliography.

Musurillo, Herbert, "Sunken Imagery in Sophocles' *Oedipus*," *American Journal of Philology* 78 (1957): 36–51.

Newton, Rick M., "*Hippolytus* and the Dating of *Oedipus Tyrannus*," *Greek, Roman and Byzantine Studies* 21 (1980): 5–22.

Scully, Stephen, "Orchestra and Stage in Sophocles: *Oedipus Tyrannus* and the Theater of Dionysus," *Syllecta Classica* 10 (1999): 65–86. Argues for the existence of a raised stage separating actors and chorus and analyzes *Oedipus Tyrannus* in terms of the spatial dynamics of the play, especially the contrast between the chorus' and Oedipus' perspectives on the meaning of the events and the gods.

Segal, Charles, "Sacral Kinship and Tragic Heroism in Five Oedipus Plays and *Hamlet*," *Helios* 5 (1977): 1–10.

——, "Synaesthesia in Sophocles." *Illinois Classical Studies* 2 (1977): 86–96.

Smith, Susan Harris, "Twentieth-Century Plays Using Classical Mythic Themes: A Checklist." *Modern Drama* 29 (1986): 110–33, especially 124–25.

Stinton, T. C. W., "*Hamartia* in Aristotle and Greek Tragedy," (1975), in his *Collected Papers on Greek Tragedy*. Oxford: Clarendon Press, 1990, 143–85. Careful study of the complexity of this term for "tragic error" or "mistake," and demonstrates the limitations of the "tragic flaw" approach to Greek tragedy, including *Oedipus Tyrannus*.

——, "The Scope and Limits of Allusion in Greek Tragedy" (1986), in Stinton, *Collected Papers on Greek Tragedy*, 454–92. Critical examination of how much of the mythical background may be relevant to a particular tragedy. Shows the significance of the absence of the family curse in *Oedipus Tyrannus* (pp. 461–64).

Torrance, Robert M., "Sophocles: Some Bearings," *Harvard Studies in Classical Philology* 69 (1965): 271–307. Broad perspective on Sophocles, emphasizing the interaction of divine justice and the character of the individual hero.

Vernant, Jean-Pierre, "From Oedipus to Periander: Lameness, Tyranny, Incest in Legend and History," *Arethusa* 15 (1982): 19–38. Reprinted in 1990 collection of Vernant and Vidal-Naquet.

INDEX

Achilles, 18, 52, 121n9
Acropolis, 7–8, 15
Adrastus, in Herodotus, 25, 121n7
Aeneid, by Virgil, 19
Aeschylus, 21, 25–28, 30, 55, 110;
  Agamemnon, 18; *Eumenides*, 43–44, 137;
  Laius, 25; *Oedipus*, 25–27; *Oresteia*, 27,
  137; *Persians*, 21; *Prometheus Bound*, 4;
  Seven against Thebes, 20, 25–28, 44, 134;
  Sphinx, 25; *Suppliants*, 74
Africa, 163
Agamemnon, 18, 32
agriculture, metaphor of, 105, 116, 139. *See
  also* plowing; seed; sowing
Agrippina, 164
Ahl, Frederick, 173
Ajax, 18, 113, 128, 168, 171. *See also*
  Sophocles, *Ajax*
Alcmaeonids, 12
Alexandria, 145
anagnorisis. See recognition; reversal
Anaxagoras, 8, 13
Andromache. *See* Euripides, *Andromache*
anger: of Oedipus, 52, 79, 90, 92; of Oedipus
  and Teiresias, 81
Antigone, 25, 33, 36, 51, 54, 57, 73, 100, 153,
  155; in *Oedipus at Colonus*, 43, 137, 139,
  140–41; in Seneca, 147. *See also*
  Sophocles, *Antigone*
Apollo, 25, 29–30, 42, 53–54, 57, 61, 66, 73,
  77, 80, 91, 94, 111–12, 119, 134. *See also*
  Delphi; prophecy; oracle
Apollonius of Rhodes, *Argonautica*, 19
Areopagus, 137
Ares, 77
Aristophanes, 29–30, 170; *Birds*, 8; *Clouds*, 8;
  Frogs, 30
Aristotle. *See Poetics*
Athena, 75; statue of in Parthenon, 8
Athena Nike, temple of, 8
Athens, in Greek tragedy, 44

Atreus, 32
autochthony, 164

Bali, 163
bird-signs, 97
birth, 100. *See also* Oedipus, birth of
Bellerophon, 49
Berkoff, Steven, *Greek*, 156
blindness: as theme, 4, 27, 83, 104, 113; of
  Teiresias, 26, 59; of Oedipus, 41, 62, 90,
  111, 113, 141. *See also* self-blinding
Boccaccio, Giovanni, *De Claris Mulieribus*,
  148
Bond, Edward, *Saved*, 156
Borges, Jorge Luis, 163
Boucourechliev, André, 157
Bowra, C. M., 169
Bronze Age, 18
Byzantium, 144

Cadmus, 164–65
Caesar, Julius, 144
Calchas, 64
calculation, 12, 76, 91, 104
castration, 41
catharsis, 145–46. *See also Poetics*
Caunus, in Ovid's *Metamorphoses*, 32
Cavafy, Constantine, "Oedipus," 158
chance, 5, 89, 147, 171–73
character, in Sophocles, 28
children, of Oedipus. *See* Oedipus
Chimaera, 49
choice, by Oedipus, 53, 61, 112, 134
choral odes, 6, 17, 59, 79, 83–84, 92–94,
  100–101, 104–5, 145; of *Antigone*, 10
chorus, 16–18, 170; as actor, 17–18; as
  character, 113. *See also* choral odes
Christ, 43
Christine de Pizan, 148
Chrysippus, 25, 33
Cinyras, in Ovid's *Metamorphoses*, 32

191

INDEX

Kore, 27
koryphaios, 16
Kunitz, Stanley, 163
Kurosawa, Akira, 60

Lacan, Jacques, 166–67
Lachner, Franz, 158
Laius, 18, 25, 31, 33, 36, 42, 51, 62; attack on
    Oedipus by, 90; in Jean Cocteau, 155;
    death of, 27, 44, 56–58, 63–65, 76, 86,
    123–26, 173; in Euripides' *Phoenician
    Women*, 31; oracle to 28, 55; in Pier
    Pasolini, 163; in Seneca, 146–47
language, 5, 32–37, 42, 67, 76–78, 96, 98
Lattimore, Richmond, 5
Laurentian Library, 144
law courts, 9, 20; and accusation of Creon, 84
laws, of gods, 92–93, 101
Lee, Nathaniel. *See* Dryden
Lenaea, 15
Leoncavallo, Ruggiero, *Edipo Re*, 158
Lévi-Strauss, Claude, on Oedipus myth,
    163–64
Livy, 164
Lloyd-Jones, Sir Hugh, 103
Longinus, *On the Sublime*, 146
Long Walls, of Athens, 8
Loraux, Nicole, 171
Lucretia, 164
Lully, Jean-Baptiste, 158

MacLeish, Archibald, 163
manuscripts of *Oedipus Tyrannus*, 6, 144–45
Manutius, Aldus, 149
Marathon, 7, 55
masculinity, 171; at end of *Oedipus Tyrannus*,
    138
Medea, 21
memory, 19, 63, 99, 109, 123–25
Mendelssohn, Felix, 158
Merope, 41–42, 89
Merrill, James, 163
Messenger, Corinthian, 16, 29, 51, 55, 60,
    62–63, 66, 94–95; recognition scenes,
    94–100, 102–4
Messenger, Second, 99, 108–11, 123
metatheater, 134, 170
meter, of Greek tragedy, 17; at Oedipus's
    recognition, 110
Middle Ages, Oedipus myth in, 148
misogyny, 172
Moravia, Alberto, *Il Dio Kurt*, 163
Moreau, Gustave, 158
Moses, 49
mountains, 59, 67–68, 84, 93; and Oedipus's
    life, 101, 118
Muir, Edwin, 163
music, in tragic performances, 17
Mussorgsky, Modest, 158
Mycenaean Age, 18–19

Myrrha, in Ovid's *Metamorphoses*, 32
myth, 20; of the hero, 49–50; of Oedipus,
    24–52; of Oedipus, in André Gide and
    Jean Cocteau, 154–56; of Oedipus,
    modern interpretations, 37–43; Oedipus
    as savior in, 43–45; and tragedy, 18–20;
    "Myth," poem by Muriel Rukeyser, 163

name. *See* Oedipus, name of
nature, 18, 75, 110; views of, 11
necessity, tragic, 129
Neoptolemus, in Euripides' *Andromache*, 32
Nero, 32, 144, 164
Niccoli, Niccolò, 149
Nietzsche, Friedrich, 37, 167
number. *See* calculation
nurture, 5, 75, 78, 91, 114, 139
nymphs, 101–2

Ode on Man, in *Antigone*, 10
Odeion, 8
Odyssey. See Homer
Odysseus, 24, 32, 61. *See also* Homer, *Odyssey*
Oedipa Maas, in *The Crying of Lot 49*, by
    Thomas Pynchon, 163
Oedipus: birth of, 60, 99; changes of mood
    in, 88, 95, 109–10; children of, 89;
    children of, in final scene, 116–20, 135,
    137–41, 173; in Jean Cocteau, 155;
    contradictions in, 36–37, 43–45, 50, 65
    (*see also* paradox); energy of, 75; exile of,
    52, 76, 85, 115, 118, 165; exposure of, 29,
    36, 54, 65, 84, 91, 103–4, 137; guilt of,
    58–59, 69n5; in André Gide, 154;
    identity of, 66, 111; recognition of truth
    by, 98–101; refusal of suicide, 111–12,
    133–35; as savior in hero myth, 43–45; as
    scapegoat, 140, 164; search for identity
    by, 4, 60; search for parents by, 81; self-
    blinding by, 60, 108–12, 123–26, 132, 134,
    138; strength of, 113–17, 133–35; and
    Teiresias, 56–57; tomb of, in *Oedipus at
    Colonus*, 43–45, 140; trials of, 49–52
Oedipus at Colonus, 4, 6, 37, 43–44, 49, 54,
    57–59, 73, 80, 131, 135–37, 139–42, 146,
    157, 158, 167, 169
oedipus complex, 38, 40–41, 159, 167
Oedipodeia, 25
oikos (household), 141
Olympus, 59, 93, 101
On the Sublime, 146
oracles, 11, 18, 24, 26–27, 42–43, 53–55,
    62–64, 80–83, 88–92, 104–5, 112, 131, 138,
    173; of Apollo, 25; order of, 61; received
    by Oedipus, 89; in Thucydides, 12. *See
    also* Apollo; Delphi; prophecy
origins. *See* Oedipus, birth of
ostracism, 165
Ouranos, in sacred marriage with Gaia, 110
Ovid, *Metamorphoses*, 19, 32